Working With Dreams

CW00971219

This book is about the practice of working with dreams. Rather than presenting a general theory about dreams, it focuses on the dream as phenomenon and raises the question how we must look at dreams if our approach is supposed to be a truly psychological one. So far most essays on, and the practice of, Jungian dream interpretation have paradoxically centered around the person of the dreamer and not around the dream itself. Dreams were used as a means to understand the analysand and what is going on in him or her. Jung's fundamental shift from his earlier person-based psychology and pre-alchemy stance to his mature soul-based psychology, informed by the hermetic logic of alchemy, has not been followed, which was already noted by Jung himself: "My later and more important work (as it seems to me) is still left untouched in its primordial obscurity."

The present study is based decidedly on the stance of mature Jung and his very different views about dreams. His most crucial insights in this regard include that in dreams the soul speaks about itself (not about the dreamer), that the dream is its own interpretation and therefore needs to be circumambulated (rather than translated into the language of psychology and everyday life), and that dream images have everything they need within themselves (rather than needing associations from the dreamer's daily life). This book discusses in detail what all this means in practice and what it demands of the psychologist. A decisive transposition away from ordinary consciousness, a "crossing to the other side of the river," is required of the consciousness that wants to approach dreams psychologically. Numerous aspects of dreams and special questions that come up in working with dreams are discussed. At the end of this book our working with dreams is situated in the wider question of the psychological task in general by exploring Jung's insistence that psychology has to transcend the "consulting room," Hillman's move "From mirror to window" and, in Plato's parable, the revolutionary move out of, and return to, "the cave."

While limited to the topic of dreams this book may also serve as an indirect introduction to an understanding of psychology as a "psychology with soul" (Jung) or as the discipline of interiority.

Wolfgang Giegerich is a Jungian analyst, now living in Berlin, and the author of numerous books, among them *What is Soul?* and *Neurosis: The Logic of a Metaphysical Illness.* His most recent works are *The Historical Emergence of the I* and *What Are the Factors That Heal?*

Working With Dreams

Initiation into the Soul's Speaking
About Itself

Wolfgang Giegerich

Routledge
Taylor & Francis Group
LONDON AND NEW YORK

First published 2021
by Routledge
2 Park Square, Milton Park, Abingdon, Oxon OX14 4RN

and by Routledge
52 Vanderbilt Avenue, New York, NY 10017

Routledge is an imprint of the Taylor & Francis Group, an informa business

© 2021 Wolfgang Giegerich

British Library Cataloguing-in-Publication Data
A catalogue record for this book is available from the British Library

Library of Congress Cataloging-in-Publication Data
A catalog record has been requested for this book

ISBN: 978-0-367-52510-1 (hbk)
ISBN: 978-0-367-52513-2 (pbk)
ISBN: 978-1-003-05824-3 (ebk)

Typeset in Times
by Newgen Publishing, UK

Contents

Sources and abbreviations

For frequently cited sources, the following abbreviations have been used:

CW: Jung, C. G., *Collected Works.* 20 vols. Ed. Herbert Read, Michael Fordham, Gerhard Adler, and William McGuire. Trans. R. F. C. Hull. Princeton: Princeton University Press, 1957–1979. Cited by volume and, unless otherwise noted, by paragraph number.

GW: Jung, C. G., *Gesammelte Werke*, 20 vols., various editors, Olten and Freiburg im Breisgau: Walter-Verlag, 1971–1983. Cited by volume and, unless otherwise noted, by paragraph number.

Letters: Jung, C. G., *Letters.* 2 vols. Ed. Gerhard Adler. Bollingen Series XCV: 2. Princeton: Princeton University Press, 1975.

MDR: Jung, C. G., *Memories, Dreams, Reflections.* Rev. ed., Ed. Aniela Jaffé. Trans. Richard and Clara Winston. New York: Vintage Books, 1989. Cited by page number.

Erinn.: Erinnerungen, Träume, Gedanken von C.G. Jung, ed. by Aniela Jaffé, Zürich and Stuttgart (Rascher) 1967.

CEP: Giegerich, W., *Collected English Papers*, 6 vols. New Orleans, LA (Spring Journal Books), 2006 ff., now London and New York (Routledge) 2020.

Transl. modif.: Appearing at the end of a citation, this indicates that I modified the particular quotation from the *Collected Works* in order to bring the English translation a bit closer to the wording and spirit of Jung's original German text.

Introduction

It is clear from the title of this book, *Working with Dreams*, that its focus is on the practical aspects of dream interpretation. It is, first of all, addressed to analysts who in their psychotherapeutic sessions with patients or analysands are confronted with their dreams and have to work with them. Writing from within the Jungian tradition of psychology, I will not offer a general theory of dreams, what they are, *ontology* and why and how they come about. I will not try to explain them, be it from the "psychic apparatus," from a person's biography or daily-life experience, from the brain and the newest neurophysiological findings, not from archetypes, let alone as the voice of God or angels. I am only concerned with the *phenomenon* "dream" *phenomenology* itself as it actually appears in human experience (especially in the context of psychotherapeutic processes) and our approach to it.

As I pointed out, the focus of *Working with dreams* is decidedly on practical aspects. But this immediately raises the question of what "practical" means in psychology. Other than science and technology, psychology cannot become practical in the sense of being solely intent upon the object, which means in our case that it cannot apply itself directly to dreams. It is constitutive for psychology that it must not forget *itself*, the psychologically thinking subjective mind, the consciousness that is doing the thinking. For this reason this book, despite being about the practice of dream interpretation, is not conceived as a practical help for the practitioner, a kind of "how-to" book of dream interpretation and is therefore not either full of case reports with dream examples or individual dream symbols, whose meaning is given. It cannot serve as a reference book on dream images. Instead, the main purpose of this book, as of any psychological study, is the training of the reader's psychological mind, the psychological preparation of the psychologist's, of our own, thinking, in this case our thinking about dreams. The central questions to be answered are: how do we have to view and approach dreams *if our access to dreams is supposed to be truly psychological?* This book is, one might say, one long meditation about the general principles of psychological dream interpretation.

The question of when our working with dreams is truly psychological and when not is crucial. If this book is concerned with the *phenomenon* "dream" and does not see dreams against the backdrop of a given overall (be it scientific or metaphysical[1]) theory, this can, of course, not mean that it and its approach to the phenomenon of dreams would be totally free of any theoretical background. On the contrary, I am writing from a decisive theoretical standpoint. The theoretical background of this book is that of a rigorous concept of psychology, more specifically, of a "psychology *with* soul" (C.G. Jung) or psychology as the discipline of interiority. The word psychology means literally "*lógos* (study, discipline, science) of the soul." But psychology, as it is conventionally understood today, has on principle given up the notion of soul (although the word "soul" may occasionally still be used tongue in cheek). This has explicitly been the case ever since Friedrich Albert Lange, who in his influential *Geschichte des Materialismus* (1866) decisively, and for serious reasons, demanded a "psychology without soul." Standard psychology is no longer the study of the soul and thus exists as a contradiction in terms. Its real topic can summarily be described as "the behavior of the (human) organism."

By contrast, *Working with Dreams* is committed to a psychology *with* soul. Saying this, of course, does not mean much by itself, since "soul" just as "interiority" are only words to which very different meanings and associations can be attached by different people. Within the space limits of this introduction it is not possible to provide an adequate explanation of what I mean by them and what accordingly the theoretical basis of this book is. I have presented such expositions of the foundation of a psychology with soul in several works; I mention here only two of them, *The Soul's Logical Life: Towards a Rigorous Notion of Psychology*[2] and *What Is Soul?*[3] To give here just a brief definition of what is meant does not make sense either. The problem is that it would be too abstract and raise more questions than it answers; in addition, it too would be open to a variety of understandings and possible misunderstandings. The reason for this difficulty is that a psychology *with* soul is too much of a foreign body within today's mainstream thinking (both in psychology and in the scientific world view prevailing today in general). To make clear what the "rigorous notion of psychology" proposed here means and involves would require our digging deeper and discussing numerous tacit prevailing presuppositions and prejudices.

That a definition and explanation of the theoretical background of this book cannot be provided here is not as bad as it may sound. It is not necessary at all to *first* have acquired a full comprehension of the theoretical stance that informs the discussions in this book because only *this* would enable one to understand the ideas it contains. It is also possible to turn this relation around and *first* read the book and *then*, in the course of and through reading it, acquire the understanding of the basic theoretical stance that informs its particular approach to dreams. Certainly, this book is about dreams, our working with dreams. But as such it is also "psychology *with* soul" *in action*, a concrete practical example of it. In fact, it would not be wrong to consider this book as a whole as an indirect introduction into this way of psychological thinking. If one is ready to follow the suggested reverse order, all one needs to do is to suspend, for the time being, the meaning of "psychology *with* soul" until what it means explains itself in the course of the discussion about how to work with dreams.

To make this suspension of the notion of "soul" easier, I nevertheless want to give two essential hints in advance. All metaphysical ideas of "soul," as they traditionally prevailed in theology, metaphysics, and popular religious thinking, must be excluded. This includes any substantiating thinking that might wish to posit "soul" as some kind of entity. My second hint refers to the "psychological difference," the terminological distinction between the "psyche" as part of the human organism or human personality on the one hand and "soul" on the other. Thinking in terms of soul is not thinking in terms of people, of individuals. Traditionally, the soul has been firmly attached to an individual, as his or her personal property. Although conventional modern psychology has given up the notion of soul, which in religion and metaphysics used to be thought of as each person's innermost personal possession and essence, it still, and even more emphatically, focuses on people, individuals, as the exclusive positive-factual substrate of psychic life. In the case of "psychology with soul" this attachment to people as substrate has to be cut, as deeply ingrained and hard to overcome as this prejudice is in ordinary modern consciousness. In order at the beginning to "suspend" one's knowing what "soul" means in psychology as the discipline of interiority, the two most important aspects to be observed are (1) that one desists from any (explicit or tacit) hypostatizing of it, and (2) keeps it free of any attachment to or subsumption under positive-factually existing people.

I mentioned that this book is written from within the tradition of Jungian psychology. This statement needs some further comment inasmuch as the question arises where one's place within this tradition is. The tradition of Jung's thought is not a fixed entity but is naturally itself subject to interpretation. Especially since Jung's work is such a rich and multifaceted body of thought, reaching from empirical association experiments to myth and archetypes, from the clinical treatment of schizophrenia and neuroses to the individuation process and to speculative thoughts about the development of the inner structure of the Godhead, from typology to synchronicity, it is apt to give rise to different "versions" of Jungian psychology, quite apart from the additional complication that each of these versions may again exist in a variety of forms depending on the different degrees of differentiation, depth, and intelligence of the minds that come up with or adhere to them.

What for my reading of Jung is essential is that I see in his work a definite development from the early to the late Jung.[4] By saying this I do not deny that there is, from early to late, a continuity in his interest in symbols, the mythic depth of life and the mysteries of the soul, and in the issue of meaning in general. All this refers to the content level. The development and discontinuity I have in mind is one on the level of the *form* of his psychological thinking. It is, above all, a shift from an initial person-based and science-based largely naturalistic thinking about the psyche of *people* (what goes on in them) and individual psychotherapy to a soul-based *objective* psychology, a *psychology* that deserves its name. In part, this new stance can be accounted for by his discovery of alchemy and by his absorbing and becoming deeply inspired by its Hermetic style of thinking. This shift allows us to speak of early Jung, by way of abbreviation, as pre-alchemy Jung and of mature Jung as alchemy-inspired Jung (much as we, *mutatis mutandis*, distinguish in philosophy between "precritical" Kant and "critical" Kant, the Kant after the "Critique of Pure Reason"). This is not only a change of specific views, ideas, teachings, but a much more fundamental shift in the general structure or logic underlying and informing particular views. It can be summarily described as a move away from a logic of substance, substrate, or subject to a logic of autonomous, "Archimedeanless" self-relation and self-expression as such, from positivity to absolute negativity (that is, to what takes place "in Mercurio" and not on the level of empirical fact), from exclusive focus on the semantic (symbols and archetypal contents) to awareness of syntax or logical form and logical transformation as form changes. The horizon and point of view of early Jung is adequately expressed in the title of his book *The Relations Between the Ego and the Unconscious* (now in *CW* 7). The standpoint is that of the ego, which keeps its "other" outside and vis-à-vis itself. Mature Jung shifted his standpoint to the soul.[5] The ego as the one side of the former "relations" simply drops out of this *clear-cut linear* relation so that the relation becomes circular, self-reflective, uroboric, the soul's relation to *itself*. Once late Jung could even exclaim: "To hell with the Ego-world!" (*Letters 2*, p. 532, to Charteris, 9 Jan. 1960). The emotional form of this momentary outburst must not mislead us to overlook the underlying fundamental and general *theoretical* shift in the orientation of his psychology.

Unfortunately, Jung himself did not systematically and explicitly work out this shift in his thinking. Nor did he follow it consistently by unambiguously revoking certain of his earlier positions in favor of his later ones.[6] "I can only formulate the thoughts the way they burst forth from within me. It is like a geyser. Those who come after me will have to get them into shape,"[7] he is reported to have said once. The fundamental theoretical shift is at work and expresses itself de facto in his later work, and also often enough comes out directly in occasional explicit dicta. He was aware of this radical change and deeply disappointed that his disciples were not able to follow him: "My later and more important work (as it seems to me) is still left untouched in its primordial obscurity" (*Letters 2*, p. 309, to Nelson, 17 June 1956), he lamented. During the last year of his life he wrote: "I had to understand, that I was unable to make people see, what I am after. I am practically alone ... I have failed in my foremost task ..."[8]

Our commitment to the psychological thinking that Jung's lifework was ultimately *heading for* must not be motivated by a wish to stay faithful to Jung as our authority. It is the other way around. The fact that in Jung's later alchemy-inspired insights psychology is for the first time trying to come home to itself is what gives Jung's late work its singular importance. Our sole authority is the rigorous *concept* of psychology. Everything Jung said must be measured by this concept.

Not everything in his work is of equal value. We always have to "test the spirits, whether they are of" true psychology.

What Jung had to say about the particular topic of this book, dreams and how to view them, is especially helpful for revealing the altered logic that permeates mature Jung's psychology where it is at its best. Just as I pointed out before that the following discussion about dreams can serve as an introduction to psychology as a "psychology *with* soul," so I can now add that it is also an indirect introduction to the psychological logic underlying the thinking of mature Jung.

First versions of the ideas contained in this book were, starting during the 1990s, severally presented in courses at various Jung-Institutes (Zürich, München, Stuttgart) and in a workshop at Sanno Institute (Tokyo) under the titles, "Working with Dreams" and "The Dream in Psychotherapy, Its Role and Significance." The former of the two early papers was published, in Japanese translation by Toshio Kawai, as one chapter in: W.G., *Shinwa to Ishiki*. Yungu Shinrigaku no Tenkai (Gīgerihhi Ronshū), vol. 3, Tokyo (Nihon Hyôron-sha) 2001. Forty years of my own practice as psychoanalyst, my work as supervisor with colleagues and training candidates, and numerous regular dream seminars or workshops provided me with an opportunity to work with dreams in the spirit described in this book and also to test, expand, and differentiate the earlier forms of my ideas about dream interpretation. The transcript of one recorded 16-hour seminar with Kyoto University doctoral candidates in psychotherapy documenting my style of working with dreams was published as a book in Japanese translation: *Gīgerihhi yume seminā* (= *Giegerich Dream Seminar*), ed. by Toshio Kawai and Yasuhiro Tanaka and with a preface and notes by Toshio Kawai, Osaka (Sogen-sha Publisher) 2013.

What induced me to look again at all my collected material about dreams and to finally undertake the work of actually writing this book was above all the lively interest in and detailed questions about the theory of working with dreams that came from the participants of a study group of psychotherapists, mostly connected with Sophia University (Tokyo), under the competent guidance of Prof. Tsuyoshi Inomata, when they came to me for several dream seminars during the last few years. The present book is an attempt to combine into a somewhat coherent form the two different first papers mentioned, numerous individual notes and additions collected over the years, and some new fundamental reflections about dreams and working with dreams.

Notes

1. With the "or" between "scientific" and "metaphysical" I accommodate the conventional idea that there is a fundamental difference between science and metaphysics. In reality, however, the scientific stance is merely one, the modern form of metaphysic.
2. Frankfurt am Main (Peter Lang) 1998, 5th edition 2020.

3. New Orleans, LA (Spring Journal Books) 2012, now London and New York (Routledge) 2020.
4. James Hillman also emphasized this change.
5. Cf. "If I shift my concept of reality to the psyche where alone it truly belongs ..." (*CW* 8 § 861, transl. modif.).
6. This is where my above analogy to the shift in Kant no longer works. Kant was absolutely clear and consistent about *his* shift.
7. Aniela Jaffé, *Der Mythus vom Sinn im Werk von C.G. Jung*, Zürich and Stuttgart (Rascher) 1967, p. 10, my translation.
8. Letter to Eugene Rolfe, November 13, 1960, quoted from Sonu Shamdasani, *Jung and the Making of Modern Psychology*, Cambridge (Cambridge University Press) 2003, p. 351. As some evidence for the justification of Jung's assessment we can consider the profession of faith by Verena Kast, a popular Jungian analyst and former President of the IAAP as well as of the Curatorium of the Jung-Institute Zürich. It is certainly only one person's statement, but it for once explicitly reveals a basic tenet that tacitly underlies the general outlook of many Jungians. Kast said: "I think that we are based in emotions because we are like animals as we are also mammals. Okay it is a hypothesis but out of this is coming our relation to the world. This is why I think early developmental psychology is important because it is the relation to the world and the body. I think in relation with the world there is an emergence of feelings and connected with these feeling is imagination, and out of this imagination we create the whole spiritual world. I know that other people say that it has to come from top down; I think it comes from bottom up" (in: Ann Casement, "Interview with Verena Kast," in: *The IAAP Newsletter.* Issue #32, 2019, pp. 265–282, here p. 272). This reductive view is, no doubt, a *possible* hypothesis and in fact nowadays the most popular one in the scientific world. But quite apart from the question whether this hypothesis is truly capable of explaining what it claims to be able to explain, it is obvious that it is a slap in the face—the reversal into the opposite—of what Jung personally stood for and, which is more important, of what is the *articulus stantis et cadentis* of Jungian psychology. One just needs to contrast Kast's naturalistic stance with *CW* 4 § 780, to cite a still relatively early example, or with Jung's conviction, expressed late in his life, that humans are "more than autochthonous *animalia* sprung from the earth" (*MDR* p. 333). Or think of Jung's concise dictum: "The spirit may legitimately claim the *patria potestas* over the soul" (*CW* 9i § 32).

Part I

What is a dream?

There have been many theories about the dream and dreaming, such as the dream as the "protector of sleep," the dream as an attempt to process the experiences of the previous day, the dream as a means to erase unnecessary information received during the previous day, the dream as wish-fulfillment, the dream as a compensation to the ego attitude, the dream as a source of religious experience, etc. We leave them all behind in order to turn to the *phenomenon* of the dream, that is, to the dream as it shows itself to people, above all in psychotherapy.

So, I do not ask the question, "What *is* the dream?" at all, inasmuch as this would be a biological, metaphysical, or philosophical question within a, let us say, "scientific" fantasy. I do not have what the Freudians call a "metapsychology." Thus, I also do not try to raise and answer the questions where dreams come from, what their true nature is, or what their meaning and purpose is. All this would be speculative. Instead my question is: how do I have *to view* dreams *if* I want to work with them successfully in a truly *psychologically* minded therapy? With Jung I can say: "I have no theory about dreams, I do not know how dreams arise" (*CW* 16 § 86) and "I take the dream for what it is" (*CW* 11 § 41, Jung italicized this whole sentence).

The dream as a conscious phenomenon: The dream as text

Here we already run into a difficulty. Modern sleep research has found an objective physiological correlate to dreams and comes up with the idea that everybody dreams several times every night and that even higher animals dream. Already Wittgenstein pondered the question (*Philosophical Investigations*, Part 2, VII) whether the dream really happens during sleep or is not much rather a memory phenomenon of the awakened person. This question need not bother us. For us *psycho*therapists the physiological side and what happened during sleep is totally irrelevant. We have to restrict our notion of the dream to the *conscious* memory of dream *experiences*. Only the *remembered* dream, and this means the story, the narrative, the images, sensations and feelings that make it up, ultimately the "text" (together, of course, with the emotional aspect of the experience) is what counts as dreams for us.

When we speak of the dream as a content of memory, the word "text" is, of course, used figuratively. But in psychotherapy it is necessary to see the importance of giving the remembered dream also the form of a written text in the literal sense. That one has to write down one's dreams is a firm conviction in the Jungian tradition of psychotherapy. The first reason is that memory is unreliable because it is not just a kind of archive, but often also productive, inventive, creating "false" memories. We even have a major example of a distorting dream memory in Jung himself. I am referring to the dream Jung had about an elderly man in the uniform of an Austrian customs official and the apparition of a crusader in a modern Italian city. It is printed in *MDR* pp. 163–165 in Aniela Jaffé's version of it, but was first recorded around 1911 or 1912 in Jung's *Black Books*, then related by Jung in his 1925 *Analytical Psychology* Seminar and then again much later told by him in the dictated notes that were to serve as the basis for *MDR*. Each of these versions is different in some, sometimes in crucial aspects.[1] As time passes and one's mood changes, as new experiences overlay what happened before, and as different issues become important, certain elements of the dream may be remembered differently from how they were remembered upon waking from the dream. Or, owing to the poetic inclination of memory, dream elements may be added, details embroidered. By contrast, thanks to the interests of the ego to maintain its habitual attitude, other elements may, quite in contrast to the original form of the dream, become assimilated to or identified with things or events known from daily life and not only lose their unique specificity and otherness, but also become banalized. The worst case is, of course, that the dream gets forgotten altogether (or should it, perhaps, be that "false memory" is, in truth, the worst case, still worse than the disappearance from memory altogether?). For all these reasons, the written dream text, recorded promptly after waking up, gives us a *document* that can serve as witness, witness even against memory itself (because the new memory replaces the original memory; it does not appear *as* a second, new memory beside it).

The second reason for writing dreams down is that it is psychologically important that the dream is not kept in the non-committal vagueness of memory, where it exists much like clouds appear in the sky that may continuously change their form. As long as the dream remains only in memory, we can tell it with these or those words on the spur of the moment, and if we tell it to two or three people from memory, the words we use and even the sequence of some of the dream events will be different each time. We also are still free to soften or alter or even conveniently "forget" embarrassing details in our presentation, indeed even in how *we* remember it. (I am not thinking here so much of deliberate changes or suppressions. What I have mainly in mind is unintentional and unwitting alterations.) By contrast, it is the duty of consciousness to take responsibility for the dreams by trying as best as it can to *capture*, as early as possible, the content of dreams in precise and determinate verbal articulation. Consciousness needs to wrestle with the dream memory and seek to find the best, most accurate linguistic expression, and not to iron out possible dream ambiguities and translate misty images occurring in it into rational clarity, but, conversely, in order to express with precision (with the "exactness of fantasy," Goethe) even the possible ambiguity and haziness of dream apparitions. In this way the dream becomes a real text, and only then has the dream become fully real: it has been wrested from the subjectivity and license of the ego-personality and become objectified. The dream having become a written text is now an objective reality, a "fact" that is no longer in my, the dreamer's, power. Instead, I am confronted with it, objectively vis-à-vis, and have to take it the way it is. This transposition from the subjectivity of the dream to its objectivity is psychologically of crucial importance.

A third reason why dreams should be written down by the dreamer is that this process of writing is in itself therapeutic. One's struggling to express the dream accurately in words and to find the best words is work, and this work is a form of devotion to this soul product and thus to the soul itself. Even the mechanical act of writing the dream down in a clean copy is such an act of dedication. In both ways, in the mental and in the mechanical activity, we also already get involved with the dream, even if only in an immediate, pre-interpretative way. On a low, simple level we already establish an inner connection between ourselves and the dream. This low level of practical contact must not be depreciated psychologically. Just as in therapy sessions it is not only the mental content of the interpretations that has a therapeutic effect, but also the atmosphere, the averbal unspoken contact between the two personalities in their realness, so the simple involvement with the dream through the mechanical act of writing, on the one hand, and the still somewhat external work at definite linguistic expression on the other, are helpful.

After these comments about the dream as "text," I repeat that psychology has to be interested only in the dream as conscious phenomenon. The fact that one may conclude from REM phases in sleep that there must have been a dream is depth-psychologically uninteresting and falls outside of the domain of psychology. Physiological observations may lead to the scientific *fantasy* or *construct* "dream," that is, to the conclusion that there must have been a dream. To use the same word for "dream" as an inference from physiological facts and "dream" as an actual psychological *phenomenon* is an equivocation. The one is a mere label assigned from outside to physiological occurrences, the other is "the real thing" experienced from within with its concrete content and emotional impact. It is much the same difference as between a movie poster and having watched the movie in a cinema. For us, only the *conscious* dream is what we mean by "dream."

This may sound paradoxical, because conventionally we are used to connecting the dream with the unconscious. Above all, Jung insisted that the dream is "a spontaneous product of the unconscious," that dreams "are direct productions of the unconscious."[2] But quite apart from the fact that we would desert the phenomenology of the dream (and even psychology as such) and slip back to the *scientific* issues, rejected above, of what the dream *is* and where it comes from, "the unconscious" as a producer, agent, or subject is itself only a fiction or construct. That we all are, to a large extent, unconscious goes without saying. *This* word "unconscious" is an adjective, the description of a possible condition of *consciousness*, not the hypostasis of a hidden agent or realm *behind* the dream as phenomenon and of it as the producer of dreams. "The unconscious" is actually the reification and positivization of our not being aware of many things. It is clear that all dreams that become the subject of therapy or of books on dreams are conscious material from the outset, not unconscious material. "A dream" is always the *remembered* dream experience and as such obviously a content of consciousness. Even the dream experience itself, although it happened during sleep, if we disregard Wittgenstein's doubt, may not be totally unconscious, but in some way conscious. Very often it is an extremely vivid experience, such as in the case of nightmares from which we suddenly awake bathed in sweat. Dreams exist only for the waking mind and happen to consciousness, primarily, however, to a sleeping one. If the dream does not become an experience, it is merely a physiological event, and as such not a subject of psychology. But if it is an experience, *it is also conscious*. The dream is proof of the strange fact that even the sleeping mind can have in a certain sense conscious experiences.

Generally speaking, the so-called "psychology of the unconscious" is not about the unconscious, but about experiences of the conscious mind!

That the reification of "the unconscious" as the producer of dreams was so dear to Jung is due to his passionate wish to construe psychology as a natural science in the modern, mainly nineteenth century sense of science, and to the naturalistic bias of his early stance, that despite his later, completely different insights, he never explicitly revoked. "The unconscious is a purely natural process ..." (*GW* 7 § 386, my transl.; the *CW* translation is misleading). Likewise, "The dream is a natural occurrence, ... It seems to be a natural product ..." (*CW* 11 § 41). Early Jung's naturalistic view of dreams must, of course, in part be seen as a reaction to Freud's theory that the dream is a mere façade, which for Jung meant that one would attribute to the dream a "possible cunning" or a "tendency to deceive" (*ibid.*). The dream as "a natural occurrence," therefore, simply meant that we cannot "assume that a dream is something other than it appears to be" (*ibid.*). Harking back to Jung's dictum that the dream is "a spontaneous product of the unconscious," we just need to delete "of the unconscious" from it to accept it wholeheartedly. Dreams appear in consciousness spontaneously. They are not of the waking mind's making. But does that make them *natural* occurrences," products of *nature*? Products comparable to hormones, semiochemicals, or excretions of the body?

It is not as simple as that. Dreams, as soon as they become conscious, have already been formed and filled out by consciousness.[3] Even Jung himself felt it

> necessary to point out once more that archetypes are not determined as regards their content, but only as regards their form and then only to a very limited degree. A primordial image is determined as to its content only when

it has become conscious and is therefore *filled out with the material of con-scious experience.*

(*CW* 9i § 155, my italics)

I need to go even one step further and claim that already the truly unconscious dream process occurs within a cultural context and is informed by it. In other words, it does not represent a *direct* archetypal experience, or rather, an arche-typal experience is in itself also a culturally formed one and is thus not an imme-diate manifestation of "pure nature." The soul is *Geist* and essentially linguistic. *Geist* and language are what they are through their reflective distance to "nature," through their having "pushed off" from it, which means that the dream as some-thing produced by "the soul" or *Geist* is not a purely natural process. It starts out as in itself always already *reflected*. However, Jung's point that the dream is not trying to disguise or deceive but *is* what it *appears* to be and nothing else is well taken. Yet it amounts to a confounding of two different issues and categories to call it a purely *natural* product.

In a paper "On the Nature of Dreams" Jung begins his discussion of dreams with the sentence: "The dream is a fragment of *involuntary* psy-chic activity, just conscious enough to be reproducible in the waking state." (*CW* 8 § 532, emphasis added according to the German original). This is prob-ably an accurate statement, but it is one that transgresses the limits of psychology. Instead of strictly staying with the phenomenon "dream," Jung *explains* its coming about, taking recourse to the idea of a "psychic activity" *behind* the dream-as-real-phenomenon, to an assumed underlying substrate or cause. But what is alleged to be behind the dream is not an empirically observed reality. It is merely a specula-tive theoretical construct, as plausible as it may be. As psychologists we need to stick to the phenomenal, experiential level. Then we can say:

When I wake up, I become aware: "Oh, I had a dream." I *had*! I become con-scious of it *as* something bygone. So, the paradoxical thing about the dream is that it only *comes into being* when it is already over, when we are already out of it. It only *is* when it is no more. It *exists* only in the perfect tense; it *is* only as the *memory* of itself. It is from the outset reflected. It has the departure from imme-diacy (immediate experience) within itself. *Within* the *real phenomenon* of the dream we have always already awakened from it. It *is* what we "tell" ourselves in an internal conversation, what we write down in our dream diary and what we report concerning it to our analyst or a friend or spouse. The fact that it only comes into being when it is already over, is *not* a kind of mishap, an unfortunate fate that befell it. Rather, it is its very nature! Its already being over is its own *internal* characteristic. It follows from this that, if we want to work psychologically with dreams, we must not literalize this characteristic, that is, pluck the "pastness" out from the dream phenomenon and project it into the literal past as an empirically real event preceding the "remembered" dream, the said "psychic activity."

The dream thus has a complex, complicated structure. As the memory of itself, it refers within itself to something that it is not immediately and that remains out

Exists
* *only*
as a
memory of
itself
comes into
being after
its existence

of reach for it. Within itself it refers to an experience that it has outside of itself. In this sense one could say that it is like other reports or memories: "Today on my way to work I missed the bus." "I had a fight with my colleague." "I fell." "There was the most beautiful sunrise today." The dream as a narrative talks about something that I really experienced. On this count there is no difference between dream experiences and other experiences in so-called real life.

The dream as the memory of a dream experience *comes* with the clear sense and knowledge that the dream experience did not happen "in reality," that is, that it is "only" a dream. Probably everyone who once awakened from a nightmare knows the relief of the insight: "Oh, it was only a dream!" In this sense, remembered dreams are fundamentally different from my thinking back of my experience today on my way to work or of the toothache that pained me yesterday so terribly. There is a difference in category that is part of the immediate phenomenology of the dream.

Ontological rupture

Normally we think that the difference between "reality" and "*only* a dream" is that the dream is merely a fiction of the mind and not real and that only normal "day" experiences are real. However, this interpretation is not borne out by the phenomenology of the dream. Just take an extreme example, the anxiety dream or the nightmare. It is utterly real, so real that you maybe awaken from it wet from sweat with a terrible heartbeat and it takes you a while to realize that the dream reality is over. Then, of course, one tends to say: "Thank God, this was *only* a dream and not reality." But this is not correct. It was absolutely *real*. No doubt about it. The dream is not less real than so-called real experience.

According to what we discussed in the previous chapter, the experienced utter reality and the physiological phenomena of being wet from sweat or having a terrible heartbeat are for us part of the dream as conscious phenomenon. The fear that comes with a nightmare, too, exists for us in memory. What we are concerned with in this chapter is the realness that is an internal moment or ingredient of the dream as remembered in the waking state, the dream as "text."

We can make this clear to ourselves by contrasting the dream experience with a novel or movie. The movie may be extremely convincing and thrilling; we may also have intense emotions, even real fear. Nevertheless, while we watch the movie and experience its powerful thrill, we know that it is fiction. This is why we voluntarily watch and enjoy thrillers. Here it is correct to say: it is *only* a movie. We know that the experienced realness of the movie action and situation is *simulated* real experience. So, in a way, it has the character of being real, but *this very reality character* is only simulated, and known to be simulated. The realness of the dream experience, by contrast, is not experienced as simulated. It is unambiguously real. There is not a duplicity of two realities as in the movie experience, where I am (1) emotionally fully *in* the dangerous movie action and (2) simultaneously comfortably sitting in the movie house where the knowledge of my sitting in the movie house is never lost, even if it may become merely sub-liminal. The dream reality, by contrast, is absolute because it is total. When and while being in the dream, this is *the* reality, *the* world. There is no other world, no sense of an alternative. The dream reality is brutally real, so real that it is precisely *not a dream while* it is being experienced (which is why I had to point out earlier that the dream qua dream only comes into being when it is over). While I had the dream last night of a dog chasing me, I was *really* being chased by a dog. I was *really* panic-stricken. The phenomenon of the dream experience is quite clear: It was not fictional.

So there is no difference as to the reality aspect between dreaming of a canyon and standing in reality in a canyon. And yet, there is the fundamental difference I mentioned. The question is what the nature of this difference is, if it is not that between the real and the fictional.

The answer has to be: the difference is one that falls into the very notion of reality itself, that is to say, "reality" falls apart into two distinct, separate realities. Both are equally real, despite the fact that they exclude each other. Our reflection upon the nature of the dream imposes on us the experience of an *ontological rupture*, as it were. And on the basis of this insight we can understand the function of the wish to interpret the dream as fictional in contrast to reality. The recourse to the notion of fiction serves the purpose of defense, namely the defense of the unbroken unity of the notion of reality. The notion of reality is supposed to be prevented from falling apart into two. The unity of our ontology is supposed to be rescued. This rescue is successful because by calling the dream a fiction or fantasy, it does not threaten the monism of our sense of reality. It is "only a dream." As a *phenomenon*, the dream is of course real, we say, but *what happens in the dream* is not real, but fictional, imaginary.

It is like with the movie. It is a real fact that now this movie is shown on the screen in the movie house, but the action in the movie is not real. Even though I am emotionally extremely involved and affected by the action of the movie, which gives the action a certain sense of reality, this reality is nevertheless an (a priori and fundamentally) *sublated* reality, a "canned," "bottled," or "bracketed" reality. This is mirrored in the subject viewing the movie. Externally, he or she stays comfortably in their seat, and the effect of the sense of reality of the movie action is as mere *Erleben* (felt experience) relegated to, and locked in, the safely encapsulated interior of the viewer. It is psychologized. The vampires in a horror movie threaten us only in a segregated inner space of free play, but do not affect the world all around us and therefore also not ourselves (our very identity) to the extent that we are living in this world. It is a merely *emotional* threat to our existence experienced as thrill, not a *logical, psychological* threat to our identity. So the distinction between fiction and reality works as a rescue of the monistic notion of reality by temporarily segregating off, within the whole realm of the real, a small fenced-in space within which the real has been temporarily suspended and the simulated reality within this fenced-in space does not undermine the basic sense—the prevailing logic—of reality.

The dream, however, does not occur within such a fenced-in space. The dream, for as long as it lasts, is the real world, the one and only reality, without the type of knowledge that the movie-goer has that all around the movie action there is real reality. When I am in the dream, I am not aware that I "only dream" while in reality lying safely in my bed asleep. The dream reality is total, with nothing outside itself. Whereas I as dreamer am middle-aged and safely in my bed, I as dream-I am really the high-school student frightened to fail in an exam, or am really at the edge of a cliff fearing to lose my footing, or really threatened by a murderer.

The falling apart of reality into two distinct realities is possible because the "I" that experienced the dream reality and the "I" that in the waking state remembers the dream is felt and known to be one and the same. I know that it is I who both experienced the dream last night and remember it now, while going about my daily business. It was really I, the same I as now, who fell down a cliff in my dream; in fact, this was one of the most vivid experiences I ever had. And in this dream I was the total "I," not a partial one, nor an optional or fictional one. It was the real me, hook, line and sinker. I experienced the dream situation with my whole being, without reserve or alternative. The unity of the "I" is the condition of the possibility of the ontological rupture. For if there were two distinct "I's" the monistic unity of reality would again not be threatened, inasmuch as each reality could be attributed to another "I." This would mean that in each case there would only be one self-consistent reality. It would be like the fact that there are many individuals or groups each with different religions or world views, each with different biographies and experiences in the world, the one, for example, having spent four years as a soldier in a war whereas the other spent the same four years as a college student, etc. The difference would not be ontological, but merely semantic.[4]

In the movie experience, there is not this identity of the "I" that we found with respect to the dream experience. The "I" that is absorbed by the movie action is a different one from the "I" that sits in the movie house and afterwards leaves the movie house. The one is, as it were, a *sublated*, only partial, fictional "I," *released* from the real reality to which it belongs and therefore free to let itself be "playfully" absorbed, as I said, by the movie action; the other one is the "I" that knows that he or she lives in such and such a house, has a family, works in such and such a profession and will have to go to work again tomorrow morning. This distinction or the sectioning off of a partial "I" within the total, surrounding "I" prevents the rupture of the sense of reality.

Our result so far is that we have two distinct realities of equal standing, but different kind. We now have to ask what this difference in kind is. With a distinction of the Romantics, we could call the one reality the "night world" and the other one the "day world." But these imaginal and phenomenal terms do not tell us much about the ontological difference. A statement by the Greek philosopher Heraclitus is more helpful: "Those who are in the waking state have one single common world, (but in sleep each person turns away from it and to his own private one)" [Fragment B 89 Diels-Kranz]. In the day world we have indeed a common world, which also implies the absolute unity of "world." Despite the fact that each person has his or her utterly individual, personal *experiences* of the world and that we each experience different semantic parts of the world and world events, we know that we have this world itself and as a whole in common. My subjective experience, in waking life, of the moon, of a landscape, of a city does not imply that this is only my personal moon, etc. No, I know that it is *the* moon, the moon for everybody, although at this moment I am perhaps the only one who looks at it from this particular spot. Even if I were the only person to witness a singular, absolutely extraordinary natural event in a lonely place on the earth, this event would, nevertheless, be known by me to be an integral part of reality (i.e., our common reality: *objective* reality). That I am the only witness of the event is contingent.

Siblings may have quite different memory images of their parents, at times perhaps so different that they are incompatible. Nevertheless, these different versions of Mom and Dad are *known* to be images *of* one and the same real father, one and the same real mother. Each image claims to be the right, the true picture. The one son contradicts the other: "but Dad wasn't like that at all."

By contrast, the moon in my dream is exclusively my own moon. Nobody else could possibly see *this* moon. The moon that other people may dream about is again exclusively their own moon. This is why it would not occur to anybody to contradict a dreamer saying: "but the moon is not like this at all, it is in truth very different" or "what you purport to have seen in your dream, cannot possibly be that way. You must have got it wrong." The reason for this liberality is that everyone a priori acknowledges that each person has his or her own dream world for which there is no objective measure.

We even have to go a step further: The moon that I experienced in this one dream is singular. Even I myself as dreamer cannot experience the same moon again in another dream. All that is thinkable is that a later dream merely cites, as it were, an image from an earlier dream. Each dream, so we must conclude, origin-ally *creates* its own world, its own self-contained reality.[5] My father that appears in my dream is always this one singular "my father" of this one dream. If I have many dreams in which my father appears, each one has its own "my father."

This means that while before I spoke of the falling apart of the notion of reality into two, we now have to realize that the dream reality exists only as a plural that corresponds to the plural number of dreams. The dream reality has the *form* of eachness and singularity. Each dream has or creates its own reality and is as such self-enclosed. There is no transition from one dream this night to a dream tomorrow. As far as the "ontology" of reality is concerned, each dream starts out from zero. Neither the elements in the dreams of all people nor even the elements in the dreams of one single individual are part of one reality.

In the waking state this is totally different. My father, that I experienced as a child or in this or that situation, is the same as the one I experienced on so many other occasions in later years, although my father may, of course, have changed considerably over years and behaved differently in different situations, and I may also have viewed him quite differently. And the same is true for all other people who see my father. He is known to be one identical being in one and the same world for all of us. So every experience in waking life is one "piece" of the one common world, the ontologically unitary and continuous reality.

In this common world there are natural unshakeable laws whose overstepping is unthinkable. I know, and everybody knows, that a human being cannot fly (without technical aid). But in dreams it may well be that he can fly, just as it may also be that he cannot. What is possible and what not is freely determined in each dream, whereas in the common world so-called natural laws rule, through which we all are bound and know ourselves to be bound.

Jung was aware that dreams are isolated elements in the life of consciousness, although he did not express this insight in terms of what I called the ontological rupture and the question of the one unitary world common to all. He only expressed it in experiential terms. He says,

ontological rupture – being

> The dream is a psychic product which in contrast to other contents of consciousness, with respect to form and meaning, apparently is not part of the continuity of the development of the contents of consciousness. At any rate, the dream usually does not appear as an integral element of conscious psychic life, but as a more extraneous, seemingly accidental experience.
>
> (*GW* 8 § 443, my transl., the transl. in *CW* is misleading)

He speaks there of the "exceptional status of the dream," which is due to the fact that "it does not arise, like other contents of consciousness, from any clearly discernable, logical and emotional continuity of experience [*Erleben*] …" So, Jung is aware of the discontinuity or disruption of the flow of conscious life that the appearance of a dream amounts to. The dream, as it were, intrudes as an alien element into the continuity of consciousness. All we need to add is the even more important, more serious ontological or logical aspect.

alien element →

Precisely when we wake up from an anxiety dream and feel "Thank God, this was only a dream!" we confirm the ontological rupture, the fact that the reality experienced in the dream is not a part of that reality which is the reality in which we are in our waking state and which *in this waking state* is known by us also to have been the uninterrupted reality in which the sleeping dreamer was while having his dream. So, it is as if the dreaming consciousness had been transported into another world, another reality, *while* the physical body stayed completely unconsciously in ordinary reality.

One important consequence of our discussion so far is that with our phenomenological approach we do not need the construct of "the unconscious" here (i.e., we do not say that the dream is the *via regia* to "the unconscious" in ourselves). No, the dream is a way that takes us ontologically or logically into another *world*, another *reality*.

Nor do we need the idea of the "collective unconscious" (Jung) as a source. The dream is not the *via regia* to the unconscious, be it a personal or a collective one.

There is no such thing as "the unconscious" as a given, existing place to which the dream as a *via regia* could and would lead. It is the other way around: this *topos* ("the unconscious") is first produced, erected, bit by bit fabricated and further elaborated, in and through one's working upon the interpretation of all the dreams during analysis, one after the other, and through one's bringing in all kinds of associations, etc. It is a true "fiction," construct, and as such not an origin (even if it is imagined as such by the psychologists), but a result, an artifact. This is so because "the unconscious" is a fantasy, an idea in the mind, not a fact or reality in the natural world. The work of analysis is the project of building up and making out such fantasies. The fact that the unconscious is imagined as, and alleged to be, a hypothetical origin does not alter its real nature as purposely produced and elaborated fantasy, a work of fiction.

My speaking of an ontological rupture should not mislead us to confuse the entire question of "private dream world" versus "the common world in waking life" discussed here with a *metaphysical* issue. It should not induce us to speculate about questions such as whether it is not perhaps even our waking life, our common reality, that is nothing but a dream (Chuang-tze), and how we could *know* that it is not merely a dream, but truly real. My concern in this chapter on the ontological rupture is strictly phenomenological. It is the analysis or comparison between the respective *internal* "ontologies" of dream and objective reality, how they themselves determine themselves and what distinguishes them. As psychologist I am, by contrast, not at all concerned with any wish to prove (or disprove) that the common world indeed is *the true* world...

The dream as interpretation

So far we have already learned that the reality that is experienced in dreams is private in contrast to the common reality of the waking mind. But this is not all we can say about its nature. Another essential difference is that whereas the components of the unitary and continuous day world have the nature of facts, real entities or events, the components of the night world or dream world are "packages" of *meaning*. Ultimately, the dream is therefore a linguistic reality, it is *sprachlich*, which here does not mean that it consists of sentences (which, as dream experience and as the dream in memory, it usually does not) but that the nature or logic of this reality is a linguistic one. "Facts" are, by definition, essentially meaning-less in the sense of in themselves not signifying anything; they simply exist; it is not their inherent nature to have a meaning the way it is the very point of the words of language to *mean* something. Facts are nothing but the established (or establishable) "that" of an occurrence, state, or thing. And the dream events are essentially not facts.

For Jung it was most important to stress that the dream was pure nature. In a first sense of this tenet of his, the point was to contradict Freud's view of the dream as an essentially distorted representation of its meaning. Freud distinguished between the manifest dream and the latent dream. The manifest dream was the result of a psychic tendency to disguise and censor the wish that was actually to be expressed in the dream. This was not acceptable to Jung. The dream as nature was for Jung essentially innocent, an unadulterated self-manifestation.

> The "manifest" dream-picture is the dream itself and contains the whole meaning of the dream. When I find sugar in the urine, it is sugar and not just a façade for albumen. What Freud calls the "dream-façade" is the dream's obscurity, and this is really only a projection of our own lack of understanding.
>
> (*CW* 16 § 319)

"The dream is a natural occurrence, and there is no earthly reason why we should assume that it is a crafty device to lead us astray" (*CW* 11 § 41). Critically, we can say that, as his example of sugar in the urine shows, there is a certain naturalistic thinking at work in these ideas of Jung's. Apart from serving the purpose of rejecting Freud's attempt to locate the actual dream meaning *behind* the façade of the manifest dream and of insisting that the manifest *is* in itself the true meaning, and, furthermore, that it is indeed the *best* way the dream thought could be expressed, Jung also wanted to have the dream understood as a natural product, a fact of nature.

This is highly problematic. Before, I said that the dream is linguistic, *is* meaning, and I contrasted "meaning" with the notion of "fact." Sugar in the urine means, of course, something to the doctor, but in itself it is not "meaning"—it does not intend to *tell* the doctor something, to inform or warn him of a problematic condition. It simply *is*. It is just a physical reality, a self-contained and *in itself* mute fact. That it has a meaning for us is the mind's productive addition. But the dream is not a piece of nature in this sense, not just a physical fact. Rather, it is in itself an expression of some meaning. Instead of merely, like sugar in the urine, being a kind of clue, indication, or sign of some prevailing condition and as such only *having* a "meaning" for those who know how to draw the right inferences from it and having it only for them subjectively, it *is* meaning—objectively and all by itself (regardless of whether there is anybody who in fact understands it or not), because it is its own innermost structure to *convey* or *express* something. It is the same as with prehistorical drawings or inscriptions. We may not be able to decipher them, to understand their meaning. We, nevertheless, know that other than natural scratches or marks in rocks such as those made by the movement of glaciers during the ice age, they are phenomena *of* meaning, having in themselves a meaning structure. Similarly, we may be absolutely bewildered by a dream and may not have the least idea of what it could possibly mean, but it is clear to us from the beginning that it has meaning quality, tells a story, or presents an image (or images). In this sense the dream is not a simple physical happening, not innocent nature in the still rather positivistic sense that Jung often implies. No, it has the higher complexity of an "about"-structure. As such it *has logos-nature*, is from the outset in itself *reflected* (having logically pushed off from simple nature or physical fact) and ipso facto is not an *immediate* reality. It does not come from the body, the human organism, but from the human mind, the soul. It is not psychic, but psychological. So while not siding with Freud's idea of a purposeful disguise and distortion, I cannot accept Jung's innocent naturalistic view of the dream either.

The reality that we call dream is not the literal dream, not the true, original dream. The full reality of the dream is always a relation, it is the actual dream events as described in the dream text *and* how this dream is experienced, remembered, and narrated by the dreamer, and how it is viewed or read by the interpreter. This "and" is the full reality, and the "actual dream" (the "pure original dream" and its objectivity) is a fiction that is only legitimate and even necessary when it is understood to be a sublated *moment within* the larger concept of the dream. We never start with the clean, pure original. And we do not have to strive for the original as the "real" truth either. We have to work with the dream text *as it stands*. We can never get back to the "true" origin, and so we should not even toy with such an idea. We always begin in the *middle*. Everything we look at has a long unknown history behind it. Any toying with a pure origin means to steal oneself away from the present real material, the only material we have. The *alchemical impulse* is to start working with the *imperfect* material as it is presently at hand. This material here. Applied to the dream this means: of course it is not the "real" dream. But such a real dream does not exist. Here, this dream text, no matter how fragmentary, how distorted through lack of memory etc. it is, this is where we have to plunge into it.

Unlike the physical facts of nature that simply are what they are, any speaking and any meaning phenomenon is "about" something and represents or expresses a certain particular *view* of what it is about and as such is inevitably interpretation.[6] For the same reason the dream, too, is from the outset in itself and essentially *interpretation*. Only because the dream is interpretation and not actual event can we say upon waking up from a bad dream: Oh, thank God, it was *only* a dream. Events in real life cannot be dismissed that easily; hard facts do not simply go away. But if the dream is in itself interpretation, then our attempt to interpret a dream is an interpretation *of* an interpretation! So the full structure of the dream is quite complicated. The dream is (1) *our reflections* about the dream as a text; it is how *we* see, how *we* interpret it. (2) The dream is the dream *text*, which in turn is the memory of the nightly dream experience itself, where the remembrance is again a (spontaneous) interpretation or reflection of what is remembered. (3) The content of what the conscious dream is the memory of, i.e., the actual dream action and dream figures in it, are, as packages of meaning and "expression" or "statement," again in themselves interpretation. Jung put it the following way: "But every psychic process, so far as it can be observed as such, is essentially 'theoria', that is to say, it is a *conception* [*Anschauung*[7]]; and its reconstruction is at best only a *variant of the same conception*" (*CW* 17 § 162, transl. modif.).

So we have to distinguish the "theoria" or interpretation as which the dream comes from the outset and what it is within itself, on the one hand, from the interpretation that we give to the dream (that is to say, that we give to what in itself is already interpretation), on the other hand. The one is, we might say, an implicit (*ansichseiend*) interpretation, absolutely "syntonic" with itself inasmuch as it is the unbroken, indissoluble identity and simultaneity of interpretation *and* what it is the interpretation of. It is both sides at once. The other one, *our* interpretation, is explicit interpretation, and for it the separation of that which is to be interpreted and the explicit act of interpretation has always already happened; the dream text is given as in itself complete object and comes, in a both logical and temporal sense, first, whereas our interpretation is essentially secondary and has what it interprets irrevocably outside and vis-à-vis itself.

The point of the insight that what is interpreted is in itself already interpretation or "theoria" is that in our way back we never come to a first origin, to pure nature, to an immediate fact that would be that which is the ultimate object of all this interpretation and reflection and precedes all "theoria." On the contrary, we are, if we want to express it in such negative terms, hopelessly caught up in interpretation and reflection.

This echoes statements by Jung that we are hopelessly enwrapped in psyche, in images, in fantasy. Jung says: "We are in truth so wrapped about by psychic images that we cannot penetrate at all to the essence of things external to ourselves" (*CW* 8 § 680) and the psyche "will never get beyond itself. All comprehension and all that is comprehended is *in itself psychic*, and to that extent we are hopelessly cooped up in an exclusively psychic world" (*MDR* p. 352, my italics). Jung's "in itself psychic" means "being interpretation, being a statement by the soul, a 'theoria'" (in contrast to the sugar in the urine as objective fact) and as interpretation, as we heard, "at best only a *variant of the same conception*" (*CW* 17 § 162, transl. modif.). Our psychological interpretations are therefore, as Jung repeatedly emphasizes using a phrase of the alchemists, an explaining "*ignotum per ignotius*," the unknown by the even more unknown (e.g., *CW* 17 § 162).

If the dream *is* a phenomenon of meaning, if it *is* fantasy, reflection, interpretation, then our thesis that it *is* consciousness is once more confirmed. It is extremely important to get this point about the dream as an in itself *conscious* phenomenon. Consciousness is the other of nature. In fact, it is the antagonist of nature. Jung, too, saw the hiatus between nature and consciousness and therefore spoke of "the miracle of reflecting consciousness." According to Jung, nature is governed by a haphazard and incidental process and he points to the hundreds of millions of years of devouring and being devoured. But in the area of the history of the mind, the said "miracle of reflecting consciousness" intervenes, or perhaps better: intrudes, as "the second cosmogony" (*MDR* p. 339), as that which

> alone has given to the world its objective existence—without which, unheard, unseen, silently eating, giving birth, dying, heads nodding through hundreds of millions of years, it would have gone on in the profoundest night of non-being down to its unknown end.
>
> (*ibid.* p. 256)

Nature in this sense is mere "fact," pure event, senseless happening, and as such without consciousness. Nature is fundamentally blind and mute (enclosed within itself, without intentionality and reflection), just think of an erupting volcano, a storm, of cell divisions in organisms, or of animal instincts ("innate releasing mechanisms").

By saying that the dream *is* consciousness (objectively *is*!), I do, of course, not wish to imply that *we* are subjectively conscious of everything in our dreams. What according to its inner nature *is* consciousness and as such is in itself reflected can of course be unconscious *to us*, just like, in the area of nature, a certain illness can *be* a virus infection without our knowing anything about viruses, or as in the area of *logos*, we may not be able to read an ancient text in an extinct language or in an as yet undeciphered form of writing, while knowing that it is something that in itself is *meant* to be read and understood. The problem of the notion of "the unconscious" as a noun is that it is the result of a not seen-through equivocation, of a confounding of (a) a description of the inner character or essence of something with (b) the subjective awareness, on the part of an ego, of this something. The statement "the dream *is* consciousness" is *mutatis mutandis* analogous to "this mountain range consists of lime-stone."

As Jung pointed out, the dream is a spontaneous and involuntary production. We do not make our dreams. As such, the dream comes to consciousness as something unexpected, surprising, and alien, a quality that gave rise to the conventional notion of "the unconscious" as the origin of dreams. The distinction between the unconscious and consciousness expresses this otherness that, in fact, exists in the relation between our dreams and our consciousness. But we must not literalize this otherness and reify it as "the unconscious," as the negation or opposite of consciousness, and as a chasm between them. On the contrary, our insight that the dream *is* consciousness requires of us to see the dream no longer naively, in terms of pictorial thinking, as a literal other, something truly external to our subjectivity, coming to it literally from outside. Rather, it is a subjectivity-*internal* other. It is from the outset an (implicit) property of the subject, consciousness's own and, as "theoria" or interpretation, comes out of its own (implicit) *thinking*.

"Ontology" of the dream-internal world

Our discussion about the "Ontological rupture" has shown that dreams are not simply distinguished from experiences in reality by being merely fictional (the way movies, fairy tales, or novels are). They are much rather in themselves absolutely real, too, only in their own way. The reality of dreams is another, second form of reality *besides* the ordinary day-world reality and is separated from the latter by a gulf. In our chapter on the dream as interpretation we gained the insight into the indissoluble identity and simultaneity of interpretation and *what* it is the interpretation of that prevails in it. This is what it has in common with works of fiction. It invents and creates itself that whose "theoria" or interpretation it is. Or, by inventing and producing what it invents, it presents an interpretation or "theoria" and not objectively existing entities; however, it presents this interpretation precisely *in the form* of an absolutely impressive, sensibly experienced reality sufficient unto itself and *not* in the form of an explicit "theory *about* ..."

In the following I want to discuss the question, how does this sensibly experienced reality of the night world, how does what shows itself in dreams, present itself to the dreaming mind? What is the "ontological" character of the night world, the form of presence of the things, persons, and events in dreams—in contrast to that of ordinary reality? It should be clear from these questions why I put "ontology" in the title of this chapter and "ontological" in the previous sentence in quotation marks. My interest is not a philosophical one; I will not present a truly ontological discussion, but a strictly *phenomenological* one.

Instead of "I had a dream," the Japanese usually say, "I saw a dream." They explicitly emphasize the visual nature of experience. What kind of seeing is the one that happens in the form of dreams, above all in comparison with the experience of external reality? Our normal seeing in daily life is characterized by the fact that there is a clear difference or distinction between the seeing and the object seen. What is seen is seen as a substantial reality, something objectively given. This means that it is seen *as* something that exists and persists independently of our seeing. For this reason I can, for example, see and look closely at a tree and when my gaze has traveled from the roots upwards to the crown of the tree I can, nevertheless, be certain that if I look down again upon the roots I will still find the same sight as the one with which I started. Or I can turn around and look at something else and know that this tree is now still standing unchanged behind my back. What is seen has its own solid being in itself, separate from the act of my seeing. It has its own firm identity and rests within itself. Its qualities are its own property. This applies even to changes, movement, and the flux of events (a running dog, a falling leaf, drifting clouds, flickering flames, a child growing up into a man): they are seen as processes upon *logically* stable, objective entities as their self-identical substrate. In fact, these processes are themselves seen as objective givens. Our day-world reality is determined by its *objectual* character, its *Gegenständlichkeit*. No matter whether thing, event, or process, everything in objective reality is seen as reliable, each according to its own nature.

This is radically different in dreams. Several aspects need to be distinguished.

1. The seeing of a dream

In most dreams, even if not in all, there is a dream-I as the figure that experiences the dream events. It is the figure from whose point of view—on a primary level—most of the other figures, things, and events in the dream are seen. But, interestingly enough, this seeing dream-I is itself one of the dream figures in the dream that is "*seen*" (to use the Japanese wording)—on a second level—by the dreaming I. It is essential to realize that the dream-I is not only a seeing and experiencing I, but also a *seen* figure, seen just like all the dream's other figures and things. It is not only subject (as which it of course feels itself), but also object.

In certain, not so common, dreams it is even more complicated in that *within* one and the same dream there is a dream-I plus an I that simultaneously sees within the dream from an external observer standpoint the whole scene, including itself as seeing and acting object (as the figure of the dream-I). In such cases, there are three levels within the dream, inasmuch as the dream as a whole (including the observing I) is also "seen." By contrast, other dreams have only one level of "seeing I or consciousness," because a dream-I as separate figure in the dream image is absent; there is only the image or scene that is seen, in the sense of "I saw a dream." I leave these complications aside and come back to the remembered dream *with* a dream-I that is at one and the same time "seeing" and "seen."

This distinguishes the dream reality radically from ordinary reality. In the latter we are, under normal conditions, only the seeing and experiencing I and as such are only and wholly involved with what there is to be seen, experienced, or done. The experiencing I is exclusively the seeing (and feeling, reacting) I, but as the experiencing and acting person in the respective scene it is not in addition at the same time observed by itself as if from outside. The experience of empirical reality is characterized by a simple subject/object opposition. Dream-reality is usually determined by a subject–subject–object structure.[8]

To avoid misunderstandings: When talking about the dream-I that is both seeing and seen, I am, as far as the "being seen" aspect is concerned, not referring to the waking I outside the dream that remembers the dream or says, Western style, "I *had* a dream" as the one by whom the dream-I is seen. Because this would be much the same as remembering from the distance of one day how one behaved yesterday in a scene in daily life. My point is that the dream-I itself is the unity and difference of its own dream-internal seeing and being seen.

2. Mutability and malleability

A female dreamer discovers a dead baby in some dark corner of the cellar. Looking at it more closely, she sees that the baby all of a sudden starts to breathe and open its eyes. What is essential here is that the first impression that the baby is dead was not erroneous and the later discovery not a correction of an initial misconception. The baby was at first really dead, and the coming back to life in the dream was not due to some Christ who possesses the power of performing the miracle of awakening dead Lazarus back to life. No, in terms of the dream there is no miracle at all. The returning life is simply a fact. There is not even any amazement, shock, incredulity, or perturbation. In the dream it is simply accepted that all of a sudden the baby is alive. Other than in empirical reality, the characteristics and conditions of dream figures as well as things are *not binding, not once and for all fixed,* so that, if at all, a change could, perhaps, only be brought about through deliberate work, laborious processing, technical means, or external causes. In the dream, the realistically impossible change from death to life simply happens without any explanation and without needing an explanation. Obviously, dream elements do not have their nature and being in themselves. They do not have to abide by their own definition and natural law; their definition is not the ultimate limit of their possibilities. The dream can change the very identity of elements as needed or desired by the dreaming "soul." They are (at times) more like clouds.

In the cited case of the dream with the dead baby, its coming to life cannot be explained naturalistically. But it can be explained psychologically. What brings life back to the dead baby is the attention given to it by the dream-I. The interested gaze, together with the dream-I's shock and emotional involvement, kindles the flame of life in the dream-baby. Maybe a special interest and emotional involvement are not even what is necessary. Maybe the mere seeing is enough. The baby's unseenness is tantamount to its being dead and the awareness of a seeing consciousness restores it to life.[9] The figure or thing that is seen in the dream can sometimes alter its very nature as a function of how it is seen by the dream-I and as a function of the latter's attitude. Subject and object are not ontologically vis-à-vis, each locked in their own finished nature once and for all given to them; there is to some extent a mutual determination of their natures.

Changes concerning the nature, conditions, or identity of dream elements do not only occur as a reflection of the attitude and behavior of the dream-I. They can also happen just like that, independently of the dream-I. Dream reality is, in principle, flexible, malleable. The properties or attributes of something that appeared in the dream can change from one minute to the next. A new moment in the dream may mean that the conditions of the "same" environment are different. One cannot, as in ordinary reality, rely on the permanence of the world's factual being-so, its unshakeable objectivity. Not even the dream-I itself is objectual; it, too, may suddenly be altered in character or nature. The reason for this amazing dream character is, of course, that dreams present an invented reality (see point 5 below) whose nature it is that in its innermost character it is interpretation or "theoria."

I do not wish to imply that the malleability of things and figures in dreams makes itself felt in all dreams and with respect to everything in a dream. Very often, persons and things retain their initial character throughout the dream. All I wish to point out is that dream reality is, in principle, not confined in its respective "definition," even if in many dreams this does not become an issue.

Other examples of this mutability: A dreamer wants to defend himself against an attacking criminal with an iron bar, but the moment he wants to hit the man the bar becomes soft and bends like rubber.—The dream-I and two companions have climbed up a wooded hillside and are now standing on top where an open plain lies in front of them. They cannot go forward because a wire-netting fence separates the wooded hillside from the plain as far as the eye can see. While they are wondering whether they should somehow climb across the fence, a man appears on the other side and asks them if they want to continue their walk on the plain. He leads them a few meters to the left, and now, all of a sudden, the fence that before had continued indefinitely, abruptly ends there and a well-trodden path leading into the plain appears.—A married woman in her mid-thirties dreams that she is a high-school student in a boarding school. Outside, she sees an unattractive boy. She hates him, but nevertheless goes out with him. Then she runs away, back to her parents' home, because she thinks that it is inappropriate for her as a married woman to go out with another man. (The dream, all of a sudden and tacitly, changed her from high-school age to her present age as a married woman.)—In the dream the dreamer lives in a small house with three rooms. He discovers a hidden door in the last room, and when he opens it, there is a huge hall with long tables fancily set for a big banquet, a hall of such a size that it actually could not possibly fit into the small house.—There is an inviting beautiful marble staircase, but when the dreamer walks up, it is all of a sudden extremely narrow and made of partially rotten wood.—"I am walking with my friend Paul and discussing with him the problems I have with my boss, but now he is Mr. Bernard, the schoolteacher I had in third grade."—It is a warm summer day in the dream, but all of a sudden the dreamer comes to an area of thick snow with lots of skiing people: the season has changed from summer to winter, without announcement and without the necessary time of several months that needs to have passed in reality between the seasons having made the change possible. The change happens instantly, without mediation.

The point of all these changes is that it is as if the floor had been pulled out from under a particular phenomenon in the dream or as if in the middle of a football match the rules of the game had abruptly been replaced by totally different rules, or as if a scene from one movie had without indication been attached to a different movie, but in such a way that the new scene appears to be a continuation of the old scene. (In other words, I am not talking here of the phenomenon of clearly marked changes of scene, which is also a possible and, in fact, fairly common feature, above all in longer dreams. I am referring to tacit changes of the character or definition of elements of one and the same continuous scene, changes that do not happen, but suddenly *have happened*, sort of behind the dream-I's back.)

Just as there is no mediation that could explain the change, so there is usually no surprise, shock, and not even an awareness of transformation. The respective change *is* now simply reality and is taken as such. This has something to do with the quality of time in dreams. As far as the described phenomena are concerned, no *comparison* takes place in the dream between the new situation and the original one. The memory of the earlier conditions is not held on to, which alone would be the condition of the possibility of the felt contrast between before and now. The dream seems in such cases to be a succession of pure Nows, each without a past from which it results, but completely fresh, as if with each Now the world had been newly created. This is why each new Now does not have to account for its nature in terms of what preceded it to make it plausible. It does not have to be consistent with foregoing descriptions of the same thing in the same dream. It is only outside the dream that *we* see the discrepancies, because *we* contain the whole sequence in memory and expect consistency.

It is not only abrupt changes without mediation or explanation that can happen in dreams. One also finds dreams in which an earlier situation is retroactively redefined or reinvented, such as in the following dream episode: *I am walking in the park near where I live. All of a sudden, I hear a strange sound coming from the underbrush. I start to investigate and find under a thick pile of leaves a wounded and probably dying dog. I am shocked and feel helpless. Further away I see two other walkers. I run to them to ask them what to do. When we come back to the place the dog has changed into a eight or ten years old boy. I ask him about his wounds. He responds: "Which wounds? It felt so cozy under the pile of leaves."*

What needs to be realized is that at first there was really a wounded dog and that later in the dream this reality, this past, is retroactively revised and changed into a just as real new truth: no dying dog, no wound, but a boy who felt well.

Of course, we should not overemphasize the dream feature of a suddenly changing fact that had been presented before. There are many dreams or developments in dreams that are perfectly consistent. What needs to be taken to heart is only the fact that we cannot expect and rely on the same kind of consistency in dreams as in what we call the real world.

Another feature of dreams that is not the same as the mutability discussed here, but in some way similar, is that in a dream you find yourself, for example, in the house in which you grew up, but it is totally different from the real house in which you used to live in childhood. Or there is your father, but he is not like your real father. That is to say, he is unmistakably *known* to be your father, but as far as looks and behavior are concerned, he is really another man. Dreams often confront the dream-I with this type of discrepancy, nay, contradiction: he *is* AND is *not* your father. Here again we must say that this is not at all experienced in the dream as a problem, a conflict. It becomes a conflict only for consciousness outside the dream.

3. Shadowiness

Dreams are typically (but not always) colorless. I say "colorless" rather than "black and white," because "black and white" would imply that in dreams we encounter in the depicted world a bold, sharp contrast of opposites and clear contours like silhouettes. Typically, dreams are not only colorless, but also specifically *pale* and vague.

It is important to note that this paleness and colorlessness are not experienced as abnormal or as a deficiency in the dream; nothing at all is felt to be wrong with, or missing from, the world as it appears in the dream on account of this colorlessness. Within the dream, this form of appearance is simply taken for granted; indeed, it is not even noticed. The colorlessness appears only to our external reflection in waking consciousness and by comparison with our experience of the empirical world in daily life. It is only our ordinary world experience in waking life that makes the things and persons shown in dreams on the whole look shadowy and somehow two-dimensional. There is in most dreams a certain flatness, maybe even thinness, of the reality shown in them, which strongly contrasts with the full, well-rounded, three-dimensional corporeality of our experience of external reality or in most works of fiction. Within the dream experience this character of the dream world in no way diminishes the sense of its reality and possible impressiveness.

Color is not always absent. Several Japanese persons have told me that they regularly dream in full color, "just as in waking life." If this should be generally so for Japanese, is this perhaps the reason why the Japanese speak of "*seeing* a dream," because it is full-fledged, sensual seeing, just as in daily life? Could this be due to a much more immediate closeness to "nature" (in the psychological sense of the word), to the unbroken *unio naturalis* in traditional Japan? In comparison with the West, it is, for example, absolutely remarkable how popular sandplay therapy is in Japan and how therapeutically effective it can be. There are amazing, wonderful sandplay therapy processes that go on entirely subliminally, *without reflection* and understanding, and without words. In Europe I heard only from one analysand that he "always" dreams in color. Interestingly enough, he is a person with a mediumistic talent, which might again point to a (partially) unbroken closeness to "nature."

On the other hand, Jung, talking about the drawings and paintings of patients in analysis, points out that,

> Mostly, to begin with, only a pencil or pen is used to make rapid sketches of dreams, sudden ideas, and fantasies. But from a certain moment on the patients begin to make use of colour, and this is generally the moment when merely intellectual interest gives way to emotional participation. Occasionally the same phenomenon can be observed in dreams, which at such moments are dreamt in colour, or a particularly vivid colour is insisted upon.
>
> (*CW* 14 § 333)

What this passage suggests is that according to Jung's experience, too, dreams in the Western world are usually colorless. This is the starting point for his further comment about the "occasional" appearance of color "at such moments" in dreams. His thesis that the appearance of color in dreams marks a transition from merely intellectual interest to emotional participation means that he understood this appearance of color in dreams on the syntactical level. His explanation makes sense especially for those dreams that are as a whole dreamt in color. Conversely, Jung's associating dreams dreamt without color with "merely intellectual interest" could be understood as pointing to the fact that for Western man, other than for traditional Japanese, the soul is generally no longer on the level of the *unio naturalis*, but on that of *reflection*. A fundamental rupture has once and for all happened (historically we can think here of the psychological change that in the Western world was brought about by the Enlightenment for the entire culture). Reflection as such can do (or has to do) without color. Color has become free, an additional attribute that is introduced into dreams only at special moments and in order to express something particular ("emotional participation," or feeling values), rather than being the ordinary form of reality in dreams in general.

Much more frequently than full-color dreams are dreams in which only one single or a few selected individual things appear in color, while the rest is without color. Then I think it is more reasonable to assume that the particular color has a particular semantic (symbolic or imaginal) meaning. It is a content in its own right. The color purple, for example, is just like certain animals or objects (a snake, a bull, an airplane, a ring, a sword, etc.) or like certain abstract shapes (e.g., triangle, square, circle) that appear in dreams expressive of some particular concrete idea or meaning. The question then would not be: "why does all of a sudden color appear in a dream?" (to which the answer, if we follow Jung's cited idea, could be: because of the greater emotional participation), but rather: "Why does 'purple' appear in this dream? What does 'purple' psychologically represent or evoke?"

The next characteristic to be discussed here further unfolds the shadowy and two-dimensional character of dream reality.

4. Lacunality

Coming back to the phrase, "I saw a dream," I now need to point out that "seeing" means something very different when applied to the dream world and all the figures, things, or events in it from what it means in ordinary waking life. When we stand in front of an imposing landscape, we see it with all its details insofar as they are distinguishable from our present standpoint. All the details are in the whole picture that the eyes at a given moment take in. Of course, not all these details will be consciously noted and individually registered. Consciousness may, in fact, only be interested in the total impression. Or, at another moment, it may exclusively focus on one particular section or detail of the whole picture. But in both cases, the entire picture with all its perceptible details is, nevertheless, in the seen picture, even if to a large extent only subliminally. It is this totality of the picture that is essential to the sense of full-fledged reality of the world in its sensible physicality. There are no gaps. There is no contextlessness of individual objects seen. Everything is inevitably imbedded in an environment, no matter how narrowed-down our specific focus upon one detail may be at a given time. The world seen *is* ultimately for us just like the way cameras see it (although a camera picture does, of course, not contain the distinction between the part of the whole picture that receives momentarily, in this now, our conscious attention and all the other parts that are only subliminally perceived). At least with pictures of the scene taken at a great distance from the lens, the camera picture shows simultaneously all parts that for us can only in successive Nows receive our special attention.

In dreams this is radically different. In them there is only partial seeing. A dream-I is, for example, attacked by a dangerous criminal. He sees a man with broad shoulders in a blue blazer, but he doesn't see his face—not because it is hidden, but because the dream simply does not show it. The dream is obviously only concerned with the type, not with the individual and his distinctive facial features. Or: A dream-I opens a door in a long dream. But what kind of door it is and whether there was a doorknob or a door handle and all such details are not part of the dream. It is just the "naked" idea of opening a door. This abstractness can go so far that occasionally a dream-I is, for example, accompanied by someone and merely *knows* that it is this particular colleague, but this person is not really *seen* in the dream. The colleague exists in the dream only in the form of the *knowledge* of his presence. Or: We may dream of a snake, but the surroundings in which it appears are not shown in the dream. It is by no means that they are merely forgotten in waking consciousness or were not in focus. No, they were simply left out. The surroundings of the snake that in waking life would inevitably also be seen, even if without any special attention to them, can in dreams be left blank, or maybe not even blank, inasmuch as "blank" would create the feeling that there is something missing. In the dream, nothing is missing or felt to be missing. This is also why my word "lacunality" for this dream quality is too negative. It seems to indicate a lack, where in reality nothing is *lacking* (or only from the point of view of waking consciousness). It is the other way around. The dream, we have to conclude, actively *shows* only what it is interested in. We have to express it in *positive* terms: The dream world is exclusively built up out of those things and aspects of things that dreams purposely *choose* to *present*. There is no omission. It is maybe a little bit like when somebody brings you a nice bunch of tulips as a present: you cannot say that it lacks daffodils and hyacinths. A much better comparison would of course be poetry.

5. "Just in time" apparition, not substantial being

The figures, objects, and world that appear in dreams must be understood to be especially (and this means: creatively) produced and presented according to an overall dream intention. This is the crucial difference to empirical reality, which is a once and for all *given* world. It is inevitably given in its entirety, which means that each particular limited experience here and now is, nevertheless, irrevocably known to be a part or segment of this total, factually given reality called "the world." That it is given also means that it has, so to speak, "bedrock" character ("objectivity") and always already precedes our ("subjective") experience of it. It exists for us a priori and we know that it will persist even if we go away, turn our attention to something else and no longer see it. It possesses substantial being independent of its being seen by us.

The dream world, by contrast, is not a priori. It emerges only in and through the process of *dreaming* and accordingly also disappears when our dreaming ends and we wake up. It is newly and freely invented on the spot. It has its origin in the momentary act of dreaming as well as in the overall dream intention and not in a pre-existing underlying substrate. That is to say, the origin of the dream world is the intention of the soul or mind, whereas seen empirical reality is merely *re*-presented by the mind. But in itself it is, of course, given to the mind and exists independently of the mind. Having its origin in the mind, the dream world (the world produced in dreams) is a product of freedom. Everything in the dream freely *gives itself*, rather than being given or being part of the given world. In each dream (sometimes even in each dream scene) we are in a new, specially created one-time reality. It only *cloaks* itself (mostly) in the form of things and figures that we know from empirical reality. But it does not need to pay heed to the laws and limitations governing the physical world, so that things are possible in it which, seen from a realistic standpoint, are "impossible" or "miraculous," for example, a person flying over a city or landscape without technical help.

The fact that the world appearing in the dream is produced, invented, and not a given world shows that dreaming is not really *seeing* in the ordinary sense. There is no clear division between a subject vis-à-vis an object. Rather, the consciousness that experiences the dream is from the outset itself involved in what the dream presents. What it "sees" is—ultimately—only *its own* product, although this intricate relationship of consciousness's involvement in its own experience, in what it sees, remains unconscious, because one and the same dreaming soul divides itself, as far as the experience in the dream is concerned, into the consciousness that "sees" the dream and the soul that produced what is to be "seen." To put it the other way around, the things and events seen in dreams are invented *as not invented* by the soul itself, in other words, as absolutely convincing, as independent sensible reality, as if truly *given*. Dreams are utterly real. There is no escape from this reality (except through waking up) and no alternative to it. This is why dreams can produce the experience of extreme fear, anxiety, terrible threat, or the unbearable physically felt oppression by an *incubus*.

As the contradiction of "invented creation" and "happening, befalling us," the reality character of dream events is that of *apparitions*, in contrast to the objective world, even if, according to Kant, this objective world is also said to be only the world as it *appears* to us. However, appearance in the Kantian sense and the type of apparition that applies to dreams are not the same. Apparition means pure appearance of its own accord: self-manifestation. I said that the elements in dreams *give themselves*. Appearance in the epistemological Kantian sense means: how *something* that exists independently of the subject appears to the subject, is logically constituted by consciousness at large, so that its transcendental idealism guarantees precisely its empirical realism and objectivity. Apparition means: something *shows* itself and shows *itself*, and this in such a way that in its showing *itself*, that which shows itself *comes into existence in the first place*, and has its existence, only in this self-presentation and only for as long as it lasts. (This is, of course, a view that is incompatible with the "metaphysical" theory of pre-existing "archetypes in themselves" that manifest in people's dreams as particularized archetypal images.)

Consciousness's involvement in what happens or shows itself in the dream sometimes even becomes partly phenomenal. The type of reaction (above all, the kind of reception or defense) that the dream-I displays to what it is confronted with can directly alter the character of the reality that it is confronted with (e.g., what appeared to be a threatening character can all of a sudden turn out to be "in reality" a helpful acquaintance familiar from conscious life). Or it can influence the direction that the continuation of the dream action takes, as if the dream-producing soul followed the dream-I's cues. And, of course, in psychology we generally proceed from the assumption that what appears in the dream is a function of the mind that has the dream: *its* reflection, self-expression. What is inside (in the logical structure of consciousness) appears to consciousness as an internal external reality: an apparition.

Dreams as apparitions are therefore not "seen" in the ordinary sense of the word, but really *dreamt* (where "dreaming" means the conjunction of producing and seeing/experiencing, the seeing of the mind's own spontaneous products). The "seeing" of dreams is *speculative* seeing (where "speculative" points to subject-objectivity or object-subjectivity). Empirical reality, because it is inexorably *given*, allows us to focus on this detail or that and let our eyes wander from one part of a sight to another and rely on the possibility to let our gaze return to a detail looked at before and find it still the same. We have the freedom of the observer of the world in front of or around us. We can choose what we look at. In dreams this is not possible, for two reasons. First, because of its apparition character and its *giving* itself, it is the dream that determines what we inescapably have to look at. And second, if the dream-I decides to focus on something particular, this act, as a dream-internal willful intervention into the dream's self-giving, may already have altered the conditions so-far prevailing in the dream and perhaps even altered the character of the very object that the dream-I chose to focus on.

Visions, delusions, and the like belong (in this regard) to the same category of "seeing." By contrast, the objects seen by people in Plato's cave are seen just like objects of sensible reality in daily life. The fact that they are mere shadows and thus poor copies of real objects (much like for Kant the object seen is an appearance, not a thing in itself) does not imply a diminished, poorer reality and quality of the mode of full-fledged *seeing*, the same way as when we look at a low-quality black-and-white print of a splendid painting our act of seeing is just as good as when we see the original painting in brilliant color. No matter what the quality, clarity, sharpness of the objects seen is, the quality of our seeing (our eyesight) stays the same. The same as what I pointed out about the seeing in Plato's cave applies to seeing movies or, nowadays, "virtual reality," such as in flight simulators. It is full-fledged seeing.

Other fantasy products (like fairy tales, myths, or poetic texts) are neither seen (like empirical reality), nor seriously experienced as absolutely real like dreams, but rather imagined, *vorgestellt*, pictorially represented *in the mind*. Other than dreams, they are consciously known to be products of the mind and to be only present in the mind as *its* own property, rather than apparitions that come to consciousness as (as if they were) real others.

6. Concepts cloaked in sensible shapes

In the foregoing section we have gained an understanding of dream images as "apparitions" in the sense of the contradiction of the mind's internally seeing its own products *as* external reality. In the section on "Lacunality" we realized that dreams display the "external" reality shown in the dream only incompletely. Only what the dream is interested in is actually represented. Although dream images have the character of sensible reality, they are nevertheless usually flat (without well-rounded three-dimensionality), pale, and colorless, somehow shadowy, as I suggested earlier. We have also had to understand that the shadowiness can go so far that a dream figure may, in fact, be present in a dream without being actually seen, that is, present only in the dreaming consciousness's *knowledge* of this presence. All these observations and insights taken together lead to the conclusion that the individual dream images (figures, things, happenings) are in truth *visualized concepts*. They are more felt, thought, known than actually seen. The dream is, as it were, "*intellectual intuition*" (in Kant's, Fichte's, Schelling's sense) in contrast to normal seeing, which is empirical perception. The dream is actually thought, ongoing thought (the process of thinking); however, thought in the *form* of sensibility (externalization, we could almost say "reification": figures, things in space, and action) rather than in the FORM *of thought*.

A particular consequence of this "conceptual nature" of the dream is that figures like a judge, a policeman, a doctor, a teacher, sometimes even father, mother *are* what their name, their concept, *says* they are. In empirical reality this is different. A judge may be open to bribery, a doctor a quack, a teacher not very intelligent or wise. Name or concept and true nature may diverge; more than that, it is the sign of reality that they never *fully* correspond. But in dreams they do fully correspond because such figures are not empirical persons, but embodied or personified *concepts*. Unless specifically shown otherwise in a particular dream (a dream could also show a crooked cop), the policeman is the true voice of the law and the embodiment of order, the teacher is truly *the* teacher, the soul teacher or the soul *as teacher*, just as the doctor is the soul doctor and what he says needs to be done, or what he does is the true cure (as unreasonable as it may appear to the dream-I). Such figures fulfill their concept.

I conclude this discussion about the "ontology" of the dream-internal world with an example: In one part of a dream, the dream-I has filled in an application form and now needs to get a signature from an official from another office before he can turn in the form. He is now with this official who carefully reads all the filled-in items, makes a few personal comments and finally signs the form.—It is to be assumed that while reading and signing the form, it is on the official's desk. But the desk is not shown in the dream, nor whether the signature is written with a fountain pen or a ballpoint pen, nor whether the official is right- or left-handed. The figure of the official himself is shown, but particular details about him, what he looks like, his facial expression, his clothing, are simply left out. He is just *known* to be a figure, but he is not clearly seen with all his physical features. What is represented is only "the official." In other words, he is the *concept* of "official," the concept that has become visible shape or *schema*, but is *not a graphically pictured* official as a particular individual. He is known in the dream to be bodily present, but he remains, nevertheless, two-dimensional and, so to speak, empty, "The Man Without Qualities" excepting the one quality of his being "the official."

Similarly, the scene presumably took place in a particular room, an office. But nothing is known about its size, about the walls, windows, lighting, the furniture, etc. By contrast, there was in this dream scene a special body sense concerning the spatial relation between the dream-I and the official: the dream-I clearly felt that the entrance to the room was behind his back and that the official was not directly facing the dream-I, but was standing a little more to the right and appeared to him in three-quarter profile.

Notes

1. I discussed this briefly in my "The Smuggling Inherent in the Logic of the 'Psychology of the Unconscious'," in: W.G., *The Flight into The Unconscious. An Analysis of C.G. Jung's Psychology Project*. Collected English Papers, vol. 5, New Orleans, LA (Spring Journal Books) 2013, now London and New York (Routledge) 2020, pp. 137–171, here pp. 139f.
2. C.G. Jung, *Kinderträume*, ed. by Lorenz Jung and Maria Meyer-Grass, Olten and Freiburg im Breisgau (Walter) 1987, pp. 19f. (my transl.).
3. Graham Hough, "Anima and Poetry," *Spring 1973*, pp. 85–96, here p. 85 f.
4. "Semantic" refers to the meaning of words or sentences. Syntactically, there is no difference between "The hunter killed the deer" and "The cat killed the mouse." The difference is only semantic. I use "semantic" here as referring to particular contents of experience in contrast to the "syntax," logical form, or (in this case also) ontology of experience.
5. We must not confuse this reality-creation with what Jung meant by his dictum, so fundamental for James Hillman, "The psyche creates reality every day" (*CW* 6 § 78). Jung spoke here precisely about the *objective* or "day world" reality that is common to all. Jung's revolutionary thesis is that even what normally appears to us as unquestionably real is, ultimately considered, not really objectively given fact, or rather *as* objectively given, together with its irreducible objective givenness, nevertheless a *product* of the *soul's* fantasy activity. Jung's interest is critically to *see through* the ordinary experience of "reality," whereas our theme here is the distinction between two different phenomenal types of reality.
6. In an earlier text I wrote: "The psychological question is not, cannot be, what and how the soul *is*, but how the soul is reflected in its manifestations. ... psychology is the study of the *reflection* in some mirror and not the study of *what* the mirror is the reflection *of*." *CEP*, vol. IV, p. 132.
7. The German word *Anschauung* (just like Greek *theôría*) implies a "viewing," "beholding" and can then, again as the Greek word, also take on the meaning of a "way of viewing" or "view," "conception," cf. *Weltanschauung*: a "way of looking at the world," "view of the world," "world view." The *CW* translation of Jung's *Anschauung* in this passage with "presentation" is not acceptable.
8. The interested reader might want to consult my discussion of the subject–subject–object structure in *CEP* vol. VI, pp. 480–485.
9. This also throws a light on the importance of consciousness and "making conscious" in therapy in general, quite apart from particular dream motifs.

Part II

Why dreams?

The significance of dreams in therapy

1. The soul's speaking

Some schools of psychotherapy do not work with dreams at all. Others may not ignore them totally when they are introduced by patients into therapy, but at bottom do not attribute much importance to them. This is altogether different in Jungian psychotherapy for which dreams are centrally important, and not only in a practical, technical sense and out of theoretical considerations; it is also inspired by a genuine heartfelt interest in dreams, if not love of dreams.

As to theoretical considerations concerning the significance of dreams, we can refer to Freud who in his *Interpretation of Dreams* stated (at the end of ch. VII. E, added in 1909): "But the interpretation of dreams is the *via regia* to the knowledge of the unconscious in psychic life," which was wholeheartedly affirmed by Jung:

> As Freud says, dream-analysis is the via regia to the unconscious. It leads straight to the deepest personal secrets, and is, therefore, an invaluable instrument in the hand of the physician and educator of the soul.
>
> (*CW* 7 § 25)

We see clearly that in these words it is still the early Jung speaking whose thinking, despite many fundamental disagreements with Freud's views on dream interpretation and psychology at large, is, nevertheless, still rather close to the basic Freudian viewpoint. This comes out in the personalistic stance, in the strictly "analytical" and merely intellectual, scientific (in contrast to "constructive") interest in discovering the "deepest personal *secrets*" and in the choice of the word "dream-*analysis*" instead of "interpretation," and in the technical, instrumental thinking that the expressions "invaluable instrument," and "physician and educator" betray. In addition, the whole concept of the *hypostatized* "unconscious" has still not been laid to rest. Above, I already critiqued both the concept of *the* unconscious and the *via regia* to it.

Notwithstanding these flaws in both Freud and Jung, there is in the theoretical assessment and personal attitude of these authors a full appreciation of the significance of dreams for psychotherapy as well as a genuine interest in and commitment to working with dreams. So far so good. But the flaws need to be overcome. And they were overcome in late Jung, although he never explicitly revoked his earlier view of dreams, and also held on to the notion of "the unconscious" for the rest of his life. Be that as it may, it suffices for our purposes to introduce one crucial quotation in which Jung's later view of dreams expresses itself in great clarity and to which we will come back repeatedly at different points of our discussion.

> In myths and fairytales, as in dreams, the soul speaks about itself, and the archetypes reveal themselves in their natural interplay, as "formation, transformation / eternal Mind's eternal recreation."
>
> (*GW* 9/I § 400, my translation[1])

The first thing to be noted is that dreams are put on a level with myths and fairy tales. There is no idea any more of personal secrets, of hidden thoughts, fantasies, wishes, or of suppressed or repressed character traits and committed deeds. The whole personalistic outlook has disappeared; more than that, the entire idea of a person, a human being, has disappeared! The dream is viewed without recourse to the individuals in which dreams happen. Instead of the logic of the personality as the *substrate* of dreams, we have here the logic of self-sufficiency and self-containment of the dream.[2] Another quote that expresses the same thought, although from a different angle, is the following: "... we are not saying anything *about* the psyche, but the psyche is always speaking about *itself*" (*CW* 9 § 483). The dream exists for its own sake. Not for our benefit. There is, in this conception, neither an author (the personality) as producing subject or mastermind behind the dream, nor a dream-external referent "*about*" whom or which the dream would provide some information. The dissociation and duality between subject and produced object as well as that between speaking dream and discussed object has been left behind. The dream *is* a self, *is* only self-relation. Just like a myth or, we might add, like poetry, it innocently, without ulterior intention or purpose, shows only *itself*, expresses *itself*. The logic that is at work in the cited Jung-passage is that of play, as also his own word "natural interplay" and the inclusion of the quote from Goethe make clear: "Formation, transformation" as "eternal recreation."

It is also important to note that in Jung's statement the archetypes are not hypostatized dream-external factors, just as the "eternal Mind"[3] is not an existing subject *behind* the dream. They are not entities. And above all, there is no metaphysics. Rather, the real "subject" is the "natural interplay," the "formation, transformation" and the "eternal recreation" (literally: "eternal entertainment") from which the archetypes and the "*ewige Sinn*" internally arise in the sense of *emergence*. The act or process comes first. The "archetypes" as typical forms and patterns emerge as crystallizations in this self-producing play. "Eternal" should likewise not be taken religiously or metaphysically. It expresses the *logic* of this natural interplay or entertainment, namely, the fact that as sheer self-relation, self-expression, and self-production it has the form or status of infinity, in contrast to all other things, beings, and events that have their causes outside and behind themselves and possibly also external purposes, purposes for others (cf. the fact that many living organisms and animals exist as food for others). For us as psychologists, all these metaphorical expressions (natural interplay, eternal Mind, eternal recreation) are different ways of paraphrasing "soul," which, of course, conversely means that "soul" is also not to be taken as an entity, let alone in a metaphysical sense, but as the *name* we give *in mythologizing fashion* to this self-producing play.

As far as the archetypal is concerned, this self-producing play must not always and exclusively bring forth from within itself the archetypal figurations that may appear in it. It is also possible that its self-production simply follows the traditional, already culturally paved "archetypal" paths or makes use of and incorporates individual, culturally available and long established "archetypal" patterns.

Returning to the question of the significance of dreams, we understand that according to the mature Jung it is "the soul" that speaks about "itself" in dreams. And *this* is what gives to dreams their particular psychological dignity, makes them precious for us. And this is also what allows us to view them as being on the same footing with fairy tales and myths, despite many differences that exist in other regards between dreams, on the one hand, and myths or fairy tales, on the other. Dreams are "the soul's" self-expression, or rather, this self-expression is what we mean by "soul." Dreams give us access, not to a person's unconscious, but to the objective soul.

Regardless of how myths and fairy tales originally may have come about, what they have become and continue to be since time immemorial—in other words, what the nature of the phenomenon myth or the phenomenon fairy tale *is*—shows that they are obviously "objective" in the sense of not having anything to do with any individual person. They are truly general, collective products.[4] They have no author. This is one of the main differences to dreams. Dreams are always some individual's dreams. This is essential to the nature of dreams, which is also why we had to stress above that in dreaming we have left the common world of the waking consciousness and each have our own personal world. With this insight we seem to get into conflict with our present observations that the dream is the product of the objective soul and that all personalistic thinking must be left behind. The situation is indeed more complicated than it is in the case of myths and fairy tales. We cannot ignore that dreams arise in individual persons and are really *their* dreams. But we can also not go back behind Jung's insight that in dreams the soul speaks about itself (and this means: not about us, not about the individual who has this dream, not about the patient).

The answer to this conflict is that dreams are that form of the objective soul's self-expression that necessarily appears *through the medium* of a particular person. What we see and experience in dreams is perceived through the medium of our own personality, our own psychic makeup, our own psychic as well as possibly real-life situation. The notion of "medium" is essential. In empirical reality it may be that we see the world around us in autumn times only through a fog as medium and at other times we look at something through colored glasses, through a milk glass pane, see ourselves in a distorting mirror, etc., or see a staff as broken when half of it is in water. In much the same way dreams present to us the objective soul's "play" more or less colored and distorted through the impure medium as which we, the dreamers of the dream, exist. We must therefore not take abstractly the idea of "the soul's speaking about itself." Dreams have a certain share of personal contamination. However, this must not mislead us to think that they are *about* the person.

As important as it is, this fantasy of "seeing through a medium" is still not satisfactory. Its fault is that it posits the objective soul in its pure form (the soul almost like a thing in itself) that in dreams is forced to appear in somewhat impaired form because of its having to pass through the human medium. Before, I quoted Jung as saying:

> that archetypes are not determined as regards their content, but only as regards their form and then only to a very limited degree. A primordial image is determined as to its content only when it has become conscious and is therefore *filled out with the material of conscious experience.*
>
> (*CW* 9i § 155, my italics)

Now it becomes necessary to give this problem a completely new formulation. Instead of assuming a pre-existing pure, empty form that is *filled out* with conscious material (stemming from personal experience), we altogether drop the idea of an empty form and of its being filled. Rather, I propose that the "objective soul" produces itself (as its speaking about itself) *exclusively in (and from within!)* the impure "medium" of concrete human individuals, which means that the whole notion of a *medium* through which we look and through which something pure can only be seen in partially distorted form, no longer makes sense. There is no such thing as the objective soul per se, just as there is no "life" per se. Life exists only in individual living creatures. We have only real dreams. As far as the phenomenon of dreams is concerned, the infinity of the soul's speaking about itself happens only in these finite events, the objective soul happens only in personal phenomena like dreams. There is nothing behind it.

What becomes apparent from the whole discussion in this section, and also from an assessment of the radical shift in Jung's own views from his early time to his mature stance, is that "the objective soul" is not a question of ontology, nor of science ("Is there in reality such a thing or not?", "Does the soul indeed speak about itself in dreams, rather than about people and what happens in them, what *they* feel, think, wish, and fantasize?"). It is *a question of logic*, of the logical constitution of consciousness. Is our consciousness as psychologists informed by the logic of the division between subject and object, cause and effect, people and their psyche, the substrate-personality and the psychic phenomena—or does it follow the uroboric logic of self (self-relation, self-manifestation, self-production)? For the positivistic, scientific stance, soul does not exist, cannot exist, which of course does not exclude the possibility that scientifically minded psychologists may occasionally still use the *word* soul, but they inevitably mean something else, a possibility that brings back to mind Georg Christian Lichtenberg's dictum: "One still says soul just as one says thaler, long after minted thalers have been discontinued."⁵ There cannot be a science of psychology—if we mean by that term a psychology with soul. One must not be misled by the prolific use of the word soul in many circles of analytical psychology nowadays and take it as evidence of the prevalence of the uroboric logic of self. One may come in the soul's clothing, but inwardly be governed by the unaltered personalistic and causalistic logic that—consciously or unconsciously— dominates the scientific mind as much as popular thinking.

2. "I do not know the answer either"

The first answer to the question, "Why Dreams?" is that they possess an inner dignity and precious value as documents of the soul's speaking. But we also had to take into account that the soul produces itself in dreams only through the particularities of individual dreamers and that these personal and situational particularities partake of the specific character of dreams. It is individuals who come into therapy. And these individuals may not be interested in dreams at all, nor interested in the soul either, and will hardly be impressed by the idea of the dignity of dreams as spontaneous expressions of the soul. They have pressing problems, painful symptoms. All they want is help, to be cured.

A second, more practical answer needs to be given to the question, "Why Dreams?" Jung once reported that "Some of my patients 'perhaps thought I knew the magic formula, but I soon had to tell them that I did not know the answer either'" (*CW* 11 § 514). The patients came with the fantasy of the healer and projected it upon the therapist. Jung disappoints the expectation of his patients. He destroys their illusion. He admits to being just as helpless as his patients. He has nothing to offer. A zero-point is reached. He stands there empty-handed.

He thus performs a radical negation: the act of his own self-negation as healer, as the one equipped with almost magical power, as well as the helper, the counselor, the knowing one, the one who has clever advice. This self-negation, which is at the same time the destruction of the patient's illusion, is the psychologically crucial act through which he becomes a true psychotherapist in the first place. This is because the therapist is not to be confused with the healer (nor with the counselor), as, above all, James Hillman pointed out with reference to the Greek meaning of *therápôn*, *therapeytês*, and the verb *therapeŷô*. *Therápôn* means first of all servant, caretaker, attendant, nurse. Only that! Nothing heroic or magnificent. "By [...] paying careful attention to and devotedly caring for the psyche, the analyst translates into life the meaning of the word 'psychotherapy'. The psychotherapist is literally the *attendant of the soul*."[6] By the same token, the alchemists thought that the artifex "is the servant of the work," the opus (*CW* 16 § 471).

By letting himself fall into his real helplessness in view of the problems of his patients Jung comes up with the second answer to our question, "Why Dreams?" For he does not end with his own self-negation. This is best made clear in other quotations:

> In the majority of my cases the resources of the conscious mind are exhausted (or, in ordinary English, they are "stuck"). It is chiefly this fact that forces me to look for hidden possibilities. For I do not know what to say to the patient when he asks me, "What do you advise? What shall I do?" I don't know either ... / In such cases, then, my attention is directed more particularly to dreams. This is not because I am tied to the notion that dreams must always be called to the rescue, or because I possess a mysterious dream-theory which tells me how everything must shape itself; but quite simply from perplexity. I do not know where else to go for help, and so I try to find it in dreams. These at least present us with images pointing to something or other, and that is better than nothing. I have no theory about dreams, I do not know how dreams arise.
>
> (*CW* 16 §§ 84 and 86)

And again:

> Anxiously [my patient] asks me, "What can I do?" And I must answer, "I do not know either. "Then there's nothing to be done?" I reply that mankind has got into these blind alleys countless times during the course of evolution, and no one knew what to do because everybody was busy hatching out clever plans to meet the situation. No one had the courage to admit that they had reached an impasse. ... / So when I counsel my patient to pay attention to his dreams, I mean: "... Your dreams are an expression of your inner life, they can show you through what false attitude you have landed yourself in this blind alley."
>
> (*CW* 10 §§ 314 and 316)

Or:

> I have often been asked, "And what do you *do* about it?" I do nothing; there is nothing I can do except wait, with a certain trust in God, until, out of the conflict born with patience and fortitude, there emerges the solution destined— although I cannot foresee it—for that particular person. Not that I am passive or inactive meanwhile: I help the patient to understand all the things that the unconscious produces during the conflict.
>
> (*CW* 12 § 37)[7]

The last sentence of this quote nicely fulfills the definition that Hillman had given of the word "psychotherapy." And the earlier sentence in the last quote about "the conflict born with patience and fortitude" recalls another statement by Hillman in his cited work (p. 117), namely that

> From the same root [as that of "pathology"] come "patient" and "patience". Both are long-enduring, and as the alchemists said, "in your patience is your soul". The eradication of pathology in the modern sense of doing away with disease, when applied to the psyche means as well doing away with tension and suffering, with the patience to endure, and eventually, with the soul.

This only as an aside.

Jung's answer to why dreams are essential is that it is precisely his perplexity and helplessness that force him to look at dreams. He, and his patient anyway, is at his wits' end. *There is simply nothing else to turn to.* But this does not mean for him that dreams present the desired answers to the patient's anxious question, "What can I do?"; they are not the way out of his blind alley. They offer nothing but *images*, and images only very vaguely "point[-] to something or other," which in turn is no more than "better than nothing."

The point to be made here is that the second answer is paradoxical. It does not really offer any positive arguments for the value of dreams, neither a eulogy nor a theoretical evaluation (Jung explicitly denies having a "theory about dreams" or knowing "how dreams arise"). It does not try to demonstrate the importance of dreams (as *objects*), how great they are, what marvelous insight are to be gained from them, what jewels lie hidden in them. Its argument *for* the devotion to dreams is on the contrary an entirely *negative* one: the confession of the therapist's own empty-handedness and helplessness and thus the absolute negation of the idea of healer or knowing counselor. By in this way ruthlessly sweeping away all hope of getting a simple practical answer ("What can I *do*?") its thrust is directed at the *subject*, rather than praising the object (dreams). It *does* something to the attitude or stance of the subject, and in this sense it is in itself a *psychotherapeutic* answer. It brutally knocks down the illusionary projection upon the therapist of "healer" and "helper." By thereby breaking the last straw at which the ego clutched in order to be able to survive *as ego*, it initiates the patient, too, into the truth of his own helplessness and brings him down from his high horse of ego-consciousness to the zero-point of unconditional surrender. No hope, no exit through "hatching out clever plans to meet the situation" (be it by himself or with the help of a therapist). The patient, too, has to bow down under nothing better and more concrete, more convincing and reliable, than the despised mere shades of dream images. He is taught to *endure* in *patience*.

Why dreams? The second negative answer is: Because they (or one's having to turn one's attention to them as the *only* possibility left) ipso facto *amount to* the ego's unconditional surrender and as such to the (at least implicit) initiation into *soul*, soul as absolute negativity.

3. Dreams versus sandplay and painting

Jungian psychotherapy frequently relies not only on dreams as the self-expression of soul. There are other products, above all sandplay pictures and drawings or paintings (as *unreflected* "unconscious" creations). The question is what, psychologically seen, is their status in comparison to dreams.

One obvious difference is that dreams are happenings. They come upon us of their own accord, often decidedly against the dreamer's will (anxiety dreams!). And the dreamer's consciousness is necessarily asleep, if the images that occur to the dreamer are supposed to be dreams. Jung, bringing out this characteristic in bold relief, said simply: "... the dream, which is not manufactured by us, ..." (*Letters 2*, p. 591, to Read, 2 September 1960). The same cannot be said about sandplay pictures, patients' drawings or paintings. They are clearly "*manufactured*" by a person, and in waking consciousness.

As one can see above all in Japan, there are numerous impressive processes of sandplay therapy. They proceed basically averbally, beneath the threshold of conscious reflection, and without interventions by the therapist—and yet are wonderfully successful. Healing may take place without reflection of the meaning of what is produced, without understanding or comprehension. The image process *contains* its meaning within itself. It does not need to become explicit. In the West, something similar can be said about sandplay therapy with young children. Keeping this in mind, we have to conclude that "manufactured by the person" can mean two very different things. It can mean that the product is the result of ego-consciousness's doing, of a conscious thinking process. But it can also mean that, despite the fact that consciousness is awake, it is, nevertheless, produced more or less unconsciously, the waking ego-consciousness being pretty much inactive. The truly active subject is the soul underneath the ego. It obviously all depends on the particular psychic constitution of consciousness. Consciousness does not have to be the modern ego-consciousness. It can also be relative unconscious, a "dreaming" consciousness.

Western man lives inevitably in a world defined strictly as absolutely meaningless positivistic facts, which at bottom allow one only to ask about their causes and effects, their internal technical functioning, and perhaps, in the area of living things, their purposiveness in terms of evolution and for survival, etc. The meaning aspect of *real-world experiences*, that is, the soul, has been absolutely excluded, eradicated as non-existing and prohibited by penalty of the verdict of unsoundness of mind. Whenever "the soul" nevertheless stirs, then this is now only a subjective problem in the "*inner*" of man, coming from *his* unconscious (where "the unconscious" is simply a personal manifestation of the meaning aspect of reality that has been *excluded* from the conscious definition of the world, just as the [possibly "superstitious"] ideas and beliefs people used to have and what has been collected in museums and scientifically segregated off under the heading of "the humanities" are the cultural meaning aspect). A radical barrier separates inner and outer, meaning and fact. Mythological man, children, and traditional Japanese (all traditional East-Asians?) live(d) psychologically, by contrast, in a world for which this barrier or rupture did/does not yet exist in its rigidity. There is/was an unbroken continuity between the soul meaning of phenomena and their factual aspect. The meaning aspect is/was not totally taboo. This explains why children and the traditional Japanese can easily let "the soul" take over when asked to produce a sandplay image. They are immediately open to the deeper meaning aspect. In the case of adults, at most only a little *abaissement du niveau mental* is needed for the objective soul to be able to assert itself and pass, so to speak, under the radar of consciousness. The radical rupture of the "psychological difference" has not happened yet; the psychic process can also be immediately psychological (expressive of soul)![8]

For Western man this is hardly possible. For him, a gulf has opened up between the psychic and the psychological. In the Western world to open oneself to "the soul" would amount to the absolute sin against the Spirit of the modern world and therefore require an almost heroic (and this also means: an ipso facto self-defeating *ego*-) act or effort. This is not to say that for Western man it is not at all possible to work in sandplay therapy. This is certainly possible in certain cases. But apart from those situations in which psychopathology has already of its own accord caused an *abaissement du niveau mental*, it is then something fundamentally different from what it is for small children, namely not a natural spontaneous form of the soul's self-expression, but the ego's practicing sandplay as a deliberate *method* and thus as something a priori fenced-in, neutralized, deprived of its innocence. A child is devoted to a sandplay as *totus homo*, absolutely seriously, unreservedly. The adult can *consciously* allow himself to step down from the level of his mature adulthood and to give himself over to sandplay by construing it as happening in the neutrality and privacy of the segregated consulting room or his own "inner" and as something that by definition does not take place in, does not touch, and does not interfere with, the "the wilderness" out there: the logic of the real world around him.

I spoke of two very different meanings of "manufactured by the person." But these two possibilities are only the two extremes of one scale. Individual sandplay pictures may have their place anywhere between these extremes. This is the problem with sandplay therapy. One can never be sure to what extent it is the soul speaking through the produced picture and to which extent it is much rather the conscious mind or the ego. It is important to get some idea of the psychic constitution of patients before offering sandplay as a therapeutic option. A hesitant, somewhat skeptical approach is advisable with adult patients.

This uncertainty does not exist in the case of dreams, because consciousness and the ego are obviously asleep. Ego-consciousness cannot be the one that invents, manufactures, produces the dream (as happens, for example, in daydreaming, mere fantasizing). It must, however, be added here that even if consciousness is literally asleep, ego-consciousness may, nonetheless, in some ways make its influence felt in dreams (most blatantly in the dream-I's dream-internal defenses, but possibly also in other ways). A complicated matter! But that does not belong to the present context. At any rate, in the case of dreams the spontaneous non-ego, pre-reflective origin, and thus the greater reliability concerning the soul as *spiritus rector* of the dream, is evident.

Much the same as about making sandplay pictures must be said about drawing or painting for therapeutic purposes and as a means to get access to the deeper soul (or what used to be called "the unconscious"). Here, too, one should not be naive and take all paintings produced in the context of therapy as expression of the soul, just like that.

I might as well add to the list of other forms of access to the soul that have been developed in the past the method of "active imagination." Here, we get an additional problem. Very frequently in the practice of psychotherapy this method is used (misused) for ordinary fantasy processes that have nothing to do with what Jung invented as the psychological method of active imagination. Therapists ask the patient to simply start fantasizing about a certain topic or image, giving him carte blanche to imagine things. Then the specific meaning of "active" that Jung had in mind is ignored. "Active imagination" requires above all two things, (a) that, under appropriate external conditions and with a specific attitude, one mentally looks, e.g., at a dream figure—merely peers without any intention of one's own!—for so long until the figure starts moving (comes to life) of its own accord, and (b) that one then tries as conscious personality to get into a conversation or interaction with this figure. Active imagination precisely does not mean to spin a yarn.

This means, however, that in the case of active imagination in Jung's sense the ego is precisely too active, first of all by starting the whole operation as a conscious method and secondly by intruding into the soul's own speaking with the ego's own concerns. This method may have its practical therapeutic or other psychic value. But it does not qualify as soul-making.

4. Listening to patients' stories as if they were dreams?

There is the idea that if the patient does not bring dreams, then at least we should *listen* to what the patient talks about *as if* it were a dream. At first glance an attractive idea. This way of listening would be a truly psychological approach to the material the patient presents in therapy.

I must also mention a number of objections or cautions.

This idea should not be used indiscriminately. There are, of course, tendencies in psychotherapy, above all in Freudian psychoanalysis, to interpret everything the patient says in a session *psychoanalytically*, that is to say, as expressive of some hidden, unconscious desire or conflict, as leading straight to the "deepest personal secrets" (as Jung had said) of the speaker. The true meaning that the speaker is unaware of lies *behind* the explicit statement. It was, I believe, Hillman who once told a joke about this in a book or paper of his. In the morning two analysts in New York happen at the same time to enter the elevator in the high-rise building where they have their offices. When they

entered the elevator, the operator said: "Good morning, sirs." Then the one analyst looked at the other and said quietly, "What did he *mean* by that?" In this
joke they try to go behind the obvious meaning to an alleged deeper unconscious truth, instead of simply answering the operator's greeting on the same
level of everyday social communication on which it was offered. We should not
forget that by interpreting psychoanalytically we break out of the communal
"language game" and the situation of human fellowship. Rather, we then behave
like detectives who try to get, as it were, "behind the back" of the patient, to
unmask his views and operate according to the phrase, "everything that you say
from now on can be used against you!"

Now it goes without saying that the idea of "listening to the patient's narratives
as if it were a dream," within a context of Jungian psychotherapy, is not at all like
psychoanalytic interpretation in the spirit of the Freudian "hermeneutic of suspicion" (Paul Ricœur).[9] It is precisely, as the wording already suggests, inspired
by what for Ricœur is the very opposite type of hermeneutic, which is driven
by "the willingness to listen" and "the vow to obedience." Nevertheless, psychological listening is still a way of breaking out of interpersonal dialogue, which
is characterized by the fact that what the person to whom one is listening says is
taken at face value. As Gadamer pointed out,

> Thus it is inherent in an authentic conversation that ... one wants to under-
> stand him (the other person), to be sure not him as the individuality that he
> is, but as *that what he says*. What is to be comprehended is the substantial
> legitimacy of his *opinion*.[10]

Listening to what the other person says in the spirit of real communication on
the social level would require one's giving an *answer*, one's own answer to the
opinion expressed by the other and on the same level on which it was offered.
Both conversation partners would be concerned about the same objective content
or issue.

We cannot proceed from the assumption that everything said by the patient is
psychologically relevant, i.e., relevant from the point of view of soul. (Of course, if
what the patient says is to be taken as a symptom, as an involuntary manifestation
of a non-ego impulse, as for example, in the case of a Freudian slip, a psychological interpretation is in place. But this may be still very much on a personalistic
psychic level and not reach into the domain of soul.) There are also statements that
have to be taken straightforwardly, or the other way around, there are situations
in therapy in which the patient must be taken seriously in what he *means*, what
he intends to express, rather than in asking what it might *psychologically* mean.
This refers to statements that provide factual information or express the person's
serious human feelings, his opinions, or intellectual commitments. They require
a simple *human* (in contrast to psychological) understanding, empathy/sympathy,
and a direct response to the objective issue at stake.

Then again, there are numerous situations in therapy that require truly psychological listening and understanding. What the special character of these situations is

and the criterion for identifying them and differentiating them from the other type of situations is not so easy to determine. It requires personal judgment about which side of the "psychological difference" is involved (the psychic, personal, human-all-too-human side—*or* the soul side). This is a distinction that, in turn, requires a developed feeling function, psychological tact and skill, and an inner flexibility on the part of the therapist, the capability and readiness to shift his standpoint according to what the situation demands. We have to learn to distinguish in practical thera-peutic reality each time anew between the two sides of the psychological difference.

In this book about working with dreams, it suggests itself to describe the essen-tial quality of those patient narratives that deserve to be listened to as if they were dreams by contrasting the patient's speaking with what we learned about dreams. Dreams are precious to the psychologist because we see them as the soul's speaking about itself. "We have not manufactured them." They do not express the dreamer's, the subjective psyche's, the I's, views. So, the crucial distinction to be made circles around the question: who is ultimately the speaking subject—is it the objective psyche or is it the person, the ego-personality? What is the *source* or origin of psychic material, the patient or the objective psyche?

Just as dreams, the patient's symptoms can also be considered to be the soul's speaking. So, all in all, we could say that we can listen psychologically to what the patient himself tells us whenever we sense that his speaking is not really *his* speaking, that he himself is not really the subject that expresses itself, but that his literal speaking is merely the place in which "the other," the "non-ego," the "soul," is speaking about itself.

Nevertheless, the special significance of dreams is that in their case we can be sure that they don't come from the ego, from the ego personality. Indeed, that they are not filtered by the patient as speaking subject as in the case of his own utterances. It is inherent in the quality and phenomenology of dreams that they are immediately felt and known by the patient himself as "other," "alien," not *his* speaking, whereas what he says to the analyst in a session as his own commu-nication and his own imaginings is accordingly also experienced by him as his personal self-expression, even if indirectly it may also be the deeper psyche that really is speaking through *his* speaking.

At any rate, it is crucial not to take a *method* for a real *object* or "prime matter," that is to say, not to confuse the soulfulness of our methodical use of a particular soulful *style* of listening to what is being said (listening to it as if it were a dream) with the actual existence of an authentic soul product. This style of listening cannot be a substitute for one's working with dreams. For in-depth soul work real dreams are indispensable, at least in the context of the modern West for which the psychic and the psychological have irrevocably separated.

When patients don't dream

Often patients say that they don't have dreams or cannot remember them. What can we do about that; what stance can we take with respect to this problem? There are a number of completely different aspects that need to be considered separately.

1   Jungian therapy is a two-person affair. There is the patient and there is the analyst. So, when confronted with the question of why a patient does not bring dreams, we first have to take a look at the patient. And since Jungian therapy as *psycho*therapy operates with the psychological difference, we need to discriminate two different possible therapeutic situations. Therefore, concerning a particular patient who does not bring dreams we have to ask: is deep soul work really necessary for this patient? Are dreams really needed for his therapy? Not everyone needs dream analysis. Sometimes there are enough problems on the ego level that need to be worked through and can also be worked through successfully on the ego level, without one's necessarily having to turn to dreams.

Jung once distinguished, for example, four stages of therapy: "confession, enlightenment, education, transformation" (*CW* 16 §§ 59ff.). I think we don't have to see them as consecutive stages. It may be better to view them as different aspects of the therapeutic process that may come to the fore irregularly at different times. But for simplicity's sake I will stay with Jung's word "stages." In all stages dreams may be additional helpful tools by bringing up certain maybe forgotten or repressed topics and memories, thus functioning technically (not psychologically) as a kind of trigger for conscious work. Nevertheless, they are not indispensable for successful work in the first three stages that Jung mentioned. They may, of course, also psychologically facilitate and support changes of attitude of consciousness. Only Jung's fourth stage, the one called "transformation," goes into the depths, requires a soul journey and thus also requires dreams. But the work on never-expressed personal secrets, embarrassing inner conflicts, etc. can be done on a conscious level. So also the work in cases of simple immaturity, a lack of adaptation to reality (this would belong to what Jung called "education") with still prevailing childish illusions or ideas of grandiosity. This would not be *psycho*therapy in the strict sense at all. This evaluation applies also to fundamentally different cases, where one is dealing with terribly painful, maybe traumatic childhood experiences that impaired the normal development of the personality. Here much *psychic* work is necessary, above all on the level of feeling (i.e., through ordinary human understanding and sympathy and a reliable relationship characterized by trust and honest care). *Psychology* in the narrower sense may not really be needed. But, again, dreams can have here an enormously supportive effect—however, not on the level of soul, but of the psyche.

Another question with respect to the patient is whether the absence of dreams is merely a matter of laziness on his part. That would then be a psychic problem to be worked out. The therapist's task would be to try to win the patient over for dream work and also to impress on him the necessity of a certain *discipline* for any serious therapeutic work.

More serious, and almost the opposite, is the situation where dreams are ignored by the patient because of an instinctive fear of an impending possible psychosis. Here the therapist should respect this fear as long as it seems still conducive.

2   A second question the therapist has to ask about the absence of patients' dreams is whether this may not be due to his own attitude and feeling, his style. Am *I* really interested in dreams, or am *I* at heart much more merely a technician in the area of psychotherapy? Do *I* love soul work, or do *I* perhaps either myself fear to go into the depths with my patient or simply do not have an authentic access to them? Much depends on the reality of the attitude of the therapist. What is his own depth, his own commitment? Does he have a developed understanding and living sense of the dimension of soul?

Patients, but also people in general, are often much more influenced by the reality and inner truth of the personality speaking about a particular topic than by the explicit statements made by the person. "In psychotherapy," Jung stated (*CW* 17 § 240, transl. altered to reflect the original), "we have gained the insight that in the last analysis it is not knowledge and the technique applied, but the personality that has a curative effect." The same is true (as Jung here also added) in the area of education, and there, with children, it is probably even more impressive. This applies, of course, also to the therapist's unspoken real relation to dreams. If the therapist does not have a genuine inner connection to dreams and if the sense of the importance of dreams does not truly live in him, the patient may subliminally sense this and not take his own dreams seriously, even if the therapist explicitly asks him to pay attention to his dreams. Conversely, if the soul level is really and strongly alive in the therapist, this may also latently inspire or "infect" the patient. The true being of the therapist's personality makes itself felt as a kind of imperceptible atmosphere in the consulting room that exerts its influence on the patient beneath the threshold of consciousness.

3   The third point concerns the way the therapist introduces the topic of dreams for therapy to the patient who does not bring dreams of his own accord. It is, of course, reasonable to explain the significance of dreams, that they provide access to deeper layers of the psyche, to those layers colloquially referred to as "the unconscious," from which also the psychic symptoms come;[11] that it is not sufficient to rely on his own conscious knowledge and ideas that the ego has, just as not on the therapist's "wisdom" and the techniques available to him; that the importance of this deeper layer of the psyche is not only a practical one in the sense of allowing us to get at the root of the problem; furthermore, that it much rather also has the character of a kind of other personality in him, of a counter-will, a "non-ego," and wants to be acknowledged and take part in one's life[12]; "That thing in you which should live is alone; nobody touches it, nobody knows it, you yourself don't know it; but it keeps stirring, it disturbs you, it makes you restless, and it gives you no peace" (*CW* 18 § 632). Furthermore, one could point out that, ultimately considered, this inner other is indeed the *soul* and that this is why it is really something precious,

something to be valued and appreciated for itself and that it is helpful, so to speak, slowly to make a friend of it. In dreams, it is *his* own soul's speaking.

The foregoing paragraph is not meant as a collection of ready-made boiler-plate text to be repeated literally to patients. What I presented in it is only an indication of the general direction and spirit in which the therapist might want to introduce the topic of dreams to his patients and provide some essential concepts that might prove useful. It probably also hardly needs to be mentioned that it would make no sense in the context of an actual session with a patient to present him with what might sound like a formal theoretical lecture. What one says needs to be spontaneous, come from one's own conviction, and fit to this particular patient and the particular therapeutic session.

Apart from such general explanations about why dreams are important for therapy, one can also give patients some practical tips, if they believe they have no dreams or have difficulties catching their dreams.

Before falling asleep at night, they could consciously ask themselves: "Will I have a dream tonight?" or "What will I dream tonight?" If one falls asleep with the topic of dreams in one's mind, it might prove helpful. By the same token, the first thought when waking up should be: "Was there a dream?" If one can remember anything at all, one should refresh one's memory and strengthen it by not merely concentrating on the conceptual content, but also reviving the concrete visual impression and sensate experience of it. One should try to really *see* the scene again, to *feel* the emotions, the sensations of the texture of things one came in touch with and the spatial feeling one had, etc.

And then, always with the precise visual and sensate impression in mind, one should jot down on paper what one remembers. It is advisable to have paper and pencil ready on one's nightstand and to begin writing while still in bed *in a semi-sleep mood*, in order to stay as close as possible to the dream atmosphere. If one gets up, turns on the full light in the room, this may have the effect of having turned a switch from night-world to day-world, from "the unconscious" to ego-consciousness, and the dream that a moment before had still been in memory may have completely vanished. So it is helpful to use a rather dim light.

For people who have real difficulties catching their dreams, it is crucial that they faithfully write down even the tiniest and probably therapeutically not usable dream fragment of an otherwise forgotten dream, even if it is merely a vague impression of something that can hardly be described in words. It needs this faithfulness and persistence to gradually get the dream activity and memory going. Such a practice concerning even seemingly meaningless fragments is also in itself therapeutic: it amounts to a humble service of the soul, of the soul's speaking, and precisely not for the sake of any practical benefit (which would be an ego interest), but simply for the soul's own sake.

Later in the day the early morning quick notes of the dream need to be written out in more detail and in fair copy, where special attention is to be paid (1) to the wording as precise as possible for the dream images with their sensual aspect and (2) to not changing anything, adding anything, smoothing out strange or inconsistent things, and filling out possible lacunas. There has to be great discipline in writing down truthfully what was actually in the dream and is still remembered. What was vague or ambiguous has to be faithfully represented as such.

The patient activity of writing down the dream in detail, searching for the best, most accurate words, and preparing a clean copy is a sign of the respect one pays to the product of the soul's speaking. Jung once threw out an analysand from therapy because he had presented him a dream on a messy torn-off piece of paper, telling him that if he, the patient, showed so little regard for what came from the soul he did not see why he, Jung, should devote himself to the patient. Quite radical. But Jung certainly had a point there!

Normally people start dreaming when in analysis, even if they had dreams only very, very rarely before.

In everything discussed so far, we have still stayed in the forecourt of our actual theme, "*Working* with dreams." We are now ready to turn our attention to this central topic.

Notes

1. *CW* 9i § 400 has "In myths and fairytales, as in dreams, the psyche tells its own story, and the interplay of the archetypes is revealed in its natural setting as ..." (The quote is from GOETHE's *Faust II* and reads in German: "*Gestaltung, Umgestaltung, des ewigen Sinnes ewige Unterhaltung.*")
2. The move performed by Jung, his pushing off from the focus on the human beings who *have* dreams to the dream itself and to the notion of the dream as the soul's speaking about itself is a wonderful expression of the "psychological difference," the difference between the psychic and the psychological, or between the psyche of the human organism, on the one hand, and the soul, on the other. At the same time, Jung's move shows us what the entrance into true psychology, a psychology *with* soul or as the study of the logos of the soul, requires: the unflinching move away from so-called "psychology" as the study of the behavior of the organism with its positivistic insistence on a factual substrate, in other words, from personalistic or ego psychology, and the intellectual courage to base psychology exclusively on *nothing* but its own *bottomless, absolute-negative* root metaphor of soul. We will come back to this topic of the psychological difference and psychology in later chapters.
3. The translation of "*ewiger Sinn*" as "eternal Mind" as well as the capitalization of "Mind" can be questioned. Goethe did specifically not use the much more likely and established phrase "*ewiger Geist*," which frequently is a way to refer to God. By using "Sinn," which also means simply "meaning" or "sense," Goethe probably wanted to avoid the immediate identification with God as a personal being. Nouns are always capitalized in German. Thus, "*ewiger Sinn*" could possibly also be rendered as "eternal sense" (lower case).
4. "Collective": supra-personal, communal, the property of the generality, the particular culture.

5. Georg Christoph Lichtenberg, *Sudelbücher*, Heft F, #575, in: *idem, Schriften und Briefe* I, ed. by Wolfgang Promies, München (Hanser) 1968, p. 539 (my transl.).

6. James Hillman, *Suicide and the Soul*, New York *et al.* (Harper Colophon Books) 1964, pp. 115 f.

7. Another Jung passage that comes to mind in this context is to be found in *CW* 11 §§ 35 and 36.

8. It would be a mistake to think that through these ideas the notion of "the unconscious" returned through the backdoor. The original and natural form of *consciousness* is in itself unconscious, that of a more or less "dreaming" consciousness. Modern ego-consciousness's fully waking *disciplined* state of consciousness is the culturally late achievement of a consciousness-internal rise above consciousness's own dreamlike state. One's entrance into true psychology requires the conquest of the insight into the "psychological difference" and one's pushing off from the psyche to soul. True psychology is a response to the modern situation. But historically the movement is one in the opposite direction. The real achievement was consciousness's conquest for itself of the status of ego-consciousness, of the psyche in contrast to soul, precisely by pushing off from consciousness's containment in soul. "Soul" and "ego" are here titles for different *forms* (logical constitutions) that consciousness can take up.

9. How far removed Jung's thinking is from the hermeneutic of suspicion is shown by his passionate refusal to see the actual dream as a façade.

10. Hans-Georg Gadamer, *Wahrheit und Methode. Grundzüge einer philosophischen Hermeneutik*, Tübingen (J. C. B. Mohr [Paul Siebeck]), 1975, p. 363 (my transl., my italics).

11. To psychologically uninformed patients one could, for example, point out that medical doctors make blood tests, check for invisible bacteria or viruses or even for DNA problems and that in a similar way psychotherapy needs material from the unconscious.

12. Jung said it wants to *mitleben*, see *Erinn.*, p. 331 (the translation in *MDR* p. 329 is inadequate). *Mitleben*: to participate in one's life as an acknowledged part of oneself, to have a real share in one's living life.

Part III

The proper attitude towards the dream

Crossing the river: The standpoint of soul

The word psychotherapy as generally used can mean two very different things.

The one is the medical or car-repair idea of psychotherapy. People have psychic disorders, and the therapists have to repair them, get rid of them. Then psychotherapy is a kind of technology, like medicine. Here above all such forms of therapy as cognitive behavior therapy have their place, but often psychoanalysis and analytical psychology are also conceived and practiced by practitioners in this way, although by comparison with technology in the ordinary sense the techniques they use are, of course, very different "soft" techniques, such as empathy, attention to transference feelings, dream interpretation, active imagination, painting from out of the unconscious.

It may sound astonishing that I include dream interpretation also among the possible *techniques* used in a psychotherapy conceived according to the car-repair model. But dreams can indeed also be *used* as means to an end, i.e., technically, without any recourse to the notion of soul. They can be used as a starting point or cue for the patient's free associations or imaginings, for reviving biographical memories, and from the therapist's point of view for diagnostic purposes, for projecting his favorite psychological theories upon particular dream images. They can also be used as a justification and support, "from the patient's own inner," for the therapist's ideas about which functions or psychic personality aspects the patient still needs to develop and what he needs to work on, furthermore, for confirming the idea of archetypes and giving therapy an aura of mystery and mythological depth.

Jung's idea of psychotherapy is an example of the other type. It is completely different from the car-repair model. Here the focus is on the soul, on the expression of the soul, and not on the cure of the patient.

A common dream motif is that the dream-I has to cross a river. The river divides one region or country on the one side from another region or country on the other side. In geographical reality rivers usually dug their bed into one tract of land cutting it apart into two. This means that we find the same type of soil and rock on both sides of the river. This is very different from the dream symbol of a river to be crossed. The dream river not only cuts in a quantitative sense one uniform whole apart into two separate pieces or sides. It establishes and marks *otherness* as such. The separation is qualitative. What is on the other side of the symbolic river is *fundamentally* different from what is on this side, indeed, it is *the* Other, more specifically the *not*-this, the *not*-familiar: the realm of absolute negativity. In this sense it is the land of soul, mythologically speaking, "the underworld," the "yonder."

The image of the river to be crossed as a dream motif is important for the dreamer's psychological development. But for us it can also serve as a helpful image for understanding psychology (and psychotherapy) itself. This image is really nothing but an imaginal representation of the "psychological difference," the difference between the psychic and the psychological, the human-all-too-human and the soul. My thesis is that psychology proper begins only when we, that is our consciousness, have crossed over the river and when our standpoint is now really on the other side. And this means: when in our way of looking at things we have left behind the side from which we came. So we have to perform this movement of a separation, a radical negation. Psychology, our type of psychology, is called depth psychology and that means it always operates with this division between, for example, "consciousness" and "the unconscious," "ego," and "soul." As indicated, this is not a harmless difference of just two different parts of the same land; the two sides are also really opposites. They clash, contradict each other. It is a different, opposite way of looking at things. → ←.

What is on the first side? The first side is, as I already hinted, the familiar world. It is the social arena of people; the sphere of ordinary, common-sense thinking; the world of objects in space and of positive facts. Of course, it is also the realm of the ego personality and all the ego feelings, ego wishes, human desires for warmth, comfort, safety, and survival, etc. All that is on the first side. And psychology begins, as I said, only when our standpoint has left all that behind. No continuity! A break, a rupture, a translocation of the standpoint of consciousness is necessary to enter psychology.

It is not enough to merely *look across* (peep over) to the other side while still standing on the old side. You have to actually *get* there and to have established your standpoint on the other side. What you see of the other side from the old side, if you merely *look* at the other side, will paradoxically always also be "ego." As long as you stand on the old side, your standpoint is ego and the ego always sees only what is ego-syntonic, an ego fantasy of what is to be seen. To be sure, you will then also be able to see "the other," but it will only be the *semantic* other, while *syntactically* this other will be seen only in terms of sameness and as "same" as being as broad as it is long. Only like can know like. The death of the old standpoint is necessary in order to have a true psychological, a soul standpoint.

This indispensable shift that the psychologist must have performed is, however, not an experiential nor an existentialist one! It is not one for the person as a whole (not a transformation of personality; it has, for example, nothing to do with Jung's "individuation process"), but it is one only for the *standpoint* of consciousness. It is an intellectual shift, a *methodological* shift. It does not refer to your own personal self-development. In a dream and thus in the inner experience of an individual, the motif of crossing a river may have something to do with a (the individual's) *personal initiation* into "otherness" on the existential and experiential level, that is, an initiation of *homo totus*, remotely comparable to that of a shaman, perhaps an initiation into the land of death or soul. But in our case it is an intellectual or methodological shift, an "initiation" (if we want to use this word here) merely into a different *theoretical* way of looking at the same things as before. It would merely be a mode change, a change of the *general* style of consciousness concerning psychological phenomena.

There are numerous statements by Jung that show that this "having crossed the river" was essential for him as a psychologist. I will cite only a few. He stated, for example: "True, the unconscious knows more than the consciousness does; but it is knowledge of the special sort, knowledge in eternity, usually without reference to the here and now, not couched in the language of the intellect" (*MDR* p. 311). What needs to be highlighted in this quote is the negations: what "the unconscious," i.e., "the soul," expresses is *not* the usual sort of knowledge and *not* couched in the language of the intellect (i.e., ego-consciousness). What it refers to is *not* ordinary reality ("the here and now"), but "eternity" as the wholly other. Again, in another context we hear from Jung that, "During the work of interpretation one must abstain from all presuppositions that smack of superstition, such as, first and foremost, the notion that the protagonists in dreams are nothing other than the same persons in real life" (*CW* 10 § 321). To consider the figures in dreams as identical with the same persons in the patient's familiar everyday life, Jung tells us, would be a case of superstition! Jung quite obviously has performed the cut between ordinary reality and the world of dreams as the world of soul. The following quote confirms the same view. After having reported an analysand's dream in which she was going to see a doctor who lived in a house beside the sea, Jung explained:

> Naturally when she dreams of the doctor, everybody is inclined to think he is myself. She is under my treatment and so that refers to me. Now it is only funny that the unconscious does not say so more definitely. Naturally anybody who analyzed dreams according to Freud's point of view would say that it was I, but I am not sure. If the unconscious wanted to convey the idea that this was Dr. Jung, it would say so; then the dream itself, which we cannot criticize, would have brought me in. But the dream says "the doctor by the sea," and the Lake of Zürich is not a sea. Therefore there is some change in the whole situation and we see that behind the impressions of the daily life—behind the scenes—another picture looms up, covered by a thin veil of actual facts. In order to understand dreams, we must learn to think like that. We should not judge dreams from realities because in the long run that leads nowhere.[1]

This text starts out with a discussion of one single specific dream image, but the concluding sentences lay down a principle for dream interpretation of general, systematic significance. The word "behind" ("behind the scenes") in Jung's text stands for my image of the river that separates two fundamentally different spheres. On this side we have "the impressions of the daily life," the "veil of actual facts," the "realities." On the other side there is the "other picture" that "looms up." It is really "other" in the sense explained above. In order to understand dreams, Jung declares categorically, the river *must* be crossed, the "realities" or positive facts *must* be left behind: "We must learn to think like that"! That staying on this side would "in the long run … lead[-] nowhere" simply means that we would miss psychology, miss "soul." A clinical approach to psychotherapy is excluded.

The psychological difference gives expression to the fact that the word "psychology" is in itself ambiguous.[2] The river I am speaking of goes right through it, and for psychology to come home to itself this divide that is inherent in itself, in the very *notion* of psychology, needs to be crossed. This is why psychology, properly understood, is not just a science, a field of knowledge, a *Fach*. A science provides knowledge that simply can and needs to be applied in practice. But psychology cannot be applied. It is not something always available, waiting to be used in the consulting room upon the suffering patient. No, it has task-character. In order to *be* in the first place, the crossing-over or pushing-off-from movement that it amounts to needs to be performed. Needless to say, "performing" does not refer to an ego action, a literal behavior. It is not something to be "achieved," not the result of an effort of the will. It happens in the inwardness of the mind and presupposes that the psychological difference has struck a deep chord in us so that, without our doing, we have already been reached by "the other side."

Having made such a strong point of the necessity to cross the river I now, nevertheless, have to remind the reader of another consequence of the psychological difference: In the practical reality of psychotherapy we must not absolutize its one side, the soul, and exclude the other side, the psyche. In answer to the legitimate question: "Can everything be seen from the standpoint of soul, or must we not also on the object side, the side of phenomena, distinguish between genuine soul phenomena and not-soul, purely factual phenomena?" we may, of course, wish to point to polytheistic mythology, which was able to see the divine at work *in* the natural, and thus at least potentially in everything. But that is no longer possible for modern man, for born man! Born man has experienced the disenchantment of the world. He lives in mere-nature.

Furthermore, as I already indicated above, I have to ask myself with each patient: does he or she really need psychology and is he able to be open for soul work or not? There are many patients who do not need soul work or are not capable or ready for this highly subtle, differentiated Jungian therapy. They merely need to learn to live a normal life. They need to adapt to reality. They need to be freed of their illusions. They need emotional support so that they can overcome deficiencies in their ego-stability. And so on. Here one needs to work on the *psychic* level, not on the *psychological* one. It would be wrong to try to work in the genuine Jungian therapy-style and think in terms of "logical movement." And second, even with those patients with whom the Jungian approach is possible and to be preferred, it is not so that every moment is one of soul-making. At times there are also other topics that need to be discussed. We must not feel under pressure to always be a true psychologist. Here, too, we must not be a stickler for principles. An inner spirit of freedom is necessary.

However, this does not give me license to do in therapy just as the mood takes me. My commitment as psychotherapist is to the soul. And two things are crucial when regarding the two possibilities of psychotherapy (the "repair idea" type vs. the truly psychological work). First, that one *knows* what one is doing in each situation and second, that one is *honest*, not calling psychology what, in reality, has nothing to do with psychology but is merely repair work or a kind of education, etc. Above all, concerning dreams one must not call something dream interpretation if one is not truly interested in the dream itself, but only in the patient, and if one uses, abuses, the dreams for certain ego-psychological purposes.

Nevertheless, even in my merely *psychic* work I would scorn *technical* approaches, particularly as they are also ethically problematic, because by using techniques upon the patient I reduce him or her to an object to be treated. Psychic work, too, should treat the patient as a subject in the spirit of freedom, and on an authentic human level, face to face. I cannot allow myself to wish to change (and this means to manipulate!) the patient. I must relate to and respect him as a truly free person, free also to have defenses or to refuse to give up his neurotic attitude.

For both sides of the psychological difference we must confirm that the therapist is not a healer, not a technician. This applies also to the question of how to cross the river. If there is in *this* my patient something that wants to cross the river or is capable and ready to do so, then I as therapist can try to support this tendency as well as help to remove obstacles. If in this patient this is not the case, the therapist cannot do anything about it. It is *not* the therapist's responsibility to make the patient cross the river. The therapist can at most only show the entrance gate. *It is the patient* or *his soul that has to do the entering*! It is his responsibility or that of his psyche. The patient (or his soul) has to do the work, not the therapist. Just as babies only learn to walk and speak through their own efforts; nobody can do it for them. It would be a mistake on the part of the therapist to want to do *for the patient* what the patient or his psyche does not really want and do himself/itself. Then the therapist is in the ego and in a technical fantasy, the fantasy of the maker or healer. Indeed, if YOU as therapist were to try to make the patient cross the river, then you would castrate his psyche. As therapists we have to respect the freedom, selfhood, and integrity of the individual. No interference in the patient's domestic affairs!

The three stances to "crossing the river" and the three forms of otherness

I started out the previous chapter with the idea that there are two fundamentally different ways to understand the word psychotherapy: the medical (clinical) or car-repair model and the Jungian idea. But if we think of the idea of crossing over the river, we need a distinction of three possibilities, because there are three possible stances with respect to this idea. The two extremes are shamanic (or analogous to the shamanic) initiation at the one end and the medical model at the other. The former implies, as indicated earlier, that the whole man, the person in his innermost essence, as *self*, crosses over to the other side. The medical or technical understanding of psychotherapy, on the contrary, means that no crossing at all over the river takes place. We have to place the psychotherapist, in the soul sense of the word, between these two extremes. I say "between" because the psychotherapist is radically different from both in some regards, while sharing something with both in another regard. That he has to cross over the river in order to be what he is supposed to be is what he has in common with "the shaman" (to use this title only as a kind of placeholder) and what sets him radically apart from the psychotherapist as medical practitioner. On the other hand, that his "crossing over the river" does not involve his self, him as the whole man, but means only a shift in the theoretical style of viewing things, so that otherwise he stays an ordinary man like everybody else, is what he shares with the technical medical therapist and what at the same time marks the difference from the shaman.

This latter point is important. Jung himself seems at times to have identified himself with the ancient role of the medicine-man in his relation "to his tribe" (that is, in Jung's case: to mankind).[3] Some of his disciples and biographers compared him to a shaman. Be that as it may (there are certainly some indications, such as his uncanny intuition, his mediumistic sides, that might possibly suggest some similarity), this is of no interest and consequence for us here. However, what needs to be clearly expressed is that to the extent that Jung indeed should have been something like a shaman or medicine-man in the ancient sense, he would *to that same extent* not have been a psychologist, psychotherapist in the sense of soul. He would have been a *healer* and left the ranks of ordinary men by having gained, and personally embodied, the superior spiritual status of *mediator* between his people and the gods or upper powers. The psychotherapist as person stays civilian man,[4] "only that!" His "crossing the river" changes the logical status of consciousness, but not his status as person and his spiritual power.

The form that "otherness" takes for the shaman is that of a cosmic supernatural realm, the world of actual spirits. The "crossing of the river" happens in his case through a literal journey, in trance, to this other world in order to attempt there to gain influence over bad spirits and acquire helpful spirits as his personal spirit guides that will also help him later to cure illnesses. The trance state is essential here. It means first that contact with the other side cannot happen in consciousness, for the waking mind. To consciousness it inevitably stays "wholly other." It means, second, that both the journey and the other side (the supernatural world and the spirits) are taken completely literally, both by himself and by his community. For the trance state is different from dreams for us moderns, since from dreams one wakes up and knows that it was "only a dream."

For psychology, the form of "otherness" is completely different. The other side needs to be reached consciously. It amounts to a transformation of the logical form of consciousness, a different style of thinking. And "the other" itself has the form of another *dimension*, the dimension of absolute negativity. The difference is not cosmic (as for the shaman), but logical.

Now turning to the other extreme (the psychotherapist who follows the medical or car-repair model), we know that he stays safely on this side of the river. But in his case, such a thing as "staying on this side" needs to be duplicated, applied to itself, in order to be understood essentially (since he is not, like Kafka's man from the country in his parable "Before the Law" merely cowardly hesitating and still waiting). We have to realize that *not* to "cross over the river" (and on principle so!) ipso facto means that for him there *is* no such river in the first place and therefore also no "other side" at all to which it might be possible and necessary to get. The idea of another side in our sense appears to him as a mystification, as a stupid superstitious fiction. The crucial point here is that the *essential* not-crossing obliterates itself, obliterates that it is a 'not crossing'.

What both for Kafka's man from the country and for the veritable psychologist is "*the* Other" as an entirely different *dimension* ("the Law" for the one, the realm of soul and its logical life, or the dimension of "absolute negativity" for the other) shrinks for the psychotherapist as technician or clinician to something on the banal level of ordinary social reality: "The other" takes on the meaning of the simple positive fact of "other human being," i.e., the patient, who is sitting vis-à-vis him in one and the same consulting room, in other words, on the same old plane. The result is the reduction of psychology as a psychology of and with soul to "people's psychology," the study of what is going on inside people, in the *psyche* (as we have to say here) of the biological organism. The only remaining sense of specific otherness is the (also merely human-all-too-human) "hidden secret" in the chest of the patient, the repressed, the unconscious, that which lies behind the façade, behind the mask or 'the manifest.' All that turns the psychologist into a *detective*. And it is the symptom, the pathology, the defects, which call for the car-repair fantasy of psychotherapy.

The elimination altogether of the notion of "crossing over the river" inevitably establishes that type of psychology and psychotherapy that is securely rooted in positivity: ego-psychology and personalistic thinking, psychology systematically focused on the patient, with the eyes on principle firmly shut to soul. This is what makes it a branch of medicine. Against first appearances, those therapies that aim for the patient's finding his "personal myth" and work with the ideas of "the numinous" and "transcendence" as their medicine also belong to this positivistic and personalistic stance. The interest in the mythic and numinous is just an external wrapping that covers the true inner core.

Psychotherapy—the making of *psychology*

In Jungian psychology we are used to interpreting myths as expressing "archetypal patterns," patterns of the soul's movement at particular moments of its logical life. The usual idea, then, is that some of these movements may occur in patients particularly in the course of a deep analysis, but maybe also spontaneously outside of any therapy process, the one pattern in one person, another one in another. During a longer therapeutic process with one patient, the movement corresponding to one myth may occur at this point, that corresponding to another myth at a later point. At any rate, the place where these mythological processes may happen is the individual. The major example of this thinking is Jung's idea of the individuation process, which is conceived as a process that goes through various stages that correspond to mythological or other archetypal forms. Despite his otherwise truly psychological and decidedly unpersonalistic stance, Jung projected the task of individuation in his high (his *psychological*) sense personalistically and positivistically onto real people and gave the impression that it is something that has to happen in and to people: "If the individual is not really changed, nothing is changed" (*Letters 2*, p. 462, to James Gibb, 1 October 1958). The individuation process is located and conceived as a process in people and as the process of *their* self-development, their becoming self. The general idea is that the ultimate goal of a deep Jungian analysis is for the analysand to undergo this process and reach his or her individuation. There is even the idea that ideally all people should "individuate" (in the particular Jungian sense of individuation).

The problem is not Jung's insistence on the importance of the individual over against modern mass society. This insistence is well taken. But *it* concerns a psychic concern, not a psychological one. The psychological theme of individuation is somehow confounded with the psychic need of strengthening the individual, and the individual is, in Hillman's sense, *literalized*.

Regardless of whether it shows merely as individual mythological or "archetypal" patterns or as an entire individuation process, I think this locating the movement that the soul undergoes in its logical life in patients, in persons, is a grave mistake: a violation of the spirit of true psychotherapy and psychology. Obviously, by thinking this way one has fallen into the clinical trap. Psychology has become people's psychology, the study of what goes on inside people.

Now, there is certainly no denying that it is by no means rare that in dreams important mythological motifs occur, also motifs that can be seen as moments of what Jung conceived as the individuation process. But then these motifs have their place *in the dream*. They are *dream* images. To conclude from this that the process *they* are *about* is a process *in those persons* is a fallacy. We can generally assert that, other than the soul in religious thinking and in metaphysics (as each person's eternal part) and other than the psyche, soul in the sense of modern psychology is not *in* people, *in* human beings at all.

Therapists may have understood that soul movements must not be construed as literal experiential or emotional happenings (i.e., happenings on the psychic level), but that as *psychological* they are strictly *logical (noetic) events*. And yet, even they may, nevertheless, at times toy with the idea that these events must happen *in people*. When, for example, in the therapy of a patient with a serious pathology, after long intensive work that included the discussion of numerous dreams and other psychic material a wonderful development took place, they might therefore try to imagine that what enabled this development and the liberation from the serious symptoms was the soul's logical movement that happened in this patient sort of behind the scenes. Itself invisible to us, it shows only in its results.

Certainly, it is very likely that invisibly behind the scenes some process has been going on of which one in the end sees the welcome results. But the point is, as a process happening in the human being, it was, of course, a *psychic* process, not a soul process, not a logical movement. This process is obviously a change in the psyche of the person, on the natural, empirical level. It may well be due, for example, to the therapeutic relationship, to the support of the patient by the therapist, to the interpretations by the therapist, or to other factors. This change has nothing to do with a psychological change. This does, however, not mean that the psychic change might not have been *facilitated* by a psychological change. If so, this psychological movement, qua *psychological* and *logical* movement, cannot be found *in people*. To look for it there is, as I pointed out, fallacious. The question is, where does a logical process happen (if it happens at all), where is the actual locus of psychotherapy in the soul sense of the word?

At this point let me introduce a story about Hodja Nasreddin. One day he lost his ring in the living room. He looked all over on the floor but could not find it. So he went out to the courtyard and searched there. Then his wife called to him: "Hodja, why are you looking in the courtyard? You lost your ring in the living room!" He answered: "Oh, in the living room it is so dark and therefore very difficult to see. Here in the courtyard the sun is shining so that it is so much easier to see such a little thing as a ring."

"The patient" is the psychological version of Nasreddin's "courtyard." For the *conventional* understanding of psychotherapy people are supposed to be where "the ring" is to be found, where the movement of the soul's logical life is to take place. The courtyard is the place of bright daylight. The patient is the obvious, visible, and tangible object of psychotherapy. He alone is a concrete empirical reality. This is, the therapeutic Nasreddin thinks, why soul has to be looked for in him.

But not what the eyes can see, but what opens the eyes, that is the Brahma, we read in the *Kena Upanishad*.

Concerning individuation, we now can say that Jung, too, located it in Nasreddin's courtyard! Despite all the thousands of Jungians and their analysands, you cannot find a single individual among them of whom one could say that they are individuated. This is *not* because they all were not good enough to achieve this goal, but because individuation in this sense simply does not take place in people in the first place. Jung tried, of course, to forestall such an objection (the objection that argues that his sense of individuation cannot be reached) by saying: "There is no linear evolution; there is only a circumambulation of the self," "the circumambulation of the center" (*MDR* p. 196 and 197), and "The goal is important only as an idea" (*CW* 16 § 400). This certainly goes in the right direction because these statements clearly remove the self and the possibility of an actual accomplishment of individuation from the empirical, positive-factual sphere. But the personalistic burdening the individual with the task of circumambulating the center and the fiction of his or her individuation remain, nonetheless.

To look for logical processes and events and thus also individuation in Jung's sense in what is obvious, in the positive-factual reality of people, amounts to a *naturalistic* standpoint. It is hard to understand that Jung with his veritable psychological sense would his whole life long not see through this fallacy. In order to do psychology, we have to overcome the naturalistic fallacy. As alchemy made it explicit, the *unio naturalis* needs to be dissolved at the beginning of the work. "Beware of the physical in the material!", the alchemists warned. Psychology requires that the "psychological difference" be realized. Our orientation has to be turned away from empirical reality, and that, first and foremost, also means away from real people. We have to learn to look into another direction. The Greek *psychê* is not in life, it comes into being only after death. And in psychology, the soul is not "what the eyes can see." And the reason why the soul cannot be seen by the eyes is not because it is allegedly "inside," so to speak, hidden under our skin, but because it is *nowhere*. It belongs, mythologically speaking, to the "underworld," it is *Geist*, "ghost," soul and not a positivity or an empirical fact. It is absolute negativity. We need to free psychology to itself.

In contrast to logical events like mythological patterns, such phenomena as alcoholism and drug addiction are indeed processes that take place in empirical reality, in the physical body of people. Their dependence, apart from its physiological aspect, is merely a *psychic* problem, and as such ultimately biological. By contrast, *psychological* processes cannot take place in people the way psychic processes do. This is why Jung frequently—and insightfully, even if, of course, metaphorically[5]—spoke of psychological processes as *background processes*.

The *psyche* is certainly personal, each individual has his or her own psyche, just like each person possesses his or her own body (with its particular characteristics, its vigorous strength, weaknesses, or ailments). In contrast to the subjective psyche the soul is objective and cultural. This was Jung's decisive discovery. The Jungian understanding of psychology is that it is in the first place the study of the objective soul.[6] The soul is *"underworldly," absolute-negative.* It is the inner Mercurial logic or *spiritus rector* of the real.

With these comments we have clearly rejected Nasreddin's "courtyard" as a place to look for soul processes or logical movements. But this does not yet answer the question what, in analogy to the Nasreddin story, the psychological "living room" is, or what the "background" or the "underworld" is. If the soul and its logical processes cannot be located in individuals, not in the empirical personality, if it cannot be found at all in positive-factual reality (in the *foreground* of "what the eyes can see"), then, of course, the suspicion might arise that the term "objective soul" must refer to a metaphysical backworld, to something that is altogether out of this world. Soul seems to belong to a no-man's land free-floating high above the sphere of human experience.

Seeing it this way would be a crude misunderstanding, for the simple reason that it would be nothing but the reversal of the positivistic stance into its opposite (the same thing, but now with a minus-sign before it) and as such still stay fundamentally tied to positivistic world experience. What needs to be understood is that with the soul as objective soul we have not only left behind the focus on empirical people and empirical reality, but also all metaphysical thinking. The soul requires the *double* negation[7] of empirical reality. It is, using Hegel's phrase, an inverted world, a *second* supersensible world: something quite concrete and yet not referring to anything positive-factual. What this is needs to be explained.

James Hillman's essential insight was that the aim of psychology is "soul-making." The term "making" in "soul-making" implies that, to begin with, the soul does not exist. It is absolute negativity. Therefore it has to be MADE, produced, in order to come into existence. From this it follows that if our task as psychologists is to *make* soul, this means that it has to become in some way *real* in empirical reality. We have a dilemma here: the soul or logical movement must be fundamentally kept apart from empirical reality and understood as a "background" or "underworldly" or "absolute-negative" process, and yet it must be made real in empirical reality (which also means that it cannot be located behind or above the world in a metaphysical realm).

How can soul and its logical movements become real without losing their "underworldly," that is, "ghostly" background quality? The answer is: soul-making is *psychology*-making and it happens in consciousness, not in empirical states or the conditions of people. It is not the making of soul *in individuals*, in patients, in ourselves, nor the cultivation of an allegedly a priori existing soul in people. Hillman took the term soul-making from the Romantics, from Blake and John Keats, and the latter, as Hillman says, clarified the phrase in a letter by stating: "Call the world if you please, 'The vale of Soul-making.' Then you will find out the use of the world."[8] So right from the outset the idea of soul-making relates to the real world out there. *It*, the world, is the place where soul is to be made, not inside people, as their self-development, not in us. However, the way it is made in the world, in the real, and thus also in dreams, is not physically, but noetically: When soul has successfully been *made*, then the result is psychology, as a psychology of soul, as truly psychological thinking and understanding. Psychology *is* the form of the SOUL *as real*, as realized. *Psychology* is the place where our therapeutic Nasreddin's ring needs to be looked for.

This is at the same time the solution of the dilemma we spoke of, because psychology is

1. in itself absolute-negative, because it consists only of ideas, images, and conceptions. It is not a positivity, not anything the eyes can see, nothing physical or embodied, nothing that we could point at. It exists just in the mind and is something logical, something noetic, just thought. As such it is "ghostly," as it were. And yet,
2. when psychology indeed happens, it is, of course, something real in the empirical, temporal world. It is, when it happens, a real event in consciousness, in the consciousness of particular persons, and as event it happens always here and now, on the earth, not in a literal beyond, in a metaphysical realm or in a literal underworld. So soul is really made when MY or YOUR style of

thinking, the logical constitution of MY or YOUR consciousness has become a truly *psychological* consciousness.

When we discuss myths as representations of particular moments of the soul's logical life, for example when I interpreted the Aktaion and Artemis myth,[9] I was not trying to present a model for understanding psychic processes in patients. What I was talking about was something completely different. I elaborated in detail what the logic of psychology or of a psychological consciousness is, that is, a psychology in the strict sense as a psychology with soul. In other words, I was speaking about *us* as *psychologists*, *psychotherapists* and how *we* can learn to think truly psychologically. Such a discussion has nothing to do with the patient or with psychological phenomenology. The "logical event" that you are looking for happens when the logical constitution of *your* CONSCIOUSNESS has become psychological, when *it* has undergone, for example, that Dionysian dismemberment that I discussed in that book. Then your understanding of the dreams and of the patient's symptoms can also be a truly psychological one. The focus must not be on the patient and what happens in him (nor on yourself as person who wishes to undergo the individuation process), but upon your own *understanding* of the material of the patient. The question is always: do I *see* what I see truly psychologically?

What does that mean practically for psychotherapy? Each therapy session has to be seen as an opportunity to create psychology anew by trying to see psychological material (the symptoms, the dreams, fantasies, etc.) truly psychologically. Each time I see a patient and am confronted with a dream is an invitation to me as therapist to *give birth to psychology* here and now through my attempt to understand the psychological material *truly psychologically*, i.e., from the point of view of soul and not in terms of practical reality. If I succeed, then I have *made* psychology (and ipso facto also made *soul*).

This implies, of course, that the meaning of the word "psychology" has become a fundamentally different one from the conventional understanding. Ordinarily, we mean by psychology a permanent body of scientific knowledge about what psychically goes on in people, as well as the knowledge about the techniques for treating people. But psychology in our sense is not a science, not a given doctrine to be *applied* to each case and to each psychic phenomenon.

When I enter a therapy session, I do not already bring with me a finished psychology. No, I enter the therapy room as ordinary civilian man or ego-personality. But then, in the consulting room, I have to *try to create*, to *produce*, psychology *from scratch* in each session and concerning each psychic phenomenon here and now through my understanding or interpretative work. Rather than being a science, psychology is performative, sheer actuosity, that is, it is *in* the doing. It is only in my and the patient's or any person's actual achieving here and now a *psychological understanding* of something. Psychology is the *momentary happening* of a person's successfully thinking psychologically about whatever the topic may be.

And psychology exists only for as long as this Now lasts, much like the taste of wine or a meal only exists while you taste them or a symphony while you actually hear it. When the actual psychological comprehension is over, I fall back into my ordinary ego-personality.

Soul can only be made in or as truly psychological insights. And even if my getting such an insight takes place *in me* and therefore is a *psychic* event, nevertheless *what it is about*, its content, the particular logical movement, is the appearance of psychology and does not happen in or to me. I am only the place where this psychological understanding actually appears. The logical movement itself is *not* my personal development. It is *its self*-development, its self-unfolding for *its own* purpose. It is sufficient unto itself. All it needs (and needs from me) is to become *realized* and actually *seen* as a truth. But having appeared in reality, it nevertheless dwells in the supra-personal and supra-empirical sphere of genuine psychological *thought* and in the sphere of *Geist*, of ideas, concepts. As such, it belongs to the generality the same way that rituals, symbols, the Catholic Mass, and Dante's *Divine Comedy* belong to the generality. It's the same way that, e.g., in mathematics, my understanding that the sum of the angles in the triangle is 180 degrees is, to be sure, *my personal* understanding, but what it is about has nothing to do with me, but belongs to everybody and nobody. Gaining psychological insights means something like one's being momentarily "initiated" into a general self-contained soul truth as a truth of the *objective soul*.

Psychotherapy needs to overcome its narrow-minded fixation on the *person* of the patient, the *personalistic* approach. It is not the person who needs to develop or needs to become "self" in Jung's high sense. It is psychology that needs to develop and become self. *It* is what needs to be advanced through more and more, deeper and deeper psychological insights. Psychology needs to be refined (distilled, sublimated) and raised to higher levels of itself through our successive psychological work. Thinking, for example, of the motif of Dionysian dismemberment the way I tried to discuss it by interpreting the "Aktaion and Artemis" myth in *The Soul's Logical Life*, we can say that each time real psychology indeed happened in a therapy session IS the moment of an accomplished Dionysian dismemberment: because in this moment of true soul-making, patient and therapist, these two ego-personalities, have *really* been dissolved and disappeared in the absolute negativity of psychology, which is now, for this moment, the real reality.

(As an aside, let me mention that by this dissolution of the ego-personalities of patient and therapist we may be reminded of the famous Zen-Buddhist cycle of pictures called the ten *oxherding pictures*. In the eighth picture, both man and ox have disappeared; there is only the circle of primordial nothingness. Formally, this is a similar situation, because in both cases the concrete empirical beings, patient and therapist or man and ox, have disappeared and absolute negativity has been reached. And yet there is a fundamental difference. In the Buddhist picture, it is total nothingness, emptiness: ontological or cosmological and semantic. In the case of psychology the negation is *determinate negation*: not nothing at all, but something that is, to be sure, absolute negativity, but nevertheless something concrete, the moment of this dream's (or any other soul phenomenon's) successful psychological interpretation as the moment of the realization of soul.)

After what I said about the task of soul-making or psychology-making as a purpose unto itself you might of course object and ask: But what about the patient? The patient does not come to therapy for the purpose of making psychology! The patient either wants to get well and be cured or to undergo self-development. Is such an approach in psychotherapy as the one I described not utterly disengaged, up in the air, merely a self-serving game?

Yes, of course: making soul or psychology is practically *useless*. It has no purpose outside itself, no ego agenda or program. It is exclusively its own purpose. So we have a real conflict of interests. How can it be resolved?

The Jungian therapist also wants to help the patient and wants him to be cured. But as *psycho*therapist he believes—and therapeutic experience also shows—that the patient *is precisely best helped* when one does not directly focus on him or her and on his or her pathology and betterment, but if instead one rather brackets and suspends this first intention, reducing it to a sublated moment within a higher intentionality, thereby attending to "the soul." The therapist's conviction is that what the patient most of all needs is to be reconnected to the autonomous life of "the soul."

The neurotic person's real problem is, after all, his frame of mind: the modern restricted, utilitarian, egoic outlook on life, the technical pragmatism. He is stuck in his ego mentality. *Psycho*therapy's concern has to be, in the first place, his regaining a wider horizon, a sense for deeper concerns than the immediate practical ones of everyday life, personal relationship problems in the narrower sense, the healing of the patient's symptoms, the solution of his problems. Therapy should be his liberation from his egoic stance, the narrowminded imprisonment in his own ego and from the purposes it is committed to. It should re-open for him an access to the soul dimension.

The central therapeutic factor is the experience of making real psychology and not the application of techniques and psychological knowledge to the patient and his disorder. Jung once said,

> The main interest of my work is not concerned with the treatment of neurosis but rather with the approach to the numinous. But the fact is that the approach to the numinous is the real therapy and inasmuch as you attain to the numinous experience you are released from the curse of pathology.
> (*Letters 1*, p. 377, to Martin, 20 August 1945)

In formal regards, this utterance confirms what I proposed here: Jung turns decidedly away from the directness of *treating* people and sees the *real therapy* in the opening-up, for the patient, of infinity.

However, that particular thing that opens up infinity is for Jung "the numinous," and this is incompatible with a truly psychological approach. Jung's opting for the numinous is due to his idiosyncratic ego-wish or need to rescue religion in modernity, or rather precisely not *religion* itself, but in truth merely the *general principle* and *abstract form*, the *zero stage*, of religion. As long as the numinous is supposed to be the real therapeutic factor, psychology would desert itself, going off in the direction of literal *transcendence*, of "religion" and "metaphysics" (in the wider sense of the word), in some way analogously to the shaman's journey to the supernatural world. The concept of "the numinous" amounts to (even if only implicit and not acknowledged) a hypostasis of this "the numinous" as something objectively existing, which is allegedly the transcendent reality behind the personal psychic experience. And on the other hand it appeals to *human emotion* on the literal experiential level, to the sense of awe of the unspeakable, to one's being *dumbfounded* and overwhelmed by an utterly incomprehensible mystery— this is its tribute to nihilism—, and forfeits sober knowing and lucid insight. If it would rely on the experience of the numinous as the main interest of its work and the real therapeutic factor, psychology would become guilty of *mystification* in an irresponsible way.

If, however, we replace the term "the numinous" by "soul-making" or "psychology-making" in Jung's above statement,[10] we can pretty much affirm it and yet stay true to our profession.

That the commitment to soul-making as psychology-making is "the real therapy" is especially true in the case of dream interpretation. For several decades I have conducted dream seminars for colleagues or training candidates. The style of these seminars has been that one participant presented two or three short dreams of one of his or her patients *without* any anamnestic data. Just the naked dreams, except for, perhaps, additional brief information about the age and sex of the dreamer (but not even that always). When, after a long immersion in the dreams on a word-for-word basis, the analyst of the dreamer was asked whether what had been found out through the dream discussion fit to his or her experience of the patient, the response usually was that the discussion has laid bare for the therapist the patient's innermost psychology and maybe even helped him or her to see the patient and the therapeutic process in a new light. What we did in each of the seminar sessions was to let the dreams—indirectly, unintendedly—reflect the psychology of the patient, rather than use what was already known about the patient for understanding the dreams.

What makes the making of psychology centrally important for therapy? The experience of the happening of psychology is liberating. The making of true psychology is the liberation of the soul, it is, alchemically speaking, the freeing of the spirit Mercurius from its imprisonment in matter, in the physical, which for the late Jung is nothing less than the ultimate goal of (alchemically conceived) psychology. And this freeing of the spirit Mercurius is also for the patient the opening-up of a hitherto unknown free-space. It *objectively* frees his consciousness, at least momentarily, from its bondage of the ego, and the personality of the patient from its entanglement in egoic desires and naturalistic conceptions. It amounts to a fundamental change of the logical constitution of consciousness. The happening of psychology is a moment of truth, of releasing soul phenomena (and thus also symptoms) into *their* truth. It is the releasement of the soul that has been submerged and buried in psychic complexes and projected on/identified with literal realities or practical concerns. When, for example, in the interpretation of a dream in a particular session, soul-making as psychology-making truly succeeds, in other words, when psychology has really *happened* as the releasement of the dream into its truth, then this IS the experience of a real moment of infinity.

It is a moment of infinity not in a grandiose sense, not as something spectacular, as an overwhelming mysterious and dumbfounding experience. This infinity is quiet and sober. Nothing unspeakable. Merely absolute-negative. The truth into which the dream is released is intellectually comprehensible, a lucid insight.

In this connection we may recall Jung's quote of Schiller's dictum: "man is completely human only when he is at play" (*CW* 16 § 98), or, translated differently as "he is only wholly man when he is playing" (*CW* 6 § 171). And what Jung adds to this: "My aim is to bring about a psychic state in which my patient begins to experiment with his own nature—a state of fluidity, change, and growth where nothing is eternally fixed and hopelessly petrified" (*CW* 16 § 99). Commitment to fixed purposes is the opposite of the freedom of playfulness. As therapist one must not have any purposes in the narrower sense of the word, but only the free, purposeless interest in what psychologically shows itself. And it is the task of therapy to help the patient gradually, through habituation in the course of analysis, to acquire this freedom for himself and towards his life.

Psychotherapy is not the treatment of patients; it is not medicine. It is not intent upon curing people. It does not wish to *do* something to the patient, trying to change him or her. It has no interest in efficacy. For then it would be (a) a technological project and (b) a betrayal of the interest in soul in its absolute negativity in favor of the positivity of visible, tangible people and practical results. One would be lost in externality. Psychotherapy is the attempt to enable the patient to *see* himself and his life psychologically. If this succeeds, it is, according to the Jungian understanding of psychotherapy, the real cure of the patient.

The dream as corpse

We have learned from the previous chapter that a therapist always starts out as civilian man and the ego-personality that he is. His job is to make soul, make psychology, and ipso facto slowly also transport himself from this common-sense position of the ego into a soul perspective. This is also and particularly the case with respect to the dreams that are presented to him. At first, he probably views them from the standpoint of everyday life. Often, they will then not make any sense, but appear as completely puzzling: just strange words, weird images. The ego cannot make heads or tails of them. They seem incomprehensible.

The dream on its part comes into being, as we said, only when it is already over, when we have awakened *from* it. It inevitably belongs to the past (even if emotionally it may still have a strong effect on us) and has lost its immediate presence and, above all, its absolute realness. We say and feel: "It was *only* a dream!" We as waking consciousness look at it from a distance.

On both counts the dream is dead for us. The psychological task is to make it come alive again. How is this possible, what does it require, and what exactly does it mean? Before we can turn to this question, I need to remind the reader that in this whole part we are not concerned with the question of a specific method of dream interpretation. This part is devoted only to the general attitude to be taken towards dreams if our work with them is to be truly psychological. I offer three images as a possible access to the question how a dream can come alive again.

My first image: The Greeks called the dead souls in the underworld *shades*, and described them as bodiless, bloodless, cold, without speech. When humans like Odysseus descended into the underworld in order to get into contact with the dead souls, they first of all needed to give the dead souls some blood to drink in order to awaken them to some sort of temporary life. We could also call the dreams shades, quite apart from the character of shadowiness that we already attributed to the original experience of dreams. When a dream is reported in a session, it is at first lifeless, bodiless, pale. Like the dead souls in the underworld, the dreams crave, we could say, for "blood," to first of all come to life for us in the analytical session, but then also to receive an input of energy to enable them to continue the soul's self-movement.

What is this input that the dream, the images, need? It is twofold. First, they need our intellectual understanding, second, they need our heart, our accompanying the dream figures and situations with our feeling. We have to feel what is blissful in a dream, feel the misery or anxiety that appears in a dream, sense the wrongness of what goes wrong, appreciate what is beautiful, and so on (of course, without any "should" or "ought"; we have to follow our true natural feelings). The intensity of genuine feeling participation is needed. This is what gives the images of the present dream the power to perhaps develop in the course of time into potential new statuses of "the soul's" life. But, and this needs to be stressed, this kind of intellectual comprehension and feeling participation is something completely different from ego wishes for an improvement or correction of, e.g., painful images. In the simple, objective pain, sorrow, and depression that we feel in view of a sad dream situation or dream ending, we release the dream into its being-so, into its indeed having been so and precisely into its being perfect the way it is, *with* all the possible "faults" in it (the anxiety and pain-causing images, the defenses of the dream-I, the wretched ending without solution, etc.), while at the same time connecting with it our conscious knowing and feeling. By releasing the dream without reservation into its having been so, we release it into its truth.

The second image for the process of making dreams come alive is that of the hen that broods an egg. Let us see a given dream to be interpreted as something like an egg that we have to sit on to brood its soul meaning out. The dream needs our patient dedication, our "body warmth" to receive the chance to reveal what is psychologically in it. The word "patient" needs to be emphasized. A hen has to sit on the egg for days on end. For us, and with respect to the topic of dreams,

patience means devoting ourselves to the dream without ego will. No insistence
on results, on "catching" the meaning. Letting it appear on its own account and
at its own time ("patient" is etymologically related to "passive"!), which even
includes the willingness to accept that our honest work on the dream may *not*
lead to the desired deeper insights into it. On the other hand, "passive" does not
mean indifferent, unconcerned, and inactive. There also has to be what I called our
"body warmth." It implies an intensity of devotion—maybe even love, the "heat"
of a "passionate" dedication, or the "thought of the heart," as Hillman might have
said ("passionate" also belongs to the same word field as "patient" and "passive").

My third image comes from a detail in a Grimm Brothers' fairy tale. This is,
as a whole, not one of the genuine fairy tales, but a somewhat farcical tale, which
includes some fairy tale motifs. The title of the tale is, "The Story of the Youth
who Went Forth to Learn What Fear Was." It is about a son who does not know
the feeling of dread or horror but thinks that it is necessary for full humanness.
Many attempts by others to frighten him all fail. Later on, he comes to a deserted,
haunted mill about which he is warned that everybody who tried to spend the
night there was found dead the next morning. He thinks this is the right place for
him. Several gruesome events happen to him during the nights at the witching
hour, but none are capable of scaring him in the least. For our purposes I highlight
only one episode.

> When it grew late, six tall men came in and brought a coffin. [...] They placed
> the coffin on the ground, he went to it and took the lid off, and a dead man lay
> therein. He felt his face, but it was cold as ice. "Stop," said he, "I will warm
> thee a little," and went to the fire and warmed his hand and laid it on the dead
> man's face, but he remained cold. Then he took him out, and sat down by the
> fire and laid him on his breast and rubbed his arms that the blood might circu-
> late again. As this also did no good, he thought to himself, "When two people
> lie in bed together, they warm each other," and carried him to the bed, covered
> him over and lay down by him. After a short time the dead man became warm
> too, and began to move.

There is, of course, a difference between the two images in that the egg is from
the outset known to be life, only life still hidden under the hard shell of the egg,
whereas the dead man in the coffin is really dead. But the difference is not so great
inasmuch as the youth in the tale is not a life-giver like God or Christ. If the corpse
can start to come alive again simply by warming it, then in the dead body the
potential of life must still have existed. The youth merely succeeded in "hatching
it out," if I may say so.

It is a marvelous image: the icy-cold corpse and the warm, living body of the
young man lying closely together in the same bed. A marvelous image for the
general attitude towards strange, hard-to-understand dreams.

One could, of course, imagine the reverse effect: the cold corpse making the
youth also cold and so depriving him of his body-warmth, his life. This would,

realistically speaking, even have been much more likely. After all, did the protagonist of the story not take, so to speak, a huge, life-size "ice cube" with him into his bed, the way others might conversely go to bed with a hot-water bottle? So the question arises: Why was the icy corpse not capable of sucking, vampire-like, the warmth of life out of the youth?

It was because the youth was the one who did not know the feeling of fear, that is to say, he was not impressed by the deadness of the corpse. He was the one who had crossed the threshold to the haunted mill and to the night-world to be experienced there. He was not one of the ordinary people who categorically refused to enter the mill, to open themselves to the night-world. (The "night" spent at home in bed, at safe distance from the haunted mill, is, of course, part of the day-world, not "night" in the soul-sense at all. The night-world requires something like the haunted mill of our tale, the crossing over the river, "*Ins Unbetretene, / Nicht zu Betretende*" ["into the untrodden / untreadable regions"][11]). This is why the fact that the man that had been brought in was a corpse did not make much of a difference for him. It could not terrify him.

This means, positively expressed, that he believed, trusted, knew from the outset that what at first sight appeared to be dead nevertheless had a spark of life within itself. His body-warmth was not just physical warmth. It was *psychological* warmth, the warmth of his unshakeable conviction that death is, as Hegel put it, a *non-actuality*. It was the warmth of having crossed the river, that is, the warmth of his commitment to soul or Spirit, of which again Hegel said: "But the life of Spirit is not the life that shrinks from death and keeps itself untouched by devastation, but rather the life that endures it and maintains itself in it."[12] The youth, who does not know what dread is, simply does not take death for an answer, death which "is of all things the most dreadful" (Hegel, *ibid.*). And this is why he is able to warm the ice block with his own body-warmth so that the dead body slowly begins to move. And why does he not know what dread is? Because he is—psychologically—already on the other side of the river.

I started out this chapter with the idea that each time we come to therapy sessions and to dream interpretation we come as ordinary ego-consciousness. We begin empty-handed and have to work ourselves up each time afresh into a status of consciousness appropriate to the soul. But now we have to add that this is only one half of the truth. It is the *intellectual* or *conceptual* side of the truth. As far as our psychological understanding is concerned, we are initially indeed at a complete loss vis-à-vis a dream. The other side of the truth is, and here we have to recall the relevant chapter above, that it all depends on whether we have crossed the river to the other side, into the haunted mill, into the land of soul, or whether we have stayed on this side of the river, with the people outside the haunted mill. Only for him who has already crossed the river can dreams (on account of their completely puzzling nature) be a *corpse* to be warmed with one's own "body-warmth" until they begin to move of their own accord, or more theoretically speaking, only then can dreams *as mere texts* nevertheless *be* the soul's speaking. Those who have not all along crossed over, as is the case with the fairy tale's "people outside the haunted mill," are on fundamental grounds not capable of ever seeing the corpse—of seeing anything as *"corpse" with* a living soul in it. All they are able to see is positive facts, facts as dead as a doornail, or words, words, words. For therapists who have their logical place "outside the mill," the issue of soul-making does not come up at all.

Not that "corpse" and "life" are the real opposites, but corpse and dead fact. Rather than warming the dream as a corpse with the warmth of a commitment to soul, the therapists who have not crossed over the river only feel the need to *explain* the dream images externally personalistically by means of associations from the patient's biography or daily-life experiences or in terms of what he subjectively feels or fantasizes *about* the images. Or they abstractly, mechanically *equate* dream images, partly, with the ready-made intellectual constructs of their psychological theory (e.g., "shadow," "anima," "persona," "the unconscious," …) and, partly, with archetypes and mythic motifs taken out of their tool chest, and they compensate the abstractness and sterility of their procedure by working themselves and the patient up into *ego emotions* about the numinosity, the mystery, and sacredness of the images and the deep mythical meaning that emerged in the psyche of the patient. "Gods and goddesses in every man and woman." This is the difference: *here* soul-making as the patient process of inwardizing oneself into a given dream and *there* the *application* of external empirical data, subjective reactions, and always already available mythological props *to* the dream. *Here* letting the dream come alive from within itself, and *there* speaking *about* the dream and its meaning.

Notwithstanding our coming as civilian man to dreams, we must always already bring something along, if psychology is to happen. We must have crossed the river from the outset, be logically already in the haunted mill, and thus bring with us the warmth of the unshakeable conviction in ourselves of the soul being in the as yet corpse-like dream. We must already be touched and claimed by the concept of soul and thus be committed to it. This is the *feeling* or *conviction* side of the truth.

We must not confuse the warming of the corpse with the crossing of the river or the entering of the haunted mill. These are two entirely different things. The warming of the corpse is a real and long-lasting act to be patiently performed in the empirical reality of dream interpretation. But the crossing over is not a doing, a project or task to be performed. It is a sudden logical shift of consciousness. There is no transition from this side to the other. Either it has already happened— or it happens not at all. The crossing over is possible only in the perfect tense (as already accomplished: one finds oneself already on the other side), not in the present (or present continuous) tense as an ongoing process.

Only like sees like; *similia similibus*: only he who logically is already in the land of "the dead," the "underworld," "the soul," is in the daily practice of dream interpretation able to see the dream as corpse and thus to make soul or psychology. "The soul" has to be on both sides. *De nihilo nihil*, nothing comes from nothing (Lucretius). It is only one youth who spends the night in the haunted mill, over against hundreds of people outside. This is so not only in this fairy tale, but also in analytical psychology. This is why Jung insisted that "Nature is aristo-cratic" and that true psychology is only for a few. "For many be called, but few chosen," that is to say, many adopt Jungian psychology as a "doctrine," but never catch fire, never are reached by the soul sense of it. They stay immune. And this, in turn, is why Jung once, when asked by Vera von der Heydt about certain views (on the role of active imagination and individuation) that were ventilated and con-troversially debated among British Jungians, felt forced to give vent to a deep sigh, seeing through "this conceptual hair-splitting,"

> Your question evidently emanates from an atmosphere in which many words are buzzing about. ... From such discussions we see what awaits me once I have become posthumous. Then everything that once was fire and wind will be bottled in spirit and reduced to dead nostrums. Thus are the gods interred in gold and marble and ordinary mortals like me in paper.
> *(Letters* 2, p. 469, 22 December 1958)

What was "fire and wind," in other words, alive, is turned into dead facts and, even worse, into buzzing, but empty words. And just as Jung once said about the Church, that it "serves as a fortress to protect us against God and his Spirit" (*CW* 18 § 1534),[13] we have to note analogously that Jungian psychology itself has become a fortress that protects its adherents against soul and soul-making, psychology-making. It can be this fortress all the more as it obviously pretends, under the names "Jungian psychology" or "analytical psychology," to *be* the very place of soul. Their immunity protects them from even getting a hunch of their staying on *this* side of the river. Because for those on this side there *is* simply no other side in the first place.

Returning to the issue of "civilian man" versus "already being in the land of soul," we need to understand that both sides are necessary: content-wise, seman-tically, and *psychically* our full awareness of our emptiness (which is the pre-requisite for being able to patiently brood the egg or warm the corpse and letting the dream of its own accord come to life for us); but syntactically, *psychologically* or logically the full presence in us of the notion of soul (that is, the presence of, as it were, nothing but the general form or mere outline of the knowledge what soul is, as well as its claim on us and our commitment to it). Both sides are really only the two sides of one coin. Together they are the whole psychological difference. They each give rise to the other, make each other possible: The corpse appears only to him who will not be overwhelmed by its icy coldness and can warm it with his own body warmth because from the outset he *sees* it already as containing the living soul spark within itself that merely needs to be kindled. And conversely, his firm conviction of the soul spark and his strong body warmth are only produced by the appearance of the corpse. It is the corpse that makes the youth capable of bringing the corpse back to life, and it is the youth who is not abhorred by death that turns what is brought to him into a corpse that carries the seed of life as its hidden potential within itself.

Now I want to give some hints about what the result of our brooding the dream, or what our warming with our own body-warmth the corpse, as which the dream at first appears, i.e., the coming alive of a dream, might practically mean.

The dream has fully come alive when we *forget* ourselves and are completely given over to the dream, when the dream is playing through us, or when its logic carries and moves us. St. Paul said: "It is no longer I who live, but Christ lives in me" (Galatians 2:20). Similarly, as far as the abstract form of this thought is concerned, not with respect to the radical existential depth that it had for Paul, the therapist could say at the end of a successful immersion in the dream: "It is no longer I who live; the dream now lives in me." (Only now, for as long as this now lasts, and merely on the level of psychological understanding.)

When we begin, there is always the sequence of many separate images that are usually alien, surprising, difficult to understand. But in the course of one's patient, step-by-step, word-for-word immersion into a dream, the dream's own teleology, its spirit, or the logical life that it is, as well as its imaginal content and substance, slowly take over. This "taking over" may be comparable to how we feel when we are in love. Or when catching fire ("Something catches my imagination"). There is the joy of an emerging insight. I turn into a hunting dog that has picked up a trail. I am caught. Something has taken hold of me.

The different motifs and images appearing in a dream can be compared to the letters of a word. In our Western languages, a child learning to read first learns the alphabet and then reads words, one letter after the other. And then all of a sudden it realizes *what word* it is. The moment that the word is realized, the letters disappear; and as long as you go letter by letter, you do not get the word. The letters by themselves do not mean anything. Only when they *zusammenschießen* (suddenly coalesce, synthesize, fuse into one meaning) and at the same time *disappear* into this meaning of the word, is the word alive.

This can also be compared to chemistry, when you have several substances in the beginning, and they slowly react with each other, and then you get a totally new, different end-product in which the substances that you started out from have disappeared. It is similar, although not as obvious, with the dream. We start out by "spelling out" the dream, circumambulating each image, but slowly the different images may come together and make a whole. What is this whole? It is the logic, or soul, of the dream. In the logic of the dream, the separateness of the images dissolves (*solutio*), they go under in the living logic of the dream. The dream has become fluid. Of course, not as obviously as in the example of chemical synthesis or in the example of synthesis of a written word from its individual letters. This is so for two reasons:

1   We are not advanced enough to achieve such a deep understanding. We can do it with words, and even in sentences where the words disappear into the meaning of the sentence. But a whole dream is probably too large a unit for us to perform this act of synthesis. (It is only God who is supposed to be able to "read" all reality, all things, events in the world, as *one word*.)

2   The dreams themselves, as they stand, are not such pure products that a complete synthesis such as with the letters of a word is possible. There can also be heterogeneous, conflicting elements left in it, disparate elements that resist integration of their independent identity into the flow of the logical movement as a whole, especially those coming from the tension between the deeper soul on the one hand and the ego interests on the other. So it is more like in chemistry when after a synthesis has taken place some residue is left that could not enter the synthesis.

This whole chapter about the dream as *corpse* may have been surprising for the reader, because do we not, after all, rightly assume that dreams have a life of their own, precisely an *autonomous* life, and that they can therefore bring about changes in persons even if not interpreted at all? It is also a well-known experience that certain dreams or certain dream images can accompany (affect, trouble, give joy to) us throughout the whole day or maybe even for months, indeed, may stay alive in our memory for years? Concerning this topic, we have to distinguish between two forms of the dream. The one notion of "dream" is the dream that happens during the night, the actual event of our dreaming the dream. Many dreams just happen, and they don't even become conscious (while some others do become conscious or at least partially conscious). *The dream as a psychic event* is, of course, not "a corpse." This dream is alive, although unconscious. It is a real experience. Even if you don't remember it, or if you are not conscious of it at all, it can still have some therapeutic, or whatever, effect in you. It can have its own life in you, keep working in you. (Dreams that have become conscious can, of course, also have an autonomous effect in you in the same way.)

But when we talk in psychotherapy about dreams, we only mean the dream that is remembered and written down. *The dream as text* is the dream as "a corpse." It is the dream written on paper. But paper is dead. It comes alive only in my or your mind, in my or your active understanding.

Not knowing as methodological starting point

When we are first confronted with a patient's dream, the initial impression is often, as I pointed out before, that the dream is completely mysterious for us, that we don't understand it at all. We feel helpless vis-à-vis it. I have heard from certain supervisees that their initial reaction to a dream is even that their mind gets frozen. They feel panicked. Jung, of course, had said that he turned to dreams "simply from perplexity," because he did "not know where else to go for help" and when patients wanted advice from him for what they could do he had to answer them that "I don't know either" (*CW* 16 § 84 and 86). For him, the dream was supposed to be the way out of his perplexity and helplessness. For us, it is precisely the dream that makes us perplexed and helpless.

This helplessness of not understanding what the dream is supposed to mean is a feeling that arises of its own accord. It is the uncomfortable condition in which we find ourselves. Not-knowing, not-understanding, is the factual truth of the situation. But now I am going to say something shocking: our factually appearing helplessness vis-à-vis a dream is not enough. Our not-knowing, not-understanding is not wrong. It is not "the obstacle," "the enemy," but conversely the potential entrance door to the dream. We have to go deeper into the not-understanding instead of fighting it, wanting to overcome it: The not-understanding even needs to be turned into the explicit methodological principle of dream interpretation, into a position deliberately to be taken by us! Jung was fully aware of this. He said:

> Even if one has great experience in these matters, one is again and again obliged, before each dream, *to admit one's ignorance* and, *renouncing* all preconceived ideas, to prepare for something entirely unexpected.
>
> (*CW* 8 § 543, transl. modif., my italics)

Rather than merely being befallen by the feeling of perplexity and not understanding, we have to actively renounce all our own ideas, make *tabula rasa*, establish in ourselves a zero point of knowing. The first reaction to our helplessness must *not* be one of trying to overcome it.

> for a long time I have made it a rule, when someone tells me a dream and asks for my opinion, to say first of all to myself: "I have no idea what this dream means." After that I can begin to examine the dream.
>
> (*CW* 8 § 533)

Only after that! The standpoint of not understanding is the *sine qua non* of a possible dream interpretation.

Why is the emptying of the mind a methodological necessity? Because only then will the dream images not be fit by the interpreter into set patterns, will our "preconceived ideas" not be imposed on the details of the dream, and the latter be pigeonholed in the system of theoretical concepts of the depth-psychological school we belong to. Only then does the dream's silent voice have a chance of being heard. Otherwise, it will be drowned out by the buzzing noise of our mind's own speaking. "It has a say now, not you," Jung said once, albeit with reference to another type of soul voice, but it applies just as well to dreams (*Letters* 2, p. 532, to Charteris, 9 January 1960). This is why our not-understanding is even helpful.

The emptied mind has to become our methodological starting point. The dream can only begin its own speaking when we start from scratch. In this sense the zero point of knowing can be seen as the subjective counterpart of the objective "corpse." The *methodical* clearing away of all already available knowledge with respect to individual dream images comes out in the type of suggestion that Jung made to analysands, e.g., to a dreamer who dreamt of a "deal table": "*Suppose I had no idea* what the words 'deal table' mean. Describe this object and give me its history in such a way that I cannot fail to understand what sort of thing it is" (*CW* 16 § 320, my italics).

The dream and its images have to be seen as *fundamentally* unknown, and we have to pass through, or even into, this unknownness. Only in this way can we possibly be "initiated" into its *inner* infinity.

Each dream and each image in it is like a person that we meet for the first time. We do not know this person. We cannot go by the face and external looks. We have to wait and see as who and as how this person will *show* him or herself to be. We start from the outside, from the external impression, and slowly get to know more and more about the person. We get to know him or her better and better—but there is always more than we know. Each dream image has its own inner infinity.

> One would do well, therefore, to treat every dream as though it were a totally unknown object. Look at it from all sides, take it in your hand, carry it about with you, let your imagination play around it, and talk about it with other people.
>
> (*CW* 10 § 320)

One initial way of holding one's own in not-understanding could be that of wondering, being puzzled, turning one's consciousness into a questioning consciousness. Starting from scratch we begin with the first few words and "take them in our hand" by asking questions. Maybe they are about the most ordinary things. But being at the zero point of knowing, that is, being like a newborn baby, we have to ask: "What is such and such a thing, what does it involve, to what sphere does it belong, what does it evoke?" and give detailed descriptions and try as best as we can to answer these questions, always speaking to ourselves quite simply as the ignorant ones—as if we had never before heard of the things or words mentioned. We might then continue: "Why does this thing appear, and what does its appearance suggest or evoke or intend?" "Is this new element not strange here? Why is it this way? Why is this *word* chosen? I would have expected such and such. What atmosphere does this word bring with it?" One can also formulate more precisely *what* one does not understand, *what* is unusual. Formulating questions is one way of circumambulating, one after the other, all details, all words and phrases, all puzzling elements. How does this new element fit in with an earlier one? In this way we need to grope our way forward through the whole dream, very calmly, with lots of patience and without putting ourselves under any pressure to come up with results (just as a *psycho*therapy that deserves its name is not after results: to get results is the trademark of the technological mind).

This not-knowing and the necessity arising from it to be puzzled and ask questions also applies to the dream-I. Who the dream-I is is also unknown. We need to *describe* accurately the dream-I in this dream and not take it for granted, in terms of our preconceived ideas, as if we knew it merely because the word "I" seems so familiar. I will comment on the issue of the dream-I later in a separate chapter in Part V.

The necessity of my going under

In the previous chapter I, as dream interpreter, have brought myself down to the zero point of knowing. It is an act of humility over against the dream. I have even made my not-knowing the very principle of my working with dreams! In the present chapter I want to continue and deepen this downwards move and go even beyond the stance of not-knowing. The latter is not really enough, for by humbling myself to the state of not-knowing I merely change one *attribute* of mine, whereas the I, the sense of me as the one who does the interpreting, still remains intact. Now I add that *I*, too, have to go under in, and into, the dream.

Of course, this does not mean to get rid of the I, of me. It rather means the de-identification of the I from the ego, with which I is usually identified in modernity above all in the Western world.[14] "Ego" in my sense is not a part or organ of the personality, an agency or complex in the psyche. We do not *have* an ego. Rather, "ego" is a particular stance, a style of thinking, feeling, and behaving (a style that is above all in sharp contrast to a soulful style). It can as such be a possible specific *self-definition* of "I," and, as I said, is nowadays the culturally prevailing one. It is a quality of attitudes, desires, orientations, etc.; and as such "ego" is, grammatically speaking, an "adjective" or "attribute," not, like "I," a "noun" (pronoun) or subject, the person as a whole as self.

Most important in our context and in modernity is that aspect of ego that has to do with the radicalization and intensification during the nineteenth and twentieth centuries of the logic of the early-modern "subject," a subject clearly standing vis-à-vis reality as its object and being the very center point from which the world is experienced as well as characterized by the inner need to feel (logically, not necessarily practically) sovereign in the sense of self-determination, autonomy, and self-assertion. Through the mentioned intensification, with which alone *the ego* came into its own, this sense of autonomy took on the form of self-centeredness, selfishness, the wish for total control under the subject's own will and, intellectually, the form of the absolute commitment to the abstract principle of identity or non-contradiction in its explanation of the world—as the *sine qua non* of its own self-preservation, the preservation of the rigid logic of absolute self-identity, as which it exists.

This stance defined by the "ego" is incompatible with true psychology. Let me use a few images to describe the counter-attitude that is conducive, nay, necessary for psychological dream interpretation. One is "swimming," another one "flying" or "gliding," a third one is "dancing." By going into the water in order to swim or float in it, we give up some of our autonomy. Instead of standing with both feet on the solid earth, we entrust ourselves to an element or medium that is fundamentally unreliable, because it does not provide a solid ground for us. When we want to step on it, want to keep our vertical upright position of standing (the ego-position), it simply yields (almost resistancelessly) so that we sink (and possibly drown). This yielding represents its having the character or status of "negativity," in contrast to the positivity of solid ground. But if we give up this insistence on standing upright and lie down flat in or on the water—despite, and against, our knowledge that it is not solid ground—it, all of a sudden, miraculously supports us. The water becomes the subject and we are the object carried by it.

To dance means similarly letting oneself be carried by the music. It is very different from walking (like going to a store to buy something or like hiking, where the movement has an external ego purpose). In dancing, the movement is its own purpose. If it is supposed to be real dancing, the music must take the lead. It must play with you. The music is the real moving subject, the dancer's body merely follows suit, has to be *in* the objective movement. This shift is what is needed with respect to dreams: Not we are to be the ones who interpret the dream the way a scientist studies some object. We let the dream take over and merely try to follow suit, in accordance with the Talmudic dictum that Jung frequently quoted: "The dream is its own interpretation." We can also think here of what Jung said about how Socrates listened to his *daimonion* and our fundamentally different modern usual attitude: "But who is listening to the *daimonion*? *We* talk but *it* says nothing, it does not even exist, ... Socrates' 'naïveté' is his greatness, ..." (*Letters 2*, p. 532). We just need to substitute "dream" for "*daimonion*." A few lines before this quote Jung had articulated with respect to this *daimonion* what for us could be said to be the principle of working with dreams: "*It* has a say now, *not* you" (my ital.).

From here we can understand why it is crucial that the dream has become a "mere text" and "corpse" for us and we approach it from a zero point of knowing. Just imagine that a particular dream (or particular images in a dream) would seem to us right away to have a clear, obvious meaning. This would have the consequence that we would, in truth, relate only to our own ideas about the dream, to our preconceived notions projected upon it. We would be unable to want to *listen* to it, to give it a chance to do *now* its own speaking. We could be compared to people who like to interrupt others in mid-speech because they think they always already know what the other person is going to say. It is precisely the dream-as-corpse idea that reverses this relation and instead of our anticipating its meaning forces us to wait and see what the dream may actually be saying.

"Anna O." coined the term "talking cure" for her own treatment. It meant, in the words of Jacques Lacan, that "the more she chattered on, the better it went."[15] Chattered! The phrase was later adopted by Freud as a formulation that captures the essence of psychoanalytic work. But a therapy in the spirit of Jung is not a "talking cure," but must much rather be conceived as the opposite, as a *listening cure*,[16] both the therapist's and the patient's learning to receive and open themselves to the soul's speaking.

Another image that we can use and that brings in an even more radical aspect than the former images is *sleepwalking*. This is how to be the I *and* to forget the ego, forget oneself and be carried by the logic of the dream. "Over against our consciousness we must learn to live as it were unconsciously," Jung once wrote,[17] and we can easily substitute for "learn to live" "learn to work with dreams." The image of sleepwalking suggests a mental state of being fully immersed in the dream reality as a reality in its own right, one's, as it were, allowing oneself to be "baptized" in it while letting it have free play. This image has the advantage that there is not, as in "swimming" or "dancing" a conscious decision to enter the water or to participate in a dance. Sleepwalking happens of its own accord. Therefore, there is no conscious struggle to overcome the ego. If we use "sleepwalking" as a metaphor for the attitude in which to work with dreams, we mean that the I (with all its skills) does the dream's, the soul's bidding. In sleepwalking there is no fear of falling. In working with dreams, too, there must be no fear of "falling": erring, making a fool of oneself, saying something stupid. Sleepwalking is not an ego-activity, but the instinct's taking over while the I is "sleeping" or while it is in the instinct's service. Another feature of the phenomenon of sleepwalking is that one must not waken a sleepwalker, because then he or she might fall: the returning I's ego attitude becomes self-conscious and wants to take the lead, wants to be in charge. Finding itself in a precarious position (like on top of the roof of one's house) that the sleepwalking *soul* brought it into, it becomes afraid, and then the sureness of its steps is gone. Sleepwalking like on the roof of a house also implies that it is truly dangerous (just like a large body of water is really dangerous). Normally, without actually sleepwalking, one would fall.

In connection with my metaphor of sleepwalking, Jung's explanation of what the status of one's interpreting myths is (provided that it is a truly *psychological* interpretation) comes to mind: "What one does is at best one's *continuing to dream* the myth and giving it a modern dress" (*CW* 9i § 271, transl. modif.). It can immediately be applied to our working with dreams too. What Jung wants to say is that in the best case, i.e., if our myth (and, we add, dream) interpretation dwells in the "dream" that the myth *is* and thus does not desert or betray the meaning, quality, and atmosphere of the myth (or dream) itself, then this interpretation is not done by ego-consciousness, not by the analytical mind of the psychologist, but by a consciousness in a dream-like state.[18] Even while we have to give the myth or dream "a modern dress," trying to put it into our own language (this is what interpretation is about), this is not to be its translation from "the unconscious" into "ego-consciousness." Our giving it a modern dress remains in the semi-conscious, dream-like atmosphere of the symbolic products themselves that we work with.[19] We heard already: only like can know like. Another time much the same idea is expressed by Jung very concisely, this time directly with respect to dreams: "Say it again as well as you can" (*Letters 2*, p. 591, to Herbert Read, 2 September 1960).

At the end of this chapter in which I have put so much emphasis on "swimming" and "sleepwalking," I must nevertheless point out that there is also a very different aspect of equal psychological importance for working with dreams (as well as psychological work in general) and one that seems to be the exact opposite of the first. It has to do with the stance of *intellectual responsibility* on the part of the psychologist towards dreams or myths, with his obligation to strive for exactness and precision rather than one's indulging in vague moods, emotional reactions, and subjective fantasies. We will come to this aspect of intellectual responsibility later when we will discuss the actual working with particular dream images. At this point I can say that the proper attitude towards the dream in its comprehensive sense is the *sustained* tension between "sleepwalking" mind and wakeful intellectual rigor.

But there is not *really* a conflict between the two. "Sleepwalking" and thought go together, because they represent the two sides of the psychological difference, "sleepwalking" is the soul side and wakeful intellectual rigor the psychic side. As therapist I have to *be* the psychological difference.

Furthermore, any true thinking requires in itself "my having gone under" and letting the matter that is to be thought have free play. For veritable thinking, just as for "sleepwalking," the same formulation Jung used once (albeit in a very different context) applies: "Try to live without the ego" (*Letters 1*, p. 427, to Anonymous, 28 April 1946). Or rather: the "Try to" in this sentence is already wrong. It is already the appeal to the ego. Where real thought happens there the ego has always already disappeared. Thought is not the application of the thinking function. It not only takes place on the *psychic* or ego level as formal reasoning. It is not only, indeed not mainly, my *doing* something to the subject matter, my saying something *about* it. Real thought is thinking the real, and this means letting the inner logic of the respective real become explicit. As such, it is itself inherently *psychological*, the unity of "sleepwalking" and wakeful intellection.

Notes

1. C.G. Jung, *The Visions Seminars*, From the *Complete Notes of Mary Foote, Book One*, Zürich (Spring Publications) 1976, Part One (Lectures October 30 – November 5, 1930), p. 7f.
2. Jung made the ambiguity explicit above all in *CW* 15 §§ 136–143 using the topic of literature. See my extensive discussion of these passages in my *What Is Soul?* New Orleans, LA (Spring Journal Books) 2012, pp. 103ff. and 108ff. The "psychological novel" is, according to Jung, useless for psychology proper because it deals only with "what the layman gets his 'psychology' from" and amounts to the realm of "clearly understandable psychology." The psychological novel can therefore well do without psychology in the strict sense (without psychological interpretation). If we take Jung's criteria as our standard and measure, we would have to say that much (if not most) of what professional psychologists do is paradoxically concerned with the layman's psychology in Jung's sense! It is ego-psychology, personalistic psychology, concerned with the psychic functioning of the organism, and not with soul. This applies not only to obvious candidates like cognitive behavior therapy, but also to depth-psychological schools, including most of presently existing Jungian psychology.
3. See, for example, *Letters 2*, pp. 586, 589, to Read, 2 September 1960 ("It is presumably the ancient functional relationship of the medicine-man to his tribe").
4. Jung contrasts the *zivilen Menschen* with the soul. ("Heaven and hell are fates meted out to the soul and not to civilian man, who in his nakedness and dullness would have no idea of what to do with himself in a heavenly Jerusalem" *CW* 9i § 56, transl. modif.)
5. Metaphorically, because soul has no place in *spatial* reality.

6. Jung frequently uses the phrase "objective psyche," but he means what I for clarity's sake call the "objective soul." If one distinguishes, as I usually do, even if not consistently, terminologically between psyche and soul and means by psyche something that belongs to each human being as its private property, then "objective psyche" would amount to a contradiction in terms: an objective subjective psyche.

7. An analogous double negation, although on a very different philosophical basis, is expressed in Nietzsche's dictum: "We have gotten rid of the true world: which world remained? The apparent one perhaps? ... But no! *Along with the true world we also have gotten rid of the apparent one!*" (My transl.). Friedrich Nietzsche, "Wie die 'wahre Welt' endlich zur Fabel wurde," in his *Götzen-Dämmerung*.

8. See James Hillman, *Re-Visioning Psychology*, New York, Evanston, San Francisco, London (Harper & Row) 1975, p. IX.

9. W.G., *The Soul's Logical Life: Towards a Rigorous Notion of Psychology*, Frankfurt am Main, Berlin, Bern, New York, Paris, Wien (Peter Lang) 1998, 5th edition 2020, pp. 203–275.

10. A statement that the way it is expressed is nevertheless probably still too bold.

11. Goethe, *Faust II*, lines 6222f., quoted by Jung, for example, *MDR* p. 344.

12. G.W.F. Hegel, *Phenomenology of Spirit*, transl. by A.V. Miller, Oxford University Press, 1977, p. 19.

13. We know the same relation in a much cruder form from the relation between the various twentieth century socialist or communist states and the ideas of socialism or communism, they preach.

14. Jung's word "*das Ich*" is in English always rendered as "the ego," which is highly problematic. "*Das Ich*" (and likewise the English "the ego") is used without clear discrimination for very different meanings, at times meaning "an agency or complex in the psyche," sometimes the person as a whole, and sometimes a particular attitude. I distinguish "ego" and "I."

15. Jacques Lacan, *The Four Fundamental Concepts of Psycho-Analysis*, London (Penguin) 1994, p. 157.

16. Cf. Greg Mogenson, *The Dove in the Consulting Room*, Hove and New York (Brunner-Routledge) 2003, Chapter 5.

17. *Letters 2*, p. 386, to J. Vijayatunga, August 1957.

18. I mentioned in the chapter about "When patients don't dream" that it is best to write down dreams right after waking up and while still lying in bed, before getting up and turning on bright lights. The reason is the same need to stay as close to the dream atmosphere as possible.

19. In other words, what is not meant is that the content or story of the myth (the dream) is fantasized *onwards*.

Part IV

The dream interpreter

Whom does the therapist address when working on dreams with a patient?

We can be quite brief in the chapter about this question, since what needs to be said here has already been well prepared in the last (or last two) Part(s) so that, to a large extent, all we need to do is pull together the relevant ideas discussed or at least hinted at before and draw the concrete, more practical consequences for the therapist's relation to the patient. The question will be what the general principles laid down above mean for the person of the analyst.

The obvious thing about the situation in the consulting room is that there are two persons vis-à-vis each other, the patient and the analyst. Two "entities" in one room. This obvious fact is seductive. What the eyes can see is also what determines the conventional understanding of psychotherapy. The latter is essentially conceived as a two-person undertaking. The patient is suffering from symptoms and comes to therapy for help, and the therapist is the one whose dedication has to go towards the patient. Therefore, therapists very often also euphemistically refer to the patient as their "client." This word comes from Latin and its basic meaning is "one who has someone (a patron) to lean to for protection," which reveals the fantasy prevalent in many conventional psychotherapy circles. According to this view the therapist's whole responsibility is to his patient as "client" and to the latter's well-being (his getting well). It is the patient who is the center and focus of the work in the consulting room. While he leans on the therapist, the latter is, conversely, really the patient's "servant" (as service provider). At any rate, the interrelation between the two persons is what the work in therapy is about, a fact that is highlighted by the psychological interest of psychoanalysts in the topic of "transference."

Against this backdrop it becomes understandable why it is the most ordinary thing in Jungian training programs or further education courses for analysts that dream seminars, *so-called* dream seminars, are conducted as a kind of case history seminar. The real topic is the dreamer, the patient, *not* the dream. The latter is reduced to a means to an end, a tool to understand the patient.

However, the obvious, that which the eyes can see, is not what is decisive for psychology. More than 40 years ago I had occasion to criticize the understanding of therapy in terms of *two* people, in an article entitled, "On the neurosis of psychology or the Third of the Two"[1]. And in the above Parts, I likewise had to reject the personalistic orientation that dominates conventional psychology. It is simply ego-psychology. But is it right to construe psychotherapy as being in the service of the patient—and not in the service of the soul? Should the word *psycho*therapy not be taken more seriously, more rigorously, namely in its literal meaning, that of *therapeía psychês* or *perì tês psychês*, i.e., as service and attendance to the *soul* (rather than to the patient or *his* psyche, his behavior, his well-being)?

To be sure, the therapist finds himself exposed to the strong influence of the wishes of the patient to get help, to get clear answers how to get out of his fix. This means particularly with respect to dreams the patient's strong desire that the analyst tell him clearly what the dream means, what concrete message it has, some suggestion that the patient can easily understand and connect with his own situation. It is supposed to make sense to him, i.e., to his ego-consciousness, to him as civilian man, and fit to his habitual mindset.

Conversely, patients often say what *they* feel about dream images, or what feelings the latter evoke in them ("how horrible," "how beautiful"). They may have definite ideas what particular images or a dream as a whole mean, occasionally even simple equation-like ideas taken straightaway from popular books on dream symbols and assumed to present the gospel-like truth about them. Or they start talking about what a dream may remind them of, freely associating with it this or that. It is also possible that they try to revise a dream by fantasizing different endings or changing details, giving free rein to their imagination.

The therapist has to learn to withstand such patient wishes and their powerful, maybe even seductive influence felt by the therapist, as well as to the dreamer's own free associations and ideas. It is a violence done to the dream *if we paint it with the colors of our[2] imagination*. The same resistance is necessary with respect to the seductive force of the obvious impression, the persuasive fact that *the eyes can see*, namely the positive fact that in the consulting room there are two persons present. An incisive cut is necessary vis-à-vis all these influences and evident "truths," a kind of radical breaking of a taboo. This cut in its radical nature is best expressed by my saying to the psychotherapist: *Forget the patient! Who cares* what the patient wants or demands or says about dreams! This negation, the performance of this ruthless break, has to be the therapist's first move if there is to be psychological working with a dream.[3]

This is, of course, absolutely shocking, indeed, outrageous. Does what I suggest not amount to an intolerable betrayal of the patient? To a cruel rejection and disregard, if not contempt, of him?

The first point to be made here is that this attack, rejection, negation is not really against the patient. It is, on the one hand, directed against "the ego" (understood as the logical structure of ego-consciousness as such). And on the other hand, it is directed against the therapist's own narcissism. It is the ego that

1   wants to insist on what the eyes can see, on obvious positive empirical facts (the two visible and bodily present persons), and on preserving the ontology of what we call "objective reality" or everyday world, the whole common-sense sphere of daily life;

2   wants to stay on the level of interpersonal human-all-too-human relations and feelings; and

3   makes the therapist wish to be the *patient's* dedicated supporter and helper, to fully understand him and to make an intimate connection to his inner.

When I said that the necessary cut I demanded was directed "against the therapist's own narcissism," I now have to qualify that it is not the narcissism of him person-ally (his private narcissism), but that of the *objective ego* (as a structure of con-sciousness) prevailing in him (as, of course, also in his patient). First and foremost, the demand for this cut is so shocking because it would amount to a self-wounding. It would be a narcissistic blow to dethrone the Two in favor of the Third of the Two, i.e., the objective soul or the dream (as the soul's speaking about itself). My respon-sibility as psychotherapist is to the soul, not to the patient (nor to *his* psyche). What is the *soul* problem? What does the soul want? What does the soul *say*—through symptoms, through dreams, etc.? These are the basic questions. As Hillman put it with reference to a sentence by Pope: "The proper measure of mankind is man; of psychology soul."[4] Forget the human-all-too-human. In dream work, our focus has to be on the dream *sensu strictiori*, the dream itself as expression of the objective psyche and not the dream in terms of the patient and his personal life. What the dream says, not what the patient says, is what we have to be interested in and committed to. Another way of saying the same thing is: The real addressee of one's psychotherapeutic interaction is the dream, and the therapist's real interlocutor is the soul who speaks through the dream, *not* the patient—even though a dream presented by the patient is as a matter of course really and only *his personal (pri-vate)* dream and not something of communal interest or validity the way myths, religious symbols, great works of literature and art were and are.

When a patient first enters the room and is greeted by the therapist, and when at the end of the session he leaves again, *then* the relationship has to be that between therapist and patient. But during the therapy session inside the consulting room this relationship has to give way to that of the psychologist to the soul (as well as, if possible, to the relationship of the patient to the soul[5]).

The distinction made in the preceding paragraph takes me to the second point of the answer to the first shock produced by the idea, "Forget the patient!" The second point is that this idea or demand has its place on one of two levels. In our psychological thinking (and practice) we need to respect, and abide by, the *diffe-rence of levels*. The difference of levels is a consequence of the "psychological difference" that constitutes true psychology. The demand to forget the patient is not as brutal as it appears on first hearing, because it does not at all refer to something that is supposed to be done on the level of literal empirical behavior and social interaction—the ego level, the level of the psychic. The cut is performed only on a higher logical, psychological level. It is a logical cut, a negation that brings about a fundamental shift in our methodological stance, our inner commitment, but does not (and should not) affect the personal relationship between analyst and patient. It should not be acted out as a behavior, but must be *erinnert*, inwardized into the constitution and logical structure of therapeutic consciousness.

The psychological difference means that the therapist has to be able to be on both levels at once; like the *Mercurius duplex* he must be *utriusque capax*. As categorical and uncompromising as the cut has to be performed on the psychological level, on the primitive human or social level the warmth of a genuine relation to the patient as person must be maintained and there must also be an honest understanding of (maybe even sympathy for) the patient's wishes, the ideas mentioned by him, his handicaps, predicaments, and complexes, even a real understanding of their (restricted) legitimacy. While not taking the patient's egoic comments and associations seriously in a psychological sense, the analyst must, of course, on the human level take his patient seriously as the human being that he is with all his comments. But this taking him and his ideas seriously on the human level does not alter the fact that the patient has come for psychotherapy and that for that very reason the therapist is authorized to represent to stance of the psychologist, the "soul doctor," the *psycho*therapist. The patient himself has, although usually unwittingly and involuntarily, given permission to the therapist to regard his first loyalty as being to the soul.

What this means practically is that the therapist needs to straddle the fundamental divide between the two levels, not in a static, but in a dynamic directional sense: from here to there. What is here referred to as the dynamic quality can also, and more precisely, be stated in different terms. The analyst needs to *straddle* the divide *as someone* who in truth has already completely crossed over to the other side (this is what was discussed above as "crossing the river"). No doubt, this is self-contradictory. But this contradiction is the way the difference of levels expresses itself: on the lower empirical level there is the "straddling," whereas on the psychological level the crossing over has always already been accomplished.

Straddling the divide means more concretely that the therapist must have a very personal, almost pedagogic skill and tact, the knack "to lead him gently upon *my* road", as Mephistopheles put it when he stated what he wanted to do with Faust.[6] That is to say, to lead the patient on *his*, the psychologist's, road, which in turn is the road of the soul, and thus to actually realize the psychological difference without doing violence to the patient. The analyst has to attempt to slowly open the patient's eyes to a more sophisticated psychological approach, without making him feel put down. This requires real skill. The therapist has to ask himself:

> How can I best make the patient understand what a psychological access to the dream is and why it is important for his therapy? What words do I need to use with *this* patient today, what style of behavior do I need to show, in order to win the patient over for the soul perspective, and *when* is the best moment, the "right time," for broaching this subject?

And tact is especially needed when it becomes necessary to show the patient that his own free associations, feelings, and fantasies are not an interpretation of or helpful for understanding the dream itself. A good idea in some cases like that might be to let the patient look at the dreams in his way and respect this as a possible way, but then suggest that one could also see another way of looking at the same dreams and then begin, in simple words, to introduce a little bit of a more psychological interpretation as a counterexample, all the while presenting it in such a way that it might be illumining and hopefully convincing to this particular patient. Slowly the patient will then—this is the goal—learn to see himself and his life in terms of the dreams, rather than wishing to see the dreams in terms of his own personality. (Of course, with patients with simple minds or perhaps modest intelligence and differentiation one can probably not hope to get into great psychological depths. There may, however, be others who merely come initially with rather abstract and merely technical ideas about dream interpretation, but who are more sophisticated, so that they can be won over to more serious dream work when one shows them what it can be like.)

I had mentioned the possibly seductive influence on the therapist of the patient's wishes. We need to realize that the seductive influence can also work in the other direction: If the work of a *psychological* dream interpretation succeeds, this will be the best advocate for the soul interest. It is also possible, and this is what is required of the *art* of psychotherapy, to make the soul perspective attractive, indeed seductive. But, as we heard already above in the chapter about "When patients don't dream," it is not only the concrete actual interpretative work, but also the personality as such, the real being, of the therapist that exerts the decisive influence. Much depends therefore, as I said, on the therapist's own authentic and firm psychological commitment, which might also indirectly affect and impress the patient. This shows through the whole style of the therapist. And if the psychologist is truly committed to the soul perspective, truly interested in the soul aspect, then he will probably also find the right words or ways to involve the patient, too, in a psychological understanding and to make this perspective convincing to him. It is not really a technical question. Psychotherapy is an art. One needs to be inventive, creative, to find the way to the heart of the patient. If there is a soul spark in the analyst, it is likely, although not certain, that the patient will also catch fire. The main factor here is the *felt presence* and *living reality* of the soul perspective in the therapist that might strike a chord in the patient. In all this, it must not be the *psychologist* who persuades the patient to soul work, but *the soul perspective itself* (shining through the personality and actual working style of the psychologist) that has the convincing impact.

Who in the therapist interprets the dream?

In the previous chapter the therapist had to become a true *psycho*therapist through the negation of the personalistic therapist–patient *relationship*. A radical cut had to be performed. The patient as such is not the true addressee of the psychotherapist's attention and obligation. Now we turn to the therapist alone. The new question is: *As whom* does the therapist himself qua *psycho*therapist devote himself to the patient's psychic material, above all his dreams?

The therapist's becoming a veritable *psycho*therapist has to be continued with a second cut, a second negation, this time a cut directed at the therapist himself. In order to be more than just an ego-personality, an ordinary person who happens to have studied psychology and now wants to apply what he learned to the patient, in order to become a professional psychologist he needs an act of self-negation, self-overcoming. He has to depart from *himself* and leave his ordinary ego-personality behind, sacrifice not only, as in what we discussed as the first move, the general *logic* of the ego that manifested in the personalistic idea of the Two, but now also specifically his own being narcissistically completely identified with himself, which is normally the initial condition of the ego-personality. He has to distinguish himself from the ego that he is (or rather is deluded to believe to be), dissolve the primitive *literalism* of his sense of self-identity, acquire a distance to himself that opens up a space in which the soul can manifest. Before, I said: "Forget the patient!" Now I add: "Forget yourself!" This is the second move to be performed.

With the two foregoing logical acts of separation the series of necessary negations has not yet come to an end. We still need to perform a third move, the downgrading and devaluation of the psychologist or psychotherapist as subject over against the dream, as we already know from the chapter on "The necessity of my going under." "Forget the analyst, forget yourself (yourself as 'I' and subject). *You* are not important. The *dream* itself is. *Its* thoughts. *Its* images." Dream interpretation must follow the logic of the Biblical "[It] must increase, but I must decrease" (John 3:30).

Here I think something Goethe said about his relation to his own poetic works comes in handy: "… just as with poems, I did not make them, they made me."[7] In this sentence a reversal takes place. What at first seemed to be the object or product (the poems) created by the subject (Goethe) turns out to have been the true subject, and conversely, what seemed to be the subject, the poet, is revealed to be *their* object or product ("they made me"). This is not only the situation in the area of poetic (or artistic) creation. It also immediately applies to dream *interpretation*. The same reversal has to take place here. The dream itself or its individual images must be comprehended as being the real subject doing the dream interpretation and must be allowed to become this true subject. It (the interpretation) is *their* (the dream's and its images's) work. They are the active agent. Not me. I am only the *place* where they can become active (provided that I do not prevent them from becoming active in me by wanting to be the subject myself).

For it is not really a simple reversal, as it at first appears. A simple reversal would retain the simple subject/object, maker/product structure, that is, its syntax, and merely exchange the roles on the semantic level. Instead, we have to see the dialectic in the relation expressed by Goethe. The poems could "make" Goethe only to the extent that he, Goethe, *made* the poems; and he could *make* them only to the extent that *they* made themselves through him. If it had not been the poems themselves that made themselves through him, his "poems" would not have been works of art, but mere ego concoctions. By the same token the dream interprets itself only to the extent that I interpret it. At the same time, my interpretation of it is only a real, a psychological interpretation of it to the extent that it is the dream that does this interpreting through me. To this we might add (in order to also bring in the additional aspect contained in Goethe's statement so far neglected in our description of dream interpretation) the observation that each dream interpretation coming about in this way also "makes" *me* to some extent. Because the dream is the soul's speaking about itself, which means that in each veritable dream interpretation I as dream interpreter am also reached (and affected) by this the soul's speaking.

The dream is the dream's thinking itself. We may here—of course, only in structural regards—be reminded of Aristotle's *noêsis noêseôs*. Jung, making use of a Talmudic dictum, said it apodictically: The dream is its own interpretation (*CW* 11 § 41). But the dream needs *us* in order to *be* its own interpretation in the first place. Only in and through us, through our working with the dream, can it become its own interpretation. The dream alone, as a "text" all by itself, does not do any interpreting at all. It, and the soul in it, only comes alive in and through the human mind. This is the complicated logic of dream interpretation. It is just as with poems. They do not exist somewhere (in heaven, in a sphere of ideal forms?) prior to being *made* by the poet. They first come into existence as the *result* of their actually having been made. There was simply nothing before. And yet this "result" *makes* them in the first place: the result sires them as its own result. This reminds us again: The soul is not an entity, always already subsisting, a soul-thing or soul-substance that has a positive existence free-floating somewhere in the universe or in people, independent of its being *made*. And yet *it* is itself the true "maker" of soul.

Ultimately, it is the soul that has to read and understand the soul's products. *Similia similibus*. "The soul" has to be on both sides.

I started out this chapter with the idea that a therapist's becoming a veritable *psycho*therapist requires the performance of a logical act of separation, a real cut. I spoke of his need to sacrifice his identification with himself, to depart from himself and leave his habitual ego-personality behind. In an earlier chapter we established the "necessity of my going under." All these formulations couch the problem in the language of the ego or at least suggest this language. *I* as subject have to do this and overcome that. *I* have to humble myself. It is *my* job, *my* duty—at least if I want to be a true psychologist.

Meanwhile, we have deconstructed this subject and recognized that the dream is the real subject. *I* am only the place where *it* can become active. Therefore I now have to add a fourth move: Forget even the wish to become a veritable psychotherapist! There must not be any high demands on oneself, no pressure, no ego-will, not even any real striving. We must not feel responsible for our work being truly *psychological* work, because there simply is no transition from ego to soul. There is no practical method for actually and directly establishing, through our efforts, the soul as the subject that interprets the dream. We always start out with and from the ego-personality. The soul cannot be commanded, it is not at our disposal. Therefore, YOU do not need to feel that you have to *get into* the dimension of soul. It is THE DREAM that *has to come to you*, open itself to you, not YOU to it. To open up the soul dimension—in *your* work—is *the dream's doing or task* (or that of "the soul" that is speaking in it).

"Forget even the wish to become a veritable psychotherapist": this fourth move is the ultimate self-depletion of the therapist as subject: he even had to give up his claim to becoming a true psychologist by totally humbling himself so that the soul might take up its residence in him.

Here we might ask: Is this, in the case of the dream, not an unachievable, utopian ideal? Far too lofty? Too elevated, too idealistic, too high a demand? Yes and no. Yes, in the sense that we will never be totally such sleepwalkers, as described earlier, when interpreting dreams. No, because we should not even try. We must not *construe* this attitude as an ideal, as something to strive for. No pressure! Never mind the ego and never mind the imperfection. We must not construe the relation of ourselves as habitual egos to the sleepwalker state as an opposition, as our relation to a distant, hard to attain goal, as the movement *from* here *to* there. This would be the wrong move. We must not try to get away from the ego, not *fight* the ego attitude: because this fighting would only be the confirmation of the ego! No striving for perfection, no struggling to actually become the "sleepwalker."

On the contrary, we must comprehend that the ego and our weakness and imperfection is a *moment* in the desirable state. The "sleepwalker" takes hold of the ego from *within* the ego! We will never get rid of the ego and will not even have to. We have to accept it, live with it, allow it to be, knowing that we are already surrounded by psyche on all sides. Hegel knew: The absolute is already there, and we are already where we ought to be. We just do not see it. This not seeing is the ego. By letting the ego *be*, we can slowly allow it to let go, to let itself be carried and moved by the soul, by the logic of what is. "Swimming" does not mean getting rid of the ego, but entrusting the ego to the water, this uncertain element. Imperfection, not knowing, not understanding are not wrong. We merely hold our place in our ignorance and not-understanding (see the message of the previous chapter). We do not think, "Oh, how embarrassing." No shame. We must not give too much weight and importance to our imperfection.

Whether YOU get into the dimension of soul is not important. The dream IS already the soul's speaking about itself. It *has everything within itself* that it needs, even if you don't see it or if you see it only as a total fog. Here the question of one's trusting the dream comes in, trusting its own completeness. Whether *we see* it or not is secondary.

One's imperfection, too, is already contained in the whole. By trying to overcome the ego and one's not-understanding, one precisely *sets up* the ego as existing outside the psyche, outside the logic of the soul. One sets the ego and the soul up *as opposites*, pulls them apart (which actually, and to begin with, are united, the one containing the other, the ego being a moment of and within the soul); one *creates* externality, the unsurmountable distance between oneself and an ideal. By trying to overcome the ego, the ego runs away from the soul, separates itself from the soul; it refuses to be a sublated moment *in* the soul. Trying to overcome the ego is the way to establish the ego, to establish it as an identity in its own right rather than a sublated moment in the fluidity of the soul's life. For the I *is* already there, is already where it thinks it should get to; it does not have to move. All that has to happen is that it has to understand better that it is already encompassed by "the absolute." It, the I, has to allow "the soul" to catch up with it, to "dawn" on the I, to make itself felt from within the I, much like a person gets *seduced* by the music into the dance. The I has to allow itself to fully and knowingly fall into its sublatedness (that has been its condition all along), into its state as a mere moment of the whole. To the extent that the I understands that it *is* already at the goal, it does not take itself as all that important any longer (which would be its ego stance): and this is the beginning of the "sleepwalker" ...

The first lines of a poem by Goethe ("*Gefunden*", "Found") read:

> I walked the woodland,
> A lonesome man.
> To look for nothing –
> That was my plan.[8]

Whatever this poem itself may be about—we can use and repurpose these beginning lines for our topic of the proper attitude towards dreams. To seek nothing and to want nothing. No ego will. Just an openness and, we might add, a kind of playfulness. No need to come up with a result. If I do not come up with a result, I don't. To seek nothing expresses not the primary innocence, but the secondary, re-acquired, reflected innocence: a methodological attitude. Freud's expression, "free-floating attention" comes to mind in this connection. Although used for the analyst's attitude to the patient, not particularly to dreams, it names quite well what we need for dream interpretation. In this way adding, however, to the idea expressed in Goethe's lines the aspect of "attention," which we would not want to miss.

Our working with dreams (as all soul work, all psychology) requires the *via negativa*, the way of negativity. We work with the imperfect, in the style of alchemy. Comprehending the imperfect as the *initial stage* of perfection. The *real* move away from the ego stance is that the I allows the ego to *be*, to stay, and not to mind that it stays. We approach ourselves with an inner freedom. A kind of *Leichtsinn*, carefreeness, "frivolity," rather than a striving for perfection.

In the *Bhagavadgita* 18th ch., verse 23, we read: "The dutiful [or necessary] deed that is done without attachment, neither out of a liking nor out of a dislike and without regard to success or reward, that is the true or right deed." Whether soul happens in us and in our interpreting work is not our responsibility. It happens or it doesn't happen. Both possibilities are all right. We can relax. If at all, it's the dream's job to become fluid. We can give up all desire to be a good therapist, a good dream interpreter. I just have to be myself, as good or poor as I really am. I must never try to be better than I am. "Be true to yourself." We each have to find OUR OWN style of working with dreams. Relentless honesty!

The therapist must, of course, not be totally inactive, not passive. He does have an important task. But this task is only to do the simple job of trying *his* best to work with the dream images. He has to faithfully, conscientiously, do his simple job of "sitting" on each dream image like a hen sits on an egg, in order to patiently brood it. A hen does not know what is inside the egg (which is why it also sits faithfully on a substituted plaster egg). And if there is a chicken in the egg, *it* will break through the hard eggshell behind which it is hidden and come out of its own accord when its time has come. This is why what we don't understand in a dream and what appears absolutely like a fog to us is precisely helpful. It is what has not always already been pigeonholed and can therefore possibly brooded or, like the corpse in the fairy tale, be warmed by our own warmth.

There is one thing that we as therapists can indeed *do*, something that is as a matter of course our full responsibility and clearly lies in our power (provided the necessary giftedness, maturity, and differentiation exist). This is *training the mind* (outside of the practice of psychotherapy and, apart from the actual working with dreams, on the level of theory). We can acquire a full-fledged intellectual comprehension of the *concept* of soul in contradistinction to ego and daily life issues and of the soul's logical life, its needs and concerns, its forms of expression. We can continually deepen and differentiate this comprehension and refine our feeling and sensibility with respect to it. Here we are not helpless. Here there is no "It happens, or it doesn't happen." It can be expected and demanded of any serious psychologist in the soul sense of the word to have acquired a clear understanding of the concept of soul. This is also the purpose of this book, which, as I pointed out in the Introduction is not intended to serve as a practical help for the practitioner, but instead to serve exclusively the purpose of training the psychological mind.

From this (the acquisition of a psychologically trained mind) it follows that there can be certain *negative* moves that one can make on a more practical level. We can become critical, work off obvious ego views and also refuse to accept any pressure, that perhaps arises in ourselves, to be obligated to understand everything in a dream and be good psychologists. But these negative moves do not mean that the soul is automatically constellated: there is, as I said, no *positive* way to get into "soul" or constellate in ourselves the soul as the true subject of dream interpretation. Here the "It happens, or it doesn't happen" has its legitimate place.

It is certainly possible to clearly sense, when we finished a dream interpretation, that it was not so successful, not really a deep psychological interpretation. Conversely, we can never be sure whether in a satisfying dream interpretation it was really the soul that was constellated as the interpreter of the dream. The soul cannot be nailed down, pinpointed. We have to leave it open. The move from the ego to the soul as an actual doing is a negative move (working off obvious ego elements). We can never positively say: now the soul is speaking from within me while I interpret the dream. And again: we must also not worry about it. It is not necessary to know. The soul has to be left alone, left to its own devices. We never become soul *literally*. We stay ego all the time. We must not even try to get literally out of the ego, out of our empirical humanness. The soul is never a positive (and positivizable) reality, not a something. It is always only the invisible depth of, and attached to, something else (imaginally speaking maybe like an "echo"). But by our training the mind we as ego-personality can perhaps become more soulful and pervious for the soul.

My interpretation

The therapist has been dethroned from his position as subject. He had to forget himself. This has been the lesson of the foregoing insights. Earlier we heard: "*It* [the dream or the soul speaking through it] has a say now, *not* you!" The therapist is, as it were, condemned to silence. But now, in a fifth move, the I returns. This move is already prepared by our above insight into the dialectic that "the dream interprets itself only to the extent that I interpret it" and that "only in and through us, through our working with the dream, can it become its own interpretation." I have to take myself as the interpreter of the dream absolutely seriously. The dream exists for me *only through me*, through and by means of my perception.

The dream is not, as the scientific, empiricist fantasy might suggest, a given object and fact to be studied objectively by filtering out all subjective reactions. Now I say: I precisely have to take note of *myself* as the subject that hears or reads the dream text. For the dream is, when I start working with it, always already nothing but *my* apperception of the dream. *The* dream per se does not exist for me. I am the lens, the glasses, through which it is seen. There is never a naked object for us, no immediacy. All observations are *my* observations and as such inevitably subjective. I perceive through myself. I am always part and parcel of what I perceive. We are always the instrument of perception and interpretation. And this is not wrong. Therefore: no false fear of being subjective. And no submission to the false ideal of "objectivity." So there is not the difference between subjective and objective, because the objective is always subjective too. The real difference is between what is *merely* subjective, exclusively *my private* feeling or idea, and what is a real reaction, in which case it is subjective-objective or objective-subjective.

The material we work with, such as a dream, is always our own subjective ideas, images, feelings etc. concerning this material, and not the objective fact. But not only that. The importance of the therapist's subjectivity extends even to his own dream *interpretations*. Here, too, there must not be any false fear of being subjective and any striving for abstract objectivity. Rather, concerning our working with dreams, our dream interpretions, we have to apply the alchemical dictum: *Oportet operatorem interesse operi* ("The operator [or artifex] must be present [or make his presence felt] in the *opus*, the work", *CW* 12 § 375) or St.

Augustine's and Luther's similar insight: *oportet me adesse*[9] ("it is indispensable that I am fully, wholeheartedly present," namely as the whole person that I am).

Dream interpretation means my showing myself, exposing myself, showing who I am, how deep or superficial my perception is, how narrow or rich and differentiated my mind and the categories I use are. To interpret means risking oneself. Coming forward: "*This* is how *I* see it." In interpreting a dream, I do not only show what is in the *dream*, but I also always unintentionally show to some extent *myself* and who I am.

Psychological dream interpretation thus requires one's letting oneself fall into one's own atomic subjectivity. The interpretation then happens as an unforeseeable event; it emerges spontaneously, produces itself, rather than being the reliable result of the application of a finished theory upon the dream or of a technique of interpretation. What does "letting oneself fall into one's own subjectivity" mean? It means to leave oneself to sink or swim in the depths of the unknownness and infinity of oneself (of I). I let this inner unknownness of myself take over and allow it to bring to light what I am made of, what was in me, but possibly unknown even to myself. In this sense, each individual dream interpretation is also a kind of "birth process": it gives birth to me, or rather to some partial aspect of myself.

My point here is not that a dream can bring to light what may have been hidden in the *dreamer*. This is, of course, also valid. No, what I am here suggesting is the completely different idea that in my interpretation of the dream of others, of patients, or of each particular motif of this dream, some aspect of who I am or some hidden possibility or dimension of mine may possibly see the light of day.

This amounts to a totally different idea about self-knowledge from the popular ideas in psychotherapy of introspection or self-reflection, self-examination. If an interpretation that I give of a patient's dream can bring to light some hitherto hidden aspect of me, then this does not come about through my looking at or into myself, but precisely through looking away from myself, namely through my wholeheartedly devoting myself to the objectively given dream text and trying my best to understand and do justice to *it*. In such a situation I am not at all interested in myself. It needs the "other," the object (the patient's dream) outside of myself to—possibly—allow some aspect of the darkness[10] of my subjectivity to surface.

This shows that the fifth move that restored the importance of subjectivity, of the I, by no means undoes the previous moves that had to do with the therapist's departing from himself and forgetting himself. Rather, this process is continued. By being wholeheartedly devoted to the *other* of a dream to be interpreted, the therapist *lets himself fall* into his own atomic subjectivity and thus relentlessly gives himself up, gives up the I's control and self-identity: abandoning himself in one and the same act to the unknownness of the objective reality out there (the patient's dream) AND to the unknownness—the absolute negativity—of his own subjectivity: a double infinity. He has lost his solid ground. I spoke before of sinking or swimming and sleepwalking. *Psychological* dream interpretation means trusting the water, the air, the absolute negativity, the bottomlessness of self. The ground on which to stand is only the *result* of a successful interpretation, not the starting point of the procedure. (This is an instance of the *hýsteron próteron* [the production of the First, the beginning, *as* the Second, *as* the result] that prevails in psychology, and the opposite of the scientific understanding of so-called psychology, where you have first to have the solid ground of a theory about the functioning of the psyche of the human organism together with a set of firm therapeutic techniques before you are allowed to start interpreting dreams on this basis.)

At any rate, the "going under of the subject" discussed earlier is not undone or reversed here. This also means that the new emphasis upon the subject (the insistence that working with dreams is always decidedly "*my* interpretation") does not give me license to interpret dreams just off the top of my head, just as I please, bringing in my subjective associations, feelings and fantasies. I as interpreting subject must forget myself. This is indispensable. My entire concentration must solely go to the dream. *It* needs to be understood. And my interpretation has to be a responsible one. What comes out of me in the way of interpretative statements about the dream elements must be measured against the dream text and stand the test. I have to be able to rationally justify, with strong arguments, why I interpret something this way and why I think that some other view does not fit to the dream at hand. What I say must make sense and convince *on the basis of the dream* (not on the basis of one's pet ideas and preferences). There has to be intellectual rigor, conscientiousness, and a committed striving for truth.

By saying that I have to strive that my interpretation of the dream is the true interpretation I land myself, of course, with the big question of "truth." The truth that we in psychology strive for is, needless to say, not truth in the abstract sense: *the* ultimate, timeless, abstract-universal truth, but it is only *absolute truth*, an expression which, however, can easily be misunderstood. What absolute truth means can in our context be best explained by citing a passage from Jung's "Prologue" to *Memories, Dreams, Reflections*. Jung wrote, "I can [...] only 'tell stories.' Whether or not the stories are 'true' is not the problem. The only problem is whether what I tell is *my* fable, *my* truth" (*MDR* p. 3). With his removing the question "Whether or not the stories are 'true'" as irrelevant, Jung rejected the abstract-universal sense of truth. But he thereby by no means gave up "truth" as such. It returns in his next sentence as "*my* truth," which is a truth that is—paradoxically—at the same time "my *fable*." It is not only the two occurrences of the italicized "my" in Jung's text that make it clear that "truth" here is fundamentally the specific, individual subject's own truth, not an "objective" ("interpersonally valid") truth, that abstracts from the subject, rising to the supra-personal level of a "consciousness at large." It is also the equation of truth and fable.

This sense of truth is "absolved" (freed) from the abstract sense of the word that prevails, in everyday as well as scientific parlance. *Psychology* has to move from ultimate to absolute truth. The latter is—how could it be otherwise?—the *coniunctio oppositorum* of the correspondence (*adaequatio*) of my interpretation to the object (the dream) AND the correspondence (*adaequatio*) of the interpretation to the subject (the therapist in his utter subjectivity: is it really "*my* fable, *my* truth"[11]). Truth does not simply reside in the object per se, in the dream considered in isolation. It is not the real meaning and inner depth hidden in the dream under its surface, under the external impression it evokes. Truth is much rather the relation or *mutual reflection* of these two correspondences, the relation between the unknown depth or infinity of the object and the unknown abyssal depth or inner infinity of the subject (i.e., not merely one side of the whole relation). The dream as "object" is not a fixed and finished entity whose truth could be discovered by analyzing it the way biologists study and analyze plants or animals. For its truth, the dream as "object" is dependent on the truth of the interpreting subject. All by itself it has no truth and no meaning.

The inner abyssal depth of the subject comes into play *only* if the subject is precisely *not* interested in itself, not using introspection, not explicitly searching his self, but uncompromisingly devoted only to the dream and forgets itself. The inner truth of the dream can only come to light if I forget the ideal of "abstract-universal truth" (using Jung's wording we could say: "Whether or not the interpretation is 'true' is not the problem.") and instead allow truth to have the character of being "*my* fable, *my* truth"—only that!

Then, as this *absolute* truth, my interpretation is truly *my* interpretation and my interpretation of the *dream*.

The *Now* of dream interpretation

We had to realize that a true interpretation of a dream must not be conceived as one-sidedly bringing to light the inner essence of the dream as the object of our study. It involves the inner essence of both object (dream) and subject (interpreter), and their mutual reflection—because the dream in isolation has no truth, no meaning. The dream as seeming "object" *needs* the subject to *be* a full-fledged dream in the first place. It is not a fixed, self-contained entity.

This process of "deconstruction" that has so far deprived the dream of its self-identity needs to be continued, but now on the side of the subject. The subject, I, is also not a self-contained, definitively circumscribed and self-identical entity. It is essentially an open, unpredictable reality. This means that my subjectivity is likewise dependent on and determined by factors *outside itself*, namely determined by the time, the concrete situation. For our theme of dream interpretation specifically, it means that "*my* interpretation" is not my interpretation once and for all. Rather, it is only my interpretation *now*. I have no control over my subjectivity and cannot guarantee that tomorrow, or after a longer period of time, I would still see the same dream the same way. Maybe *my* interpretation a month later would be quite different. The dream (the same dream text) would have become a completely different one.

This impossibility of ever arriving at *the* final interpretation is well known from hermeneutics. Great works of literature and art (e.g., Homer's Iliad, Sophocles's or Shakespeare's tragedies, Goethe's Faust), great historical figures (Caesar,

Napoleon, etc.) have been interpreted quite differently at different times and are being and will be in the future subjected to new insights about them dependent on the spirit of the respective age. It is not always the case that earlier interpretations are shown to be untenable and replaced by new and better ones, nor that new information not available before about the works or persons has surfaced, although both these possibilities can of course also occur. But the insight to be gained in our context is that for a new age, in a new situation, the same work *is* a different one. Its truth is not supratemporal.

The same is the case with dreams and dream interpretation. But whereas in the case of the change from one historical age to another there is a new generation of interpreters who devote themselves to the same work, I am here concerned with the differing interpretations of one and the same individual (and of one and the same dream) at different moments of time or under different conditions.

Just as the written dream is not *the* original dream, but the dream version as it appeared to memory to the best of the dreamer's knowledge at the moment of writing, so our interpretations of dreams in therapy are inevitably bound to the Now of this particular dream-work session. This now is not only "my personal" now. It also includes the environment, the external conditions, for example, the social situation of dream interpretation. It is one situation when I am all by myself and read a dream text sent to me by letter or email, and a very different one when I am with the dreamer of this dream. In a therapy session with one particular patient a dream might evoke an interpretation that is partially or completely different from an interpretation of a dream with basically the same content and form in a session with another patient. The atmosphere in the session, the particular form of the therapeutic relationship, the heaviness or type of the patient's pathology and psychological problem, the presence or absence of resistance in the patient, his own greater or lesser openness to soul, all this functions as imperceptible influences upon *my* apperception of this dream. Similarly, in dream seminars: the same dream text may induce in me quite different interpretations with one group of participants than with another.

That this is so, that *my* interpretation is influenced by the concrete quality of the Now should not merely be the way it factually is. Before, I insisted that the dream interpreter must let himself fall into his own abyssal subjectivity. Now I add that we also need to let the very concept of our own subjectivity fall into the eachness of its Now. We have to learn to consciously, methodically, integrate this awareness into our attitude and thus, as I indicated, to consciously, relentlessly abandon ourselves to the infinity and unpredictability of the *now* of each dream discussion. We must not try to reach the correct, intersubjectively and timelessly valid interpretation, but conversely leave ourselves to sink or swim in the respective Now. And here, to this abandonment to the Now, much the same applies as what was said above about "*my* interpretation"—about the dialectic of this self-abandonment and about the dialectic of absolute truth (in contrast to "abstract universal truth"), only with respect to the eachness of each Now. Yes, let the Now take over, but without explicitly turning your attention to it. The *depth* of the Now determines your thinking precisely when your conscious attention goes exclusively to the dream. And yes, commitment to truth, but the only question is: is it the truth *of my real present*, of this concrete situation, and only in this sense also my *fable*? *Today* I have to give my best with respect to the dream, my best from within this actual Now. I must not wish to leap over myself and over my real Now of dream interpretation into the fiction of a timelessly true interpretation.

Included in the lesson of the Now is the insight that my subjectivity is not merely *in* me, confined within the borders of "me" as my solipsistic self-identity, let alone my genes. *My* subjectivity is a relation: it extends into what is not I, into my surroundings, into the world, and is partially shaped by all this.

A dream is, likewise, not the abstraction of "the dream text," not the dream in isolation, but the concrete experience and perception of the dream images in this concrete moment. The dream *is* in reality the *relation* between the abstract idea of the dream as literal text and the mind that tries to understand it *at a concrete qualitative moment of time*. The real dream has event character, not entity character. We must not *eject* the dream *out of* the moment of our thinking about it. We must not posit it as existing prior, outside, and independent of our thinking about it. The dream exists—for the practicing psychologist—*only* in our remembering it, hearing it, reading it, thinking about it, feeling something about it—always in each actual Now. It is much like a work of art. A painting in a museum that is not seen and appreciated by a human mind is a dead object and not a work of art. It turns into a work of art only in the moment when a mind actually *views* and *appreciates* it as art. A piece of music is only what it is when it is played *now* by this particular musician.

What was discussed in the last few chapters or maybe even this whole Part IV on the dream interpreter could be considered to be nothing but an unfolding and spelling out of the inner complexity of what I meant by the terms "swimming" and "sleepwalking" introduced earlier.

Notes

1. Originally published in *Spring 1977*, this paper is now to be found in my book, *The Neurosis of Psychology. Primary Papers towards a Critical Psychology*, (= W.G., *Collected English Papers*, vol. 1) New Orleans (Spring Journal Books) 2006, pp. 41–67.
2. "Our" is comprehensive; it includes patient and therapist (as ego-personalities, civilian persons).
3. With my view I contradict directly Jung's admonition, "Never apply any theory, but always ask the patient how *he* feels about his dream-images. For dreams are always about a particular problem of the individual about which he has a wrong conscious judgment." But interestingly enough, Jung's next paragraph begins with a kind of retraction. "But today I am going to contradict myself and break all my rules. I am going to interpret a single dream, not one out of a series; moreover, I do not know the dreamer, and further, I am not in possession of the associations." His excuse or justification is: "If a dream is clearly formed of *personal* material you have to get the

individual associations; but if the dream is chiefly a *mythological* structure—a difference which is obvious at once—then it speaks a universal language, and you or I can supply parallels ..." (*CW* 18 § 248 f.). This justification is only partially convincing. True, concerning personal material in dreams we need *information* that the patient has and we don't have. But information is not "what *he* feels about his dream-images." The assertion that only dreams with an obviously mythological character speak a universal language unduly limits the notion of universal language to strictly archetypal images. There is no reason why personal material in dreams cannot be a form of what Jung here calls "universal language." We must not literalize this term, not construe it positivistically. We see Jung here at the crossroads. His strict rules in the first quoted passage represent his early personalistic stance. In the second and third quotes his later stance is foreshadowed, even if only still bashfully. Jung has at this point not yet freed himself to the insight that treating dreams as images, as the soul's speaking, does not need any excuse and not the binary opposition of the literally mythological vs. the personal.

4. James Hillman, *Re-Visioning Psychology*, New York *et al.* (Harper & Row) 1975, p. 189.
5. It is, in fact, the general goal of psychotherapy that the patient can acquire a distance to himself as ego-personality and gain an authentic relation to soul.
6. "Ihn meine Straße sacht zu führen." Goethe, *Faust*, line 314.
7. Joh. W. von Goethe, *Kampagne in Frankreich*, Aug. 30, 1792, my transl.
8. Translated by A.Z. Foreman. https://poemsintranslation.blogspot.com/2010/12/goethe-found-from-german.html, accessed March 2019. The original German: "*Ich ging im Walde / so für mich hin, / und nichts zu suchen, / das war mein Sinn.*" What has been translated in the second line as "A lonesome man" actually means "completely casually, unconcerned, 'just like that'."
9. This is what Luther (in his *Disputatio de iustificatione*, 1536, WA 39 I; 96,6) added by way of commentary to a statement by St. Augustine (in Sermo CLXIX CLXX, 13, *Opera omnia* [Migne V, p. 923]): "*qui creavit te sine te, non salvabit te sine te*" ("he who created you without you, will not save you without you"). For the page references of these quotes I am indebted to Prof. Martin Brecht, Münster.
10. "Darkness" here means simply unknownness, opacity. It does not refer to something like "dark secrets."
11. It would not be *my* truth if I merely applied standard theoretical concepts to the dream, putting every dream in some pigeonhole that my psychological theory provides.

Part V

Interpreting the actual text of dreams

After having explored some aspects of what a dream, as such, is, of why dreams are therapeutically important, what the general attitude to dreams should be, as well as what the role of a dream interpreter in the context of a psychology *with* soul is, we are at long last ready to turn to the theme of the dream text itself, that is to say, its contents, the story it tells, its images, and how to work with all this. In the spirit of this book, which is devoted to the topic of "*Working* with dreams," our purpose cannot be to discuss specific dream images or symbols and their meaning on a semantic level. We have to be concerned with general ways to understand and practically approach dream images *as such*, regardless of what their particular content or meaning may be.

Before beginning with my own discussion I want to recommend to the reader above all the various writings by James Hillman (not only those directly devoted to the discussion of "image" and the imaginal as such,[1] but also most of his other texts because they contain numerous examples of an insightful working with particular images) and Pat Berry's ground-breaking essay, "An Approach to the Dream," in her *Echo's Subtle Body*, Dallas, Texas (Spring Publications) 1982, pp. 53–79.

"Object level," "subject level" and the objective psyche

An important part of Jungian ideas about dream interpretation is the distinction between an interpretation on the object level from one on the subject level.

The object-level interpretation would imply that the dream refers to and is about some aspect of external reality, for example persons in real life. It would have a referent outside itself. For this reason, this type of interpretation is not really acceptable from a psychological point of view. For one thing, it would violate the psychological difference. By viewing dream figures as external referents we would construe the dream story as taking place in the social arena, in literal reality, which, in turn, would have the consequence that the dream-I too would be apprehended from outside as just another figure taken from external reality, i.e., an existing human being or citizen ("civilian man"), as one of the people moving in the outside world. Furthermore, this type of interpretation would reduce the dream as a whole to a "sign" and deprive it of its symbolic nature.

The difference between sign and symbol or image is that the sign has a referent and is merely an instrument for pointing away from itself *to* that referent, while the symbol/image points only to *itself* and means only itself. It does not *have* a meaning, it *is* itself the meaning that it has. Therefore it is self-contained and self-sufficient. It is true simply because it exists, a statement that I modeled after Jung's sentences (*CW* 11 § 4 and 5), "The idea is psychologically true inasmuch as it exists." "An elephant is true because it exists." No otherness and no instrumentality! The symbol and the dream are selves or, as we just heard, "living entities." The remarkable things about Jung's statements are (1) that he conceives truth as an existence, like an entity, whereas normally we think that truth is a possible quality of propositions, statements, or opinions *about* something real and consists precisely in the *adaequatio rei et intellectus*, i.e., in a special relationship (namely one of correspondence or equality) *between* the *two*, and that (2) existence (something that exists) can be true because it *is* in itself meaning, it *is* psychological, soulful! A real elephant as "fact" is not really true, whereas the elephant as an image or symbol is true.

So it was necessary to reject the object level of interpretation. What remains is the subject level. Although an interpretation on this level is much more on the way to being psychological, if we look closely, it turns out that it is not acceptable either. Why? Because it ultimately also points to an external referent, namely to the ego personality. It is, of course, true, "my inner father" or "my internal shadow figure" are not out there, in external reality. They do not have a material existence; they are already figures, images, ideas, i.e., *meanings* in themselves. Nevertheless, they are conceived as components of "me," i.e., of the ego-personality, part of my make-up, and thus subsumed under the I as its attributes. I as human being am the external referent of all dream images, because I am their substrate. With this type of interpretation, use is made of something that is external to the dream and that is a literal, factual reality in contrast to a purely symbolic or imaginal reality. The ego-personality is here the empirically real container of all the components that the dream images refer to or express in this type of dream interpretation.

So, the problem of the subject level interpretation is that the psychological difference, the difference between man and soul, is also not heeded. Psychologically it does not make much difference if we support the notion of external reality one way or another, be it by focusing on the dream figures and elements as the persons, things and events out there in the social world and in the physical world of nature in the way of object-level interpretation, or be it by viewing, in the manner of subject-level interpretation, the dream images as inner figures and components *of the personality of the dreamer* as the ultimate substrate of the dream. In either case our thinking remains an "ontologizing" one rather than a psychological one, and in either case the natural positivistic worldview of what we call "the ego" remains unchallenged. For the psychological mode, the dream has *everything* it needs within itself and points only to *itself*, whereas for the "ontologizing" mode the dream has the essential reality it refers to outside of itself.

With both modes of dream interpretation, we would still stay outside of the door to psychology. Both are decidedly personalistic, only concerned with different aspects of the psyche of the human organism, the one, if I may compare the human being with a nation or state, with its *foreign affairs*, the other with what falls into the domain of the *Home Office*, the *interior ministry*. This political comparison throws a light on this kind of approach: with its practical-management aspect it is clearly ego-psychological. The soul as the constitutive root metaphor of psychology has not yet been sighted.

Psychology requires the standpoint of the *objective* or *autonomous soul*. In order to reach it with respect to the dream, we need to cut the dream loose from both the positively existing person of the dreamer and from the external world, in which the dreamer as biological organism and civilian man lives, and interiorize it into itself. We have to locate it as a priori being "on the other side of the river" (see the chapter on "Crossing the river," above). As mentioned and critiqued before, the dream has been viewed as the *via regia* to the unconscious, by Freud, Jung and Hillman. Here now I can add to my critique of this idea that the dream is not a *via to* … at all, neither to the unconscious, nor to "the other side of the river." Why? Not only because this would reduce the dream to a means to an end and instrumentalize it for our, the ego's, purposes, but also because from the outset it *is* already on the other side. It is the objective soul's speaking about itself. It does not want to lead anywhere. It is a soul *thought* that conversely has *come* from the other side into consciousness, and come of its own accord.

Before we can explore more closely what the dream, interiorized into itself, is and what this involves we need to address a very common mistake in dream interpretation.

Trap: Dream interpretation as the dream's translation into the terms of one's psychological theory

As long as we start out with a customary personalistic orientation, we are also likely to have some kind of general theory about the personality, about psychodynamics and the nature of people's unconscious desires, about the "family romance," and about various clinical illnesses, etc. We are, accordingly, in danger of listening to the patient's material with a view to *matching* what is in the material, in the dream, with our theories. We mechanically translate the patient's specific personal details into, or subsume them under, the general terms of our psychological theory. We treat the dream as *logically* known. It is only unknown in *empirical* regards. This means: we try to *identify* dream elements as particularized variants or examples of the concepts or constructs of our theory. We thereby put, for example, the patient's dream into one of the always already available boxes with which our therapeutic mind is filled. Then it is the particular box that becomes the important thing, not the specific content inside the box (the real phenomenon itself that has been put into the box). The box need not and must not be opened.

Another way to describe this matching type of interpreting would be to say it is like sticking labels on things. Again, the label would then be more important than the object to which the label has been applied. By thinking this way, we ultimately say that the dream consists only of *already known* elements, known building blocks. Similarly, one can use the method of *amplification* in such a way that one approaches the dream with a *given repertoire* of knowledge about myths and symbols and then relates this dream motif to that knowledge. Then there cannot be anything truly new. What is still unknown is merely *which* building blocks are in this particular dream and in what *combinations* they occur. This is exactly the opposite of what I said about meeting a person for the first time. This person is then really *new* to me, completely unknown. Dream interpretation should follow this model. It must be an adventure, an expedition into the unknown.

To approach the dream with "boxes" or with "labels" is the way of positivity, the attempt to positivize the meanings of the individual images, to reduce them to *known* and *closed* meanings ("closed" like a book with seven seals). They have become so-called meanings, "meanings" that do not really *mean* any longer. Instead, they turn into objects to operate with. They become instrumentalized, instead of being what opens the eyes for new dimensions. In principle, syntactically, there is not really much of a difference between a patient's being convinced that a given dream image has this or that fixed meaning according to a *dream book* or a *smartphone application for dreams*, and a therapist's putting the labels of his *theory* on this image. Semantically, the latter may be far more sophisticated and based more on actual practical experience and serious theoretical thinking. But the operation or method is the same in both cases.

Jung was very clear about this type of approach. His view is best expressed in the following quote, of which we already know its second part:

> Stereotyped interpretation of dream-motifs must be rejected [...]. Even if one has great experience in these matters, one is again and again obliged, before each dream, *to admit one's ignorance* and, *renouncing* all preconceived ideas, to prepare for something entirely unexpected.
>
> (*CW* 8 § 543, transl. modif., my italics)

The crucial pair of opposites here is: "always already known" versus "entirely unexpected" (and in this sense *really* new: coming as a surprise that can open one's eyes). They also imply two opposite directions to move. In the one case the therapist pulls the new element (e.g., the patient's dream) to himself, incorporating it into the structure of his theory. This activity is like filing the dream (or its diverse images) away in the theory as the therapist's filing cabinet. In the other case the move goes in the exactly opposite direction: here the therapist has to *enter* the dream as something new and unknown, with a view to exploring it, getting to know it, and with the readiness to be taught, to let his own consciousness be expanded or reformed. We call this activity of entering the dream or interiorizing oneself into the dream *thinking*. Dreams need to be thought. Thinking is the way into the previously unknown depth. Referring back to our image of the closed book we could say that thinking is one's opening the book and reading, studying, it. Our above crucial pair of opposites can now be reformulated as: "filing away" versus "thinking."

A prominent idea is that theories and techniques must be "applied" to individual cases. "Application" seems to suggest the therapist's moving *to* the case, the patient, the dream, and not the other way around, a pulling them to himself. But this is, of course, only the first appearance. In reality, all applications of our theories to something amounts to our filing it away and subsuming it under our already existing knowledge.

If we as therapists are supposed *not* to apply our theories to individual dreams, if we are even told by Jung to *renounce* all our preconceived ideas and firmly establish ourselves in our ignorance, we might think that theoretical knowledge about psychology is altogether unnecessary and we could devote ourselves to dreams as theoretically innocent babes in the woods. Of course, we need long and thorough training and lots of psychological knowledge. We have to have learned a lot: about mythology, symbolism, religions, the history of ideas, psychological and psychopathological phenomenology, about the whole range of the forms of human feelings, emotions and behavior, the dynamics of people's relations to each other, etc. One has to have a rich experience of psychotherapeutic processes and have worked with many, many dreams.[2] *But*: what is very important when, after all that, interpreting a dream is that one has to let go of all one's knowledge. You have to forget all theory, all acquired knowledge and make "not knowing" your starting condition, as we said. Jung's advice to his pupils was: "Learn as much as you can about symbols and forget it all when you are analysing a dream" (*CW* 18 § 483).

What does "forgetting" here mean, what is this type of not knowing? Forgetting is actually a natural process and cannot be willed or commanded. Here, however, we have in mind precisely a deliberate, methodically produced forgetting, as Jung's word "renouncing" indicates. This means that what is forgotten is not literally forgotten, totally gone. It is merely pushed aside or removed from the actual foreground of consciousness. Consciousness has made itself independent of it. What we have here is a sublated forgetting and a sublated ignorance!

Let me illustrate this idea of sublated forgetting with the example of a virtuoso violinist. In order to have gotten to where he now is, he must have undergone years of hard, disciplined training, with many hours of practice every day. His fingers and arms needed to be trained. They had to learn to move absolutely reliably in an exactly prescribed way and in the necessary, often incredible speed and precision. The point of this training was that his limbs could move in the desired way quasi *automatically*, without his explicit conscious attention. We could say that the point of the training was to make itself forgotten. No conscious concentration, no literal command to each finger for each stop that it has to go to is necessary. The technique of playing is simply not an issue any more. It has disappeared in a deeper, subliminal, unconsciously performing level in him. This is virtuosity. The violinist is then free to devote himself totally to the musical quality of the piece he is playing, to the soul of the music. He has "forgotten" the whole mechanics of playing. It is no longer he as body who plays the music; the music plays itself through him, through his mind and heart, using the *trained* muscles of his fingers, which simply follow suit; the fingers have to perform the way the music wants and, as I said, quasi automatically.

In much the same way one's psychological knowledge has to disappear into the subliminality of the background of consciousness, not because this knowledge is unimportant, but because it must not remain an external and prior structure, something given and existing outside the dream.[3] Nicholas of Cusa developed the idea of the *Docta ignorantia* (learnèd ignorance). I leave aside what it means in his thinking and concentrate here only on the phrase itself. It is *docta* ignorantia, that is to say, first one has to have learned the knowledge before one can forget it. But if I have in this sense, with an intentional purposelessness, "forgotten" it, then it is no longer really I who interpret the dream, but it is that dream which interprets itself through me, through my mind and soul—and through the way my mind and soul have been psychologically trained and are structured.

The logic of the dream is like light, and I am (my mind is) the prism in which this light is broken. This is what *thinking* the dream means.

Getting started: Beginning with the *subject*. Circumambulating the dream

We now come to the heart of the Jungian view of dreams as concrete texts with specific contents, images and meanings. It is important to find the right entry into this topic. There are so many ideas and statements about dreams with which we could start. I think the proper beginning, that is to say, our beginning with what at the same time is also the inner logical starting-point of the Jungian view of dreams itself, is Jung's declaration: "In dream analysis I proceed on principle by circumambulating it …" (*Letters 2*, p. 293f., to Jacobi, 13 March 1956, transl. modif.[4]). Another time he explained the change in his way of proceeding over against his style of working with dreams during his earlier Freud-inspired days,

> I no longer followed associations that led far afield and away from the manifest dream-statement. I concentrated rather on the actual dream-text as the thing which was intended by the unconscious, and I began to circumambulate the dream itself, never letting it out of my sight…
>
> (*CW* 18 § 430)

Jung *circumambulates*: he does something, he performs a movement around the dream. Of course, this is not a literal movement in spatial reality. It is a logical movement, and in this sense the word "circumambulation" is used metaphorically. It describes with one image the fundamental attitude toward dreams.

The remarkable thing here is that this beginning does not really start with the object, the dream itself as the analyst's "object of desire," not with his getting involved with the dream itself, with trying to "comprehend" or "interpret" it. It *starts* solely with the subject itself: with an activity performed by the subject, more particularly: with its doing something *to itself*, namely getting *itself* into a circular motion. To be sure, this motion circles around the *dream*. But precisely only around it: without touching it, trying to grasp and conquer it intellectually ("analyzing it"), or doing anything *to* it. A distance is kept towards it. It is entirely left alone, free, intact. The dream is, no doubt, in the center, but it is not the object and focus of the subject's attention or interpretative claim. In circumambulating, the subject is first of all busying itself with itself. This is the constitutive act of a *psychological* approach to the dream, which needs to be explained a bit more in the following.

To circumambulate is especially known from ritual practice as one's walking or dancing around an object of worship. For Jung, the dream is not an object of worship, but his own circumambulation, nevertheless, amounts to metaphorical ritual, a ritual practice on the level of methodology, and the distance at which the dream is kept from or by the subject is one of respect.

Why does the psychological approach necessarily begin with the subject, with the subject's own movement? This is absolutely contrary to both daily life and the scientific attitudes which from the outset sound the (cognitive) attack on the object, that is to say, are directly intent upon it. They operate within the binary subject/object dichotomy. The sciences are based on methodical filtering out and eliminating, as far as possible, the subjective aspect, reducing it to an abstract-universal consciousness at large, so as to end up with hoped-for pure objectivity. Jung's beginning with the subject's circumambulation, therefore, marks a radical shift (or rather a downright reversal) in orientation, his stepping out of the conventional dominant stance of (above all Western) man towards the world, that stance that is perhaps best epitomized by what Lothar Schäfer called "The Bacon-Project,"[5] emphasizing the *interventionist* character of the Baconian epistemic approach. Psychology, in order to be what it is, has to begin with the subject and take it seriously (instead of trying to eliminate it). We could think here also of the fact that the profession of the analyst starts with the student analyst's own training analysis, with himself. But this comparison is superficial and would also be directly misleading. The analyst's own training analysis is mainly concerned with "introspection," with the subject's one-sided, direct interest in *itself*. Introspection and the effort to gain self-knowledge are psychic and personalistic, not psychological. They are the simple reversal into the opposite of the scientific focus on the object in its pure objectivity within the subject/object disjunction and as such do precisely not leave the *logic* of scientific investigation. They confirm it and only exchange "the subject" as the new quasi scientific *object*.

Circumambulation leaves this logic altogether. It is neither concerned with one-self (one's own subjectivity, one's inner life) nor concerned with the abstract object. This whole dichotomy has been left behind. Instead, it is the subject's getting busy to patiently move around the object. In this sense it is neither subjective nor objective, neither one's one-sided focusing on oneself nor on the object; in fact, it is not primarily any direct, "aggressive"[6] *focusing* (in the Baconian sense) on any-thing at all. The subject is certainly highly involved, very active, but not directly with respect to any object, in this case, to the dream. And yet at the same time, its movement goes around the dream, thereby explicitly putting *it* in the center of the subject's own doing and honoring it, giving it prime importance.

The circumambulating subject "does its thing," its own thing, namely moving (around the dream). In doing this, it does not directly focus on the dream. On the other hand, its "doing its own thing" is not solipsistic, self-centered. Its movement has precisely an *objective* center outside of itself, and its whole purpose is to be concerned with this center. The relation to the dream is in this sense indirect. Circumambulation is one's explicit, and yet not subjective and direct, but instead objective and factual devotion to the dream. It is crucial to understand this contra-diction: whole-hearted appreciation, dedication, devotion *to* the dream—and yet no direct focusing on and no subjective–emotional fraternization with the dream, but keeping a respectful, austere distance to it.

What does this mean? Working with dreams, if it is psychological, does not mean thinking or talking *about* the dream in order to explain ("catch") its meaning. "About" would mean that the subject has the object that it is thinking about in front of itself, separated by a fundamental gap. By concentrating on the object, it wants to get technically practically useful information about the latter. It is the stance of the ego. The about-structure means the position of *external reflec-tion*, an approach to the dream decidedly *from outside*. According to the ordinary naturalistic stance, analyst and dream stand vis-à-vis each other in simple linear opposition.

For the circumambulating subject, however, the dreams are not an object of its study to be milked for technically (therapeutically) useful information or for some gratifying "higher (archetypal, maybe even 'sacred') meaning," and not the "other" *over there* in front of itself. They are *within* the circle described by it. The strict opposition of and alienation between subject and object has disappeared. By circumambulating the dream, the latter is surrounded on all sides, so to speak *embraced* by the subject. Because the subject is now all around the dream, an intimate connection between the dream and the subject has—logically, objectively—been established, the dream is no longer wholly other, "out there," no longer external object, mere positive fact, but within the subject's own sphere. As strange and difficult to understand as the dream may semantically and psychic-ally[7] appear to consciousness in its imagery, logically or structurally it has, never-theless, in some sense already become the subject's own—although, and this is crucial, inasmuch as it is at the same time left entirely free, it has by no means been appropriated and pocketed by the subject or turned into something in the subject's "inner."

So we had better retract the expression, "the subject's own." It is not the literal subject itself whose "own" the dream has become. Rather, the dream has been inwardized into the *objective status* of "within-ness." Only the *relation* between the subject and the dream has become redefined. The dream stays other, which includes also on the practical level that it remains hard to understand. In addition, it is also respected as other and as vis-à-vis, but it is no longer positive-factual other and mere object of our investigation. As strange and ununderstood as the dream may still be, the "within"-structure that it now has means that it can and must now be seen *from within*. The stance towards the dream (or the logic of the relation to it) has become totally different. The circumambulating psychologist cannot go back to thinking or talking *about* the dream. He speaks *with* it. The dream is now seen and appreciated as *(other) subject*! The psychologist asks the dream questions and waits for and listens to the dream's answers. It is a conversation between two partners—fundamentally different from the scientific subject/object, therapist/dream relation.

Circumambulation is that "ritual" that wrests the dream from the status of absolute logical otherness ('object') and allows it to be experienced as other subjectivity and selfhood. It performs this transformation by drawing the dream *within*, interiorizing it into the logical sphere of the subject and thus into the sphere or *logic* of subjectivity as such (not into the person!).

The realm that is surrounded by the circular logical movement with the dream at its center is the new dimension of *interiority* ("within-ness"). It is logical interiority. And it is the subject that by circumambulating creates this inner logical (not psychic, not empirical) space. But it is also conversely the object, the dream itself, that makes that circumambulation possible in the first place and turns the dream from mere object into encircled *center* in the first place: both sides, circumambulating motion and center, are equiprimordial, they produce and constitute each other.[8] And this interiority is the dimension of soul.

To express the same once more in a slightly different way: The real beginning of it is a *decision* on the part of the psychologist, the therapist: the decision to circumambulate a dream. One does not have to do this. And in fact, most analysts don't do it, never will do it. But this decision to begin one's work with dreams by circumambulating them turns the dream from a mere positive-factual object "out there," in ordinary empirical reality, into something that has itself the character of interiority and as such has become a presence of soul. It now has been transposed to, and has its place in, the land of soul. And the psychologist himself has thereby "crossed over the river" to its other side.

The decision to circumambulate is only possible if the therapist has already been reached by the soul dimension to begin with. It is not an ego decision at all. You cannot decide to make this decision. If it happens, it happens *of necessity*, not of the ego's free choice. You have to *have crossed* the river in order to be able to start circumambulating, just as, conversely, only by your circumambulating is the soul dimension made possible, is there a river to be crossed, and is a real dream something that deserves, as well as invites and requires, circumambulation. It is much like what we heard from Goethe: "just as with poems, I did not make them, they made me." The decision is mine only if and because it makes me. I have to *be* this decision.

The encircling movement firmly surrounds and encloses the dream. The latter is, as it were, imprisoned. The circle described by the interpreter's circumambulating movement represents a logical border. The dream cannot get out. This reminds us of what the alchemists did with a prime matter that they possibly found *in via ejectus*, contemptuously discarded on the street. They picked it up from "the street" and put it into their retort, the alchemical vessel. As Jung pointed out, "As the *vas Hermeticum* of alchemy, it was 'hermetically' sealed (i.e., sealed with the sign of Hermes); it had to be made of glass, and had also to be as round as possible, since it was meant to represent the cosmos [*das Weltall*], in which the earth was created" (*CW* 13 § 245). Why was it sealed? What needed to be prevented at all cost was two things: first, that the always *fugitive* spirit Mercurius (which was imprisoned in the matter, but was supposed to be freed from the matter by the alchemical *opus*) might escape altogether, so that the production of the *lapis philosophorum*, the ultimate goal of the *opus*, would no longer be possible, and secondly, that anything from outside might intrude and adulterate the prime matter. "Above all, don't let anything from outside, that does not belong, get into it…" (*CW* 14 § 749).

Jung believed himself able to interpret alchemy as an implicit psychology of the unconscious, a modern *psychology* still in the medieval *guise* of an operation with chemical substances, i.e., psychology projected into or upon matter. Be that as it may, it is clear that while the alchemists worked with literal substances enclosed in a literal alchemical vessel this is no longer possible for the modern mind. The modern mind has left the form of naturalistic thinking. It has been catapulted onto the level of logical form. Nevertheless, the *logic* of substance or prime matter and *vas Hermeticum* also constitutes psychology as a psychology with soul, but substance has become "distilled" and elevated to a fundamentally higher level. For the alchemists in their search for the spirit Mercurius, the retort was a physical object made of glass. But it has now become sublimated, vaporized, deliteralized: it now has the distilled form of a (logical) movement around a (likewise mental or spiritual) object, a psychological phenomenon such as a dream. The *vas Hermeticum* is now nothing else but the subject's act or performance of the logical or methodological "ritual" of circumambulation.

By moving around the dream, the subject itself becomes, has to *be*, the alchemical vessel in which the matter, here the dream, is enclosed. The subject no longer *has* a vessel as a permanent instrument, like the medieval alchemists did, it has to *be* the vas and, because this new "*vas*" is a specific attitude, the subject has to constantly uphold it, keep it going. By describing the circle around the dream through his own continuous movement, he *is* the living periphery of the circle, just as the center *qua* center exists only through his circling movement. Periphery and center, though clearly different, are nevertheless the Same; they are the one reality called "circle": Identity of identity and difference. This explains why when working with dreams the beginning has to be made with the subject. Just as the dream has become interiorized (a "within"-structure), so it is also crucial that the subject be actively involved (rather than staying aloof vis-à-vis the object "over there," like a scientist). The subject has to have to be the (not one-time, momentary, but) *ongoing*, *continual* beginning and thereby really invest *itself*—with a certain personal dedication, even self-abandon—to what it circumambulates. It has to establish an inner connection at the feeling level to the dream. Here we recall the already cited alchemical dictum, *Oportet operatorem interesse operi* and Luther's *oportet me adesse*. The beginning can no longer be externalized, reified (as a literal vessel), or viewed as a single point in time. It has come home to the subject as its own doing, performance—its *being*. The beginning is irrevocably "in here," in the subject, in interiority.

I said that the dream is, as it were, imprisoned in the enclosure of the subject's circumambulating movement or, metaphorically, in the hermetically sealed alchemical vessel that this circumambulation amounts to. "Imprisonment" lets us think of exertion of power, violence, suppression, deprivation of freedom. But first of all, by circumambulating the dream the subject commits and binds itself exclusively to the dream (for the duration of its working with the dream), just as the dream, conversely, is exclusively enclosed in "the retort." And second, I had already occasion to emphasize that the circumambulating subject leaves the object, the dream, totally free, does not touch its integrity. On the contrary, the circumambulation even expressly *frees* the object from its initial status of positive-factual object and allows it the status of a subjectivity of its own. Now we can add that the hermetic closure of the circle, the dream's "imprisonment" in it, is what performs this transformation and what protects the dream's subjectivity and selfhood from the enormous power of nowadays prevailing naturalistic thinking in terms of the subject/object dichotomy. The alchemist's placing chemical substances, the prime matter, into the hermetically sealed retort rescued nature from the reductive thing-ontology and the goal-oriented, instrumental-technical apperception of it and restored it as something to which man could have a personal relation.[9] The moment anything from outside would be let in, the dream would instantaneously be reabsorbed into the domain of positive-factual objects, and the subject, the therapist, on his part would automatically find himself again on *this* side of the river, in his habitual definition as ordinary ego-personality or civilian man. It is the hermetic closure that *reproduces* the dream as a soul reality, makes it *objectively* have its own *subject*-quality, and guarantees it freedom from positive-factualness. It is what makes possible the revolutionary change from thinking and talking "about" the dream as an object of *our* investigation to talking "with" the dream as a speaking subject.

With this insight we can go on to the next chapter.

Turning to the "object": The *dream* as subject and self

In the foregoing chapter we have, as it were, witnessed the actual transformation of the dream from an external object and positive fact into a subject and soul reality, a transformation also of the therapist's general position to it from "about" to "with," which became possible through the performance of the logical "ritual" of the subject's circumambulation of the dream. We now have to turn away from the subject and give our attention to the former object, to the dream itself.

At the very beginning of this book, in Part I, we saw that the dream is an interpretation of an interpretation of an interpretation. And the *negative* way to express this result was to say that we are hopelessly caught in interpretation. This negative way of describing the situation results from a particular orientation, namely from looking out hopefully for some starting point or, the other way around, for a resting point that is *not* interpretation any more, but pure being, pure nature or facticity and thus the ultimate *object* of all this interpretation. This whole orientation is an ego perspective, the day-world perspective, that serves the basic interest of "survival" in the widest sense of the word. It is informed by the undialectical, binary opposition of subject and object, subjective consciousness and objective or natural world. As an ego orientation, it is a soul-less, an unpsychological orientation. The longing to get to something that is no longer consciousness, no longer reflected, no longer interpretation, but immediate fact, and as such is something at which our thinking would finally arrive as a sound foundation, is a "naturalistic" or ego longing.

How do we get from this orientation to a psychological orientation? There is no need for a violent rejection of the naturalistic or ego orientation, no need for painful sacrifice and enormous effort. All we have to do is to allow our insight to come home to this orientation of consciousness, to let it take its own medicine, to let it be affected in the sense of "feedback" by its own result ("Self-application").

If the very phenomenon that is the ultimate object of our dream interpretation, namely the dream experience during sleep, is itself already interpretation, and if we cannot possibly find anything that it *would be the interpretation of*, then our linear forward orientation toward the uninterpreted immediate fact as the object of interpretation is bent backwards and becomes a uroboric circle, and the dream itself can be seen as a self-contained, self-sufficient phenomenon, i.e., as a self.

What does "the dream as a self" mean? It, first of all, means that it is a totality, enclosed within itself and self-sufficient. When interpreting the dream, I have to treat it as a world unto itself. And this means a fundamental closure. This is why we have to heed the admonition contained in the golden rule of dream interpretation for which Jung relied on an alchemical adage, "Above all, don't let anything from outside, that does not belong, get into it, for the fantasy image has 'everything it needs' [*omne quo indiget*] within itself" (*CW* 14 § 749, transl. modif.). The dream is self-sufficient, complete within itself. James Hillman stressed much the same point (within a special context). In his *The Dream and the Underworld* he stated, "nothing has to be introduced by anyone from anywhere, because the opposite is already present. Each dream has its own fulcrum and balance, compensates itself, is complete as it is."[10] For the duration of my working with the dream there is *only* the world conjured up in and by the dream. Nothing exists outside the dream. Whatever exists, exists *within* the dream and *by virtue of* the dream. Only then am I truly *in* the dream.

Also, the dream is a closed, self-contained Now. There is no outside past and no future. All past and future that still exist are the *internal* past and future of the dream itself.

A world closed unto itself implies two different things. First, the fact that it excludes everything else and has nothing outside of itself gives it conversely its fundamental openness, that is to say, opens it into being a *world*, a totality. In this sense a dream is like a poem.

And second, it prohibits us from toying with what has been called "fake (or fictitious) possibilities" (Stekeler[11]). Just as *all* characteristics that, for example, Conan Doyle ascribed to his figure Sherlock Holmes are the latter's necessary and essential qualities, so, conversely, if Doyle did *not* say anything about Holmes' grandparents, there *is* nothing to be said about his grandparents; in fact, the very idea of "Holmes' grandparents" is not allowed (despite the fact that in ordinary reality everyone has or had grandparents). In the discussion of dreams just as of myths and fairy tales, we must not, on the basis of common-sense truths and ordinary experience of life, speculate about what could possibly have been done by the dream-I in reaction to a certain situation, what childhood traumas might have formed the dream-I or the protagonist, what desires might have motivated him, *if* this information is not explicitly given in the dream or story. "Only the material that is clearly and visibly indicated as belonging to the dream by the dream-images themselves should be used for interpretation" (*CW* 18 § 434), says Jung and warns:

> Here the interpretation must guard against making use of any other viewpoints than those given by the content itself. … [a correct interpretation] will essentially be an *amplification* of the same image. … A scientifically responsible interpretation which proceeds along the line of the image it wants to interpret does not merely have the status of a tautology, but expands the meaning so that it becomes a general conception (amplification).
>
> (*CW* 17 § 162, transl. modif.)

The alchemical vessel has to be firmly closed and sealed with the seal of Hermes.

So, all knowledge that I have concerning the dream must come from within the dream. If it is, nevertheless, seemingly external knowledge (amplifications, associations), it must have come to me as the dream's gift to me, as an idea or association or memory that arose in my consciousness from out of the dream and thanks to the dream. This applies to any information that I might adduce from my knowledge of mythology and symbols, of personality theory, of pathology, etc. just as much as from my knowledge of the biography of my patient, his complaints, the diagnosis of his illness, the previous sessions we had and the previous dreams. The *otherness* of this my knowledge that I adduce to the dream must have been decomposed, worked off. The knowledge must have been melted down. It has been melted down because I made the zero-point of knowledge my methodological starting point. All specific knowledge has been "forgotten" with methodological intention, so that, when it reappears during my working with dreams it reappears as the dream's *own* and *integral* association, as inspired and evoked by the logic of the dream as *its* living and liquid core and not by *my* consciousness. Then it is certainly not something that "*does not belong.*" If it were not the dream itself that brought back the memory of this bit of knowledge, it would remain soulless and external knowledge.

Imaginally speaking: we stare through the glass of the retort at what is enclosed within it (the dream), and turn our backs on the outside world all around us. Only what is in the alchemical vessel counts.

Here we have to halt for a second. Our language used here, our thinking in terms of "excluding," "turning our back on the outside," prohibiting letting anything in from outside and "staring *at* the content of the retort" all betray that we ourselves are still outside and only talk *about* interiority. We still operate with "inside" *and* "outside" and ipso facto demonstrate that syntactically the outside world still exists and exerts its influence. Warnings against letting anything in from outside are a defensive reaction and show that an ego effort is called for (or felt to be needed) to enter interiority. But the psychologist cannot stare through "the retort" at the dream, because his circumambulating means that he has to *be* the retort himself. There is no "glass wall" between him and the dream, and along with the literal glass vessel the possibility of "staring at…" has also disappeared. This is the first point. The second follows from it. The moment what has been established is truly interiority, this interiority is no longer defined in opposition to externality. It has become *absolute*: absolute interiority, that is to say it does not border on any outside, nor refer to nor exclude anything external. It is infinite. A totality. A world unto itself. Psychology does not privilege—on the semantic level—the one of two alternatives and exclude the other. To have truly arrived in interiority, the whole opposition between—or the syntax or logic of—inner and outer has to be left behind.

If the dream has everything it needs within itself and as long as we think psychologically, it must not be conceived as caused by something else, by external conditions, nor be viewed as a reaction to something, e.g., to events of the previous day. For the *psychologist*, the dream is not a processing of experiences, not—and here I contradict Jung—a compensation for anything![12] Nor can it be the result or expression of the personality as substrate. If it were that, then it would not have everything it needs within itself. It would not be enclosed within the retort, i.e., within itself. As a self it is spontaneous in the deepest sense: *sua sponte*. Thus it is, as it were, *causa sui* (Spinoza): it even has its origin within itself, namely as the *meaning* that it is—or rather, that it *does* ("to mean" in a verbal sense). Because it *is* meaning, conveys a meaning, the dream is essentially a speaking.

This comes out most clearly in a dictum by Jung that I introduced already very early in this book:

> In myths and fairytales, as in dreams, the soul speaks about itself, and the archetypes reveal themselves in their natural interplay, as "formation, transformation / eternal Mind's eternal recreation."
>
> (*GW* 9/I § 400, my translation)

Similarly, Jung said another time: "As you know, we can treat fairytales as fantasy products just like [we treat] dreams, by conceiving them as *spontaneous statements of the unconscious about itself*" (*CW* 13 § 240, transl. modif., my italics). The dream speaks about itself! This also means: not about us, not for our sake! But above all, it means that it is a *speaking*, a talking, a communication, a text! It is not an object. The dream is a linguistic phenomenon, not a psychic or biological product (like spittle, sweat, urine, an excretion).

When Jung speaks of *the soul* as speaking about itself or *the unconscious* as making spontaneous statements about itself, we need to understand that he is making use of a mythologizing language. The dream is not an expression of the soul or of the unconscious, as if soul and unconscious were existing entities that produced the dream. No, there is not a soul as real subject that in addition to its existing as a subject at times also speaks about itself through dreams (the way a patient may indeed literally speak about himself to his analyst). There is only the *speaking itself* that takes place in the dream, and this SPEAKING, this self-sufficient—I am tempted to say: free-floating, at any rate subject-less—act of *saying* and *meaning* something, *is* itself what we mean by "soul," with nothing behind it as its author or speaker. We must not superstitiously believe in "the soul" as something mysterious behind the scene, the hidden director, scriptwriter, producer, or "factor" (in the literal sense of the Latin word: "maker"). And, conversely, we must not conceive of the dream as a literal object caused (produced) by the soul as a subject in terms of the logic of cause and effect or subject and object. What in mythologizing parlance we call soul is, contrary to Schiller, *only* what appears, *only* what shows itself, *only* the psychic phenomena: the dreams, myths, fairy tales, fantasies, the psychic symptoms, the religious conception and rituals, the works of poetry and art and philosophy, etc. "The soul" comes only into being in "its" *products.* If we thought otherwise, the dream would (1) not be a self, we would (2), in violation of our methodological principle, escape from within the dream (from the retort) to something external, and we would (3) ipso facto be guilty of a metaphysical hypostasis.

The idea of the soul's speaking about *itself* introduces the topic of the dream as self-relation, self-reflection, as uroboric. "all the dream-images are important in themselves because they have their meaning in themselves" (*CW* 8 § 471, transl. modif.). This is epitomized by the Talmudic saying already familiar to us and repeatedly insisted on by Jung, the saying that "the dream is its own interpretation" (*CW* 11 § 41; 18 §§ 172 and 569. *Letters 2,* p. 294, to Jolande Jacobi, 13

March 1956). Jung could also have referred to the similar figure of thought to be found in Luther, who said that the Bible is *sui ipsius interpres* (its own interpreter), and applied it to dreams.

I want to stay with the Talmud statement for a while. One has to listen carefully to what it entails. (1) The dream *is* interpretation. This is what I discussed already above when I rejected Jung's idea of the dream as nature. (2) It is, as such, not really, or at least not primarily, in need of *our* interpretation. On the contrary, if it is its own interpretation, it is first of all and intrinsically a *manifestation, revelation*. It is a *speaking*. It shows something, makes it known. *The dream speaks.* This fact that the dream is speaking, is saying *something*, presents a *view* or *idea* about something, is what makes the dream be a subject in the full sense, alive: It is a living image. (3) But what the dream presents and reveals is only *itself*. It is not like a messenger who brings a message about some other thing, it is not like a textbook that instructs us about some subject and that thus is no more than an instrument for making this subject known to us. A messenger and a textbook are intermediaries. They do not have their purpose within themselves, but in that which they are about or to which they point. This is why the dream's speaking cannot be compared to the patient's speaking in therapy about himself either. His speaking has also has its referent (the patient himself) outside of itself. The dream, however, is its own *self*-presentation, *self*-expression, similar to how persons and animals are not in need of our interpretation, but present themselves as what they are. It is more like a jewel that radiates and only points to itself having all its value and importance within itself. If it has everything it needs within itself, this also means that as far as interpretation is concerned it is not an interpretation *of* something else, but that it is itself that which its interpretation is about. The dream is self-display. It does not have a referent or object. It *is* itself its own referent. We could also say, it even has within itself its referent or that of which it is the interpretation or, even more precisely, it has it *as* itself, which once more confirms its uroboric, self-contradictory nature.

There is, however, a complication concerning the idea of the dream as its own interpretation. A dream, considered as a text in the sense of positive fact, does, of course, not at all interpret itself. It does not do anything. It is written on a piece of paper and just sits there mute. If it is to interpret itself, *we* must circumambulate it, which also means that by forming this hermetical circle around it we close it with respect to what is outside. But true circumambulation means more. It means, positively, our dedication to the dream, dwelling with it, abandoning ourselves to it, interiorizing ourselves into it. As we already heard: *Oportet operatorem interesse operi*. There is a dialectic here. We can only interiorize ourselves into the dream if it is apperceived as its own interpretation. Conversely, the dream can only be its own interpretation through our having abandoned ourselves to it. *It* speaks and interprets itself only in and through us.

Jung said, "*I take the dream for what it is*" (*CW* 11 § 41 [right after "the dream is its own interpretation"], Jung's italics). This is in total contrast to the Freudian idea already discussed that the "manifest" dream disguises, obscures and conceals the "latent" dream content or dream thought. For Jung, "The 'manifest' dream-picture is the dream itself and contains the whole meaning of the dream" (*CW* 16 § 319). If the dream is not a façade that has behind itself what it is actually about, if for Jung it *is* qua *manifest* dream the latent dream thought, then the dream is really pure *Schein*, appearance, however, not in the "nothing but" sense of façade, deception, falsehood, but in the affirmative sense of *Scheinen*, shining forth, manifestation, display—without a "solid substance" *behind* it *whose* manifestation it would be. Exactly in this sense Jung had said: "I doubt whether we can assume that the dream is something other than it *appears* to be" (*CW* 11 § 41, my italics), and we can connect this with another statement from *Memories* (not about a dream but some parapsychological event), "This experience has to be taken as it is or seems to be" (*MDR*. p. 191, transl. modif.). As it *seems* to be! No going back behind the appearance to an external cause, referent or other explanatory factor, no longing for a factual, reliable basis. The *Schein*, appearance, is all there is and it is that which we have to dwell with. The *telos*, the end result, the *phaínesthai*, is uroborically its own beginning and origin!

All this shows that in Jung's mature thinking the logic of difference and otherness is excluded. What prevails in Jung's thinking is, on the contrary, the logic of center, circularity, and sameness[13] and thus also of absolute interiority. Jung refuses to go back behind what shows itself to an external cause, a mysterious hidden speaker, an external referent, a concealed actual truth.

What is also excluded is the logic of *différance*, deferral, together with its privileging the future. In some quarters of psychoanalysis there is the idea that the innermost subjectivity or soul needs yet to speak and express itself (such as through the patient's free associations) and in this speaking to betray itself. But from a Jungian point of view concerning dreams, the soul *has* always already spoken. Meanings are already there (even if maybe not apperceived and understood). They are present in the dreams, and also, for example, in the psychological symptoms. The last point is also why Hillman, too, could conceive of pathologizing as soul-making. Nothing needs to be sought, longed or striven for. Jungian psychology follows the logic of presence, a fulfilled present. Above I introduced the image of "brooding" for the Jungian mode of working with dreams (or, for that matter, with psychological phenomena in general). But brooding makes sense only if there is already an "egg" to sit on that "has already everything it needs within itself." The logical *movement* that is still necessary (and is expressed in the image of brooding) is from implicit presence to explicit presence.

Now we understand why the dream is self-enclosed and what self-enclosure actually amounts to. Real self-containment is not a literal locking up of something in a vessel or prison. It is rather the inherent consequence of the fact that the dream *is* meaning. Only if we succeed in seeing the dream as *meaning*, as self-presentation, is the dream self-sufficient for us. If the dream were a fact of nature, a physical thing, it would not mean anything in the sense of *being* meaning (it could at most *have* a meaning *for* some subject, or be assigned some meaning).

It is because the dream is a *logos* or *Geist* phenomenon that it is uroborically enclosed within itself. And therefore, if we want to see the dream psychologically, we must raise ourselves from the level of naturalistic thinking in terms of things, objects, facts existing in the dimensions of space and time to the level of *logos*, of language, of meaning. We also understand why the dream must be its own interpretation. Because only as such does it have *logos*-structure in the first place, does it mean anything in the sense of *being* meaning in contrast to being a *sign* of something else or meaning something else.

"The dream is interpretation" means that it is not a positivity, like objects of nature are for us. Rather it is essentially, by definition, something *secondary*, because an interpretation always presupposes something that it is the interpretation of. But this essential secondariness is the first beginning of the dream, inasmuch as the dream *is* interpretation. In this sense, the dream is a true *hýsteron próteron*. It is self-contradictory. This is its *logos*-structure. And we have to raise our consciousness to the level of this self-contradictory structure in order to be able to do justice to the dream and look at it psychologically. As long as we do not succeed in achieving this, we at bottom really remain "physicists," even while believing to be psychologists. What *makes* the psychologist is not that he turns to human emotions, desires, dreams, imaginings instead of to animals, plants, continental drift, galaxies and nebulae as his objects of studies. It is his capability to *see* psychologically.

This is difficult only because usually in modern times we cling to a naturalistic, positivistic thinking in terms of things and a unilinear cause-and-effect logic. But the dream is not a thing that in addition to being what it is also *has* a meaning. It is not like a sign-post on the road that first of all is a physical object, a positivity and second *has* a meaning, namely the function of showing us the way. No, the dream does not have a meaning, it *is* meaning or interpretation. It begins as interpretation, and this interpretation has exclusively within itself that which it is about. It begins as the secondary which within itself *creates* the primary, its own primary.

Inner infinity and the wildness of the living image

It is natural for us to cling to something that positively exists outside the dream. We get so easily seduced into identifying a motif, e.g., father or mother in the dream, with the object in empirical reality by the same name. Here a passage from Jung may be helpful, although it does not go far enough. Jung says: "It may seem strange that I should attribute a character of a so to speak indeterminable content to the relatively fixed symbols." And in contrast to the early Freudians for whom most symbols, but especially of course obviously sexual images, had an unambiguously sexual meaning, he states,

> Instead of indulging in a dogmatic conviction based on *the illusion that a known word implies a known positive thing* [my italics],[14] I therefore prefer

the view that the word symbol refers to an unknown quantity, hard to recognize and, in the last resort, never quite determinable. Take, for instance, the so-called phallic symbols which allegedly are supposed to stand for the *membrum virile* and nothing more. But [and this is the important point for us] from the standpoint of the psyche the *membrum* is itself a symbol [*Sinnbild*] ...

(both quotes CW 16 § 340, transl. modified)

The image of a sexual organ in a dream does not mean the sexual organ, much like the *lapis* in alchemy is explicitly a stone that is not a stone. Sexual scenes in a dream do not mean literal sexuality. They only mean themselves. Similarly, women in a dream do not mean literal women, men not literal men. "They do *not* 'mean' ..."! Nothing in the dream means a positive entity or empirical reality. It only means itself. It is *tautegorical*.[15]

The psychological is the field of logical negativity. Jungian psychology means dwelling with the unknownness and the not-understood, persevering with it, indeed, *guarding and protecting its unknownness*! We heard already: "Even if one has great experience in these matters, one is again and again obliged, before each dream, *to admit one's ignorance* and, *renouncing* all preconceived ideas, to prepare for something entirely unexpected" (*CW* 8 § 543, modif.) Again Jung said: "One would do well, therefore, to treat every dream as though it were a totally unknown object" (*CW* 10 § 320). Totally unknown! Precisely what seems familiar, what seems to refer to facts or meanings known from one's knowledge of the patient's life or of mythology, must be given the status of being totally unknown. Jung goes even further. It is not only our *not-yet* knowing and not only *our* ignorance. In the last analysis it is even downright impossible to know what the truly deep soul images mean; the unknownness is fundamental, inherent: "The reader should not imagine that the psychologist is in any position to explain what 'higher copulation' is, or the *coniunctio*, or 'psychic pregnancy,' let alone the 'soul's child' " (*CW* 16 § 465). For us, this means that ultimately the images mean *nothing*—as long as under "something" we understand something positive, something to be identified with known items. This is why Jung adds, "Nor should one feel annoyed if the newcomer to this delicate subject, or one's own cynical self, gets disgusted with these—as he thinks them—phoney ideas and brushes them aside with a pitying smile..." (*ibid.*). The dream image is logically negative: an unknown quantity, never quite determinable! A dream image speaks only about itself, and as such it is, for the circumambulating psychologist, something like a vortex or a black hole that has a powerful pull down deeper and deeper into itself, into its unknownness, its inner infinity.

The practical consequence to be drawn is expressed in another of Jung's statements:

In our working with dreams we must never forget that we move on treacherous ground where nothing is certain but uncertainty. I would almost be inclined to call out to the dream interpreter: "Do anything you like, only don't try to understand!" – simply for the purpose of preventing him from premature interpretations.

(*CW* 16 § 318, transl. modif.)

Don't try to understand! We could call this the alchemy of dream interpretation. No premature understanding! *No translation* from the unknown into something known, i.e., into the vernacular language of the ego. Above all no identifications, no "equal signs" of the type "oblong things = penis or phallus." Therefore we must not only "stick as close as possible to the dream images," as Jung demanded (*CW* 16 § 320), we must even stick to their inner unknownness, or rather, one's truly sticking to the image *is nothing else but the preservation of its unknownness and inner infinity*. Any further work with dream images has the task of slowly penetrating into this unknownness, of brooding it, circumambulating it further, getting more familiar with it *in its unknownness*. When Jung had spoken about the dream to be viewed as totally unknown object, he continued: "Look at it from all sides, take it in your hand, carry it about with you" (*CW* 10 § 320). And he elucidated the act of circumambulating a dream by adding: "as one turns an unknown object round and round in one's hands to absorb every detail of it" (*CW* 18 § 430).

This *mental* turning an unknown object round and round or circumambulating it is what we call thinking. We need to *think* dream images, not merely *imagine* them.

By turning an unknown object round and round in your hand you do not end up with a "translation" of it, with an "interpretation" that gives you its "meaning." All you do is to make yourself more familiar with it, while at the same time leaving *it* intact in its inner unknownness and infinity. The same is true for a chicken brooding an egg. It leads to a new chick, not to an interpretation or explanation. The chick is in itself just as unknown as the egg was. What in my image is the chick, Jung called with respect to the unexplainable soul images (such as "higher copulation," the *coniunctio*, or "psychic pregnancy" and the "soul's child") "*psychological facts*." We would do better to consider them, like the chick, as living soul substances, objective, autonomous psychological realities with their own personality and dynamic, enclosed within themselves, like animals in the wild. "Psychology deals with ideas and other mental contents as zoology, for instance, deals with the different species of animals" (*CW* 11 § 5).

"Rose is a rose is a rose. Loveliness extreme" (Gertrude Stein [1922]). *This* is not the rose as a positivity. It is the rose that is fully interiorized into itself, with nothing outside of itself: sheer self-expression. It is loveliness extreme because it is only blooming from within, revealing its inner infinity. Here one might also remember a verse by a German mystic, Angelus Silesius: "*Die Ros ist ohn Warum; sie blühet, weil sie blühet, / Sie acht' nicht ihrer selbst, fragt nicht, ob man sie siehet.*" ("The rose is without a why [or: a 'wherefore']—it blooms because [or: 'while, as long as'] it blooms./It pays no attention to itself, asks not if it is seen.") It simply shows itself.

Psychology's turn against interpretation in the sense of translation into something known and understandable and thus from the soul language into the language of the ego means that truly psychological interpretations (i.e., the result of our brooding, circumambulating, or warming the corpse through our own body warmth) is, and *means* to be, no more than explaining *ignotum per ignotius* (the unknown through the even more unknown). The intactness of the personality and inner infinity of the "wild animals" as their meaning must be preserved. "From this standpoint, the dream images are important *per se*, inasmuch as they bear that meaning in themselves that is the sole reason for their appearance in the dream in the first place" (*CW* 8 § 471, transl. modif.). "*Per se*" and "in themselves"! The dream is a "psychological reality," a living being, not a sign that transports a meaning.

This has important consequences for therapeutic work with patients. Often dreams are interpreted as indications that the dreamer should work on his inferior function, integrate this or that shadow aspect, get into a better relation with his anima, overcome his resistance to the unconscious, etc. But if dream images are seen as alchemical substances, as psychological realities with their own personality and inner unknownness, the patient should not, does not have to, do anything. He does not have to "get the idea," not subjectively comprehend and apply to himself what he understood in the sense of his "working on himself." This would only be ego work. No, all he has to do is to turn the dream images as an unknown object round and round in his hands, circumambulate them again and again, warm them as so many cold corpses with his own body warmth. Psychologically, it is exclusively the images in the soul themselves that do all the therapeutic work.

The patient with a truly psychological disorder cannot heal himself merely with the help of clever interpretations by his analyst. The images themselves have to come alive in him. *They* heal, once they have been hatched out and turned from egg into living animal, that is, when they—the soul thoughts or soul truths that they represent—have ceased being dead mental objects ("corpses") and have come alive in the patient and thus turned into active agents. The healing takes place on the other side of the river. When Jung wrote, "Over against our consciousness we must learn to live as it were unconsciously" (*Letters 2*, p. 386, to Vijayatunga, August 1957), he certainly did not want us to become more unconscious. But in our context we could say, he wanted to let the psychological realities on the other side of the river *do their thing* (in us). No pulling the dream thoughts over onto *our* side, the side of consciousness, in the sense of their appropriation by us. "Do anything you like, only don't try to understand!" Leave them on *their* side. *They* must increase, but ego-consciousness must decrease.

Let me add here a comment about the concept of "integration." A patient had a dream in which a person turns into a terrible, bloodthirsty, mangling monster. Several other indications made it likely that this monster was the first immediacy, in which this dreamer was confronted with his own unconscious, suppressed powerful masculinity. The idea of the therapist was that the dreamer would have to slowly integrate this monster, which would, of course, mean that simultaneously the monster might in future dreams be transformed into more acceptable images of masculinity.

But I think that "to integrate" precisely does not mean for the dreamer to take the monster into himself, but conversely to *release* the monster, to set it free, to release *it* into *its* selfhood, its truth, its *concept*. In other words, not wish to incorporate it egoically into his own personality and to appropriate it, but to release it into objectivity. The dreamer should not put himself into the center. In ancient times such ideas would have been "integrated" by going to the temple of the pertinent god and presenting an offering to him, i.e., "out there," *objectively.* Today we could say that what is needed is to give "the monster" (and thereby the psychological reality embodied in this dream image) a place in the objective *logic of consciousness.*[16]

Actually *working* with dreams

My statement, "Leave them on *their* side" might sound as if we were condemned to passivity. But this is, of course, not at all the case. We are called upon to seriously work with the dreams. How else could the "corpse" be warmed, the "egg" be hatched out? The point here is only that the spirit of working with dreams has to be our interpreting *ignotum per ignotius*, or, as Jung once put it:

> We have simply got to listen to what the psyche spontaneously says to us. What the dream, which is not manufactured by us, says is *just so.* Say it again as well as you can.
>
> (*Letters 2*, p. 591, to Herbert Read, 2 September 1960)

All we have to do is to "say it again," *tautologically* or *tautegorically*,[17] but, and this addition is important, "as well as we can."[18] It is not a senseless repetition, a kind of parroting. We certainly have to try *our best* to articulate in *our own* words what is in the dream, to unfold what is implicitly inherent in each image. This would be our *productive* contribution. And "our best" does not merely refer to the technical skill side of the task, but also to our wholehearted investment of ourselves in the act of "saying again." Only in this way do we add our body warmth to the "corpse" or "egg." At the same time, the implication of "as well as you can" is that "our saying it again" will never be *fully* up to what "the psyche spontaneously" has said.

In order to be able to unfold what is implicitly inherent in each image we must turn the dream and each image, indeed each word and phrase, "round and round in our hands," treating them as unknown objects. That is to say, we try to spell out the meaning of the words as if we had never heard them before and needed to be provided with a kind of detailed dictionary explanation. We thereby circumambulate each word or phrase and image. Furthermore, we also try to bring out their own connotations, implications and associations, the sphere they belong to, the feeling quality as well as, possibly, any sensual feel they bring along with themselves, and whatever else they may evoke or suggest in the context of the dream. We start at the beginning and go through the dream step by step, consecutively. It is important to pay attention to the diction, the style of the language, to anything that is noteworthy concerning the word order, the grammar, the logic of the sequence of phrases and sentences, possible inconsistencies or contradictions, etc. By familiarizing ourselves in this way with the dream in depth and getting actively involved in it, we also more and more dig ourselves into it; we interiorize ourselves into it, and if we are lucky, the reward may be that slowly internal connections between all the elements of the dream, at first perhaps confusing and incoherent, become visible and a sense of what the particular dream is really about emerges. The story and image become a thought.

It is very patient and painstaking work, not grandiloquent (not indulging in much mythic meaning, symbolic depth, and sacred aura), but very modest, down to earth, with a loving attention to detail.

Jung said, "We have simply got to listen to what the psyche spontaneously says to us." Listening means passive reception. The dream is speaking, not we. We only have to listen. But the detailed work with the individual words and images of the dream that I described, i.e., our having become active, is itself nothing but the way of listening. Listening is thus also an intensive activity. Jung called it "saying again." The word "saying" in this phrase refers to the active side, the "again" to the passive side (to our not adding anything of our own, on the contrary, our even preventing anything from outside, that does not belong, from getting into it).

By the same token, our "saying again" is not in conflict with "It has a say now, not you!" Because we are not saying anything of our own, but merely unfold what *it* has said.

It is very important to take note of everything in the dream. It will not do to pick out only the one or the other striking and personally impressive image and reduce the dream to being about it, while ignoring the rest. It would be especially wrong to select those parts that confirm one's own preconceived ideas about the patient, or one's pet theories, or one's "premature understanding." A certain discipline is indispensable when working with dreams, a critical strictness, a degree of rigor. It is serious *work*. Dream interpretation requires in this sense a kind of craftsmanlike scrupulousness. No wild speculation. We have to stay very close and obedient to the text.

Part of the craftsmanship is an attention to the *exactness* and *sensual precision* of the images. Goethe pointed out that for a person educated in the exact sciences it is difficult to imagine "that there could also be an exact sensuous imagination."[19] And it was especially James Hillman who stressed the importance of the sensuality of the image and the specificity of images. Hillman therefore also rejected the widespread Jungian idea of dream *symbols* in favor of the poetically seen image. It happens so easily that the idea of symbols gets unwittingly accompanied by the notion of those "fixed meanings of symbols" that Jung had already denied with his declaration that the final standpoint "recognizes no fixed meaning of symbols.

From this standpoint, the dream images are important per se, inasmuch as they bear that meaning in themselves that is the sole reason for their appearance in the dream in the first place" (*CW* 8 § 471, transl. modif.). At any rate, it will not do to lump all sorts of different images together under one abstract-universal concept, for example: horse, cow, dog, monkey, cat under "instinct" or "body," or, as Erich Neumann was wont to do, bowl, cup, cooking pot, vase, bucket, crate, coffin, grave under "Great Mother." Each particular image has to be honored in its specificity.

Part of the exactness of the dream image is its *objective feeling* quality, which should be captured with the greatest possible precision and refinement. Objective feeling or soul feeling must be radically distinguished from subjective feelings ("What *we* feel," "what the patient feels"). With "what *we* feel" we are talking only about ourselves, about what we register as going on in ourselves, above all whether we like a certain thing or not, and often also what emotion is evoked in us (fear, panic, joy, delight). But objective feeling refers to the feeling quality that the object, in our case, a particular dream image, has, or what "the soul" feels about it. Soul or objective feelings are *cognitive*, not emotional. They capture a quality. We are familiar with such objective feelings outside of dreams. For example, steady, calm rainfall represents the objective feeling of being soothing, moody, and a bit melancholy. Or take melodies, they may be happy, vivacious, or joyful; but they can also be mournful, depressive, others are dramatic and heroic, such as a march. In therapy it is important to try to teach the patients to slowly abstract from their own feelings, so that in dream work they become able to distinguish between ego feelings and soul feelings. The psychological training of the patient is a very important function of therapy. That one feels perhaps disgusted by a rat or cockroach in a dream or is terrified by a snake or a potential rapist is not very interesting. This is natural and just what the ego feels. The objective feeling of a snake in a dream is something completely different.

Another aspect of our dream work is that it should be rational. One should have arguments for why one sees this quality or meaning in a given motif or a whole dream. One should be able to defend one's view with good reasons on the basis of the text of the dream—or else admit that another view presented by someone else is, in fact, more appropriate. I am responsible for what I say about an image, responsible *to* the image! What I say is not up to me. There is an obligation.

Beyond this one's having to have good reasons for what one says about particular dream elements, the fact that our work should be rational also includes in a much wider sense our making use of the intellect, of rigorous thought, in our approach or, as Hillman once put it,

> an effort of intelligence that leads us into the dream, the effort of following its imaginatively deformative leads, where exegesis is exitus, leading life out of life, where dream interpretation is not a life science but a death science, like a philosophizing which too was once considered to be a leading of life towards death.[20]

What really leads into the depths is *thought*. Hölderlin once said with respect to a very particular topic, namely about Socrates and Alcibiades, "He who has thought what is deepest loves that which is to the highest degree alive." In our context we might instead say: He who loves dream images, will want to *think* them most deeply. Depth can only be thought. Thought is always sober and excludes sentimentalism as well as emotionality. And, this is most important, it is, as we could almost say, "tautegorical" in Schelling's sense, for what is thought in a particular case is only as deep as *your actually thinking* it is. It is not "about" anything, but it, qua thinking, *is* itself *what* it thinks. This is in complete contrast to the fundamental disproportion or duality that exists between people's inflated entertaining and indulging in *ideas about* deepest things (gods or God, mythic meaning, the sacred, etc.), on the one hand, and the shallowness of the minds that feel justified to entertain those ideas, on the other. The word "entertain" is suggestive. With its reference to "entertainment" it points to the self-gratification for which these ideas are being instrumentalized. It is unethical to entertain *ideas* or imagine *images* that you are not able to actually *think*. Strutting in borrowed plumes.

Discerning the proper horizon of and context for individual dream elements

Concerning individual dream figures, objects, or events three cases must be distinguished and discriminated. The first case is that of dream elements that clearly refer back to the dreamer's personal memory and conscious knowledge of his ordinary life situation or the social arena in general: "my sister in law," "a boyfriend when I was in elementary school," "my boss when I worked for XY company," "the bicycle I got as a present for my twelfth birthday," "the first apartment I lived in after moving out from my parents' home," etc. Numerous dreams contain such elements. As psychologists we do, of course, not understand such images on the "object-level." Nevertheless, it is clear that they belong to the strictly personal sphere of the dreamer and are mainly of merely psychic, not psychological interest. Often the whole dream may be on this level, so that what it is concerned with is the psyche of the person, the person's complexes, character, relationship problems, shadow aspects and so on. In such cases *psychology as such* is not needed to discuss such dreams.

It is, of course, also possible that the dream introduces such elements known from real life but, nevertheless, leads into much deeper waters. Jung, for example, had a dream that began with his (real) father, but the dream father was from the outset very different from his father in reality, namely a custodian of the sarcophagi of famous great personages in a crypt and a distinguished scholar. But not only that. In the continuation of the dream this altered father, as a real psychopomp, led Jung as dream-I into a sphere that had nothing whatsoever to do with the real-life reality in which Jung himself lived, namely ultimately "into the highest presence" (*MDR* pp. 217 ff.). This dream is, of course, of psychological significance and not only concerned with Jung himself as personality and *his* psyche. Whenever figures or things known from real life appear altered in some way, this may be a hint that the dream intends a transition from the everyday life sphere into soul country. However, even if there is this intention, it may not, and in fact frequently does not, leave the psychic realm very consistently. Whether and to what extent it does needs to be determined in each actual dream afresh.

The second case includes those images that clearly have a realistic cast, but do not explicitly refer to particular persons, objects, or events known to the dreamer from his biography or from his present life situation. As an example we may here mention again the dream of an analysand of Jung's in which she was going to see a doctor who lived in a house beside the sea. In order to defend his view that the doctor did not in a transference sense refer to him as her analyst, Jung made the point that the dream showed a different situation over against his own reality, since Jung's house was not one beside the sea.[21] As well as this point is taken, it is not the crucial one. The real point is that the dream says "a doctor." It does not identify the doctor as a particular person, but only defines him as one who lived in a house beside the sea. Here we must apply what we learned from Pirmin Stekeler about "fake (or fictitious) possibilities." *Who* the doctor is is not mentioned, and ipso facto not only not relevant but also a false question. This doctor does not *have a personal identity*. He is "a doctor," that is to say, the pure function of doctor, doctor as such. He is not a human being who in addition to his being an existing man also happened to have studied, and now practices, medicine. According to what we learned in the chapter "Concepts cloaked in sensible shapes" in Part I above we can say: He is the *concept* "doctor" and nothing more. The same applies to many other such figures, the policeman, the guide, the door-keeper, the teacher. With the appearance of "concepts" we have left ordinary reality and entered the land of soul. Dream or dream parts in which such seemingly embodied concepts appear have to be understood within the horizon of the soul. The dream in such a case has already all along "crossed the river," so that for us the necessity arises to view it from the other side, from the standpoint of soul, not from the point of view of commonplace reality, just as Jung pointed out in connection with the dream about the doctor beside the sea:

> we see that behind the impressions of the daily life—behind the scenes—another picture looms up, covered by a thin veil of actual facts. In order to understand dreams, we must learn to think like that. We should not judge dreams from realities because in the long run that leads nowhere.

The *unio naturalis* must have been dissolved. In our detailed and diligent work with the dream text we must look at the dream as well as at all individual images in it "from within," from the soul side, not "from outside." We need to follow the dream's "imaginatively deformative leads, where exegesis is exitus, leading life out of life," as Hillman said.

Now we come to the third and last group of dream elements I spoke about. With them we are also, and even to a higher degree, in soul country from the outset.

What I have in mind is elements of a clearly mythological, archaic or uncanny character (and feel). Whereas the concepts discussed in the second case are mostly self-explanatory, only needing perhaps a brief definition or description, because the functions that they represent are basically familiar from ordinary reality and to ego-consciousness, the case with the third group of figures, events, or objects is much more difficult. They have no equivalent in our modern world and in empirical reality. So they are totally alien on the semantic level, almost like "extraterrestrials" for us, and completely puzzling, baffling.

This has two reasons. First, they have their place "on the other side of the river," in the wholly other world described in myths, fairy tales, religious dogmas or performed in cultic rituals; second, history (above all the Enlightenment and, thereafter, the cultural rupture coming with the Industrial Revolution) has radically cut us off from tradition, tradition that not only used to provide general familiarity and knowledge about this wholly other region, but also offered the indispensable soul horizon for doing justice to them. This makes us fundamentally helpless. Even if we can intellectually maybe reconstruct some of the lost knowledge, such restored ("archaeologically" dug up) knowledge simply does not fit into the logic of modern consciousness. It will necessarily remain an alien body within it and *cannot be integrated*. We live, as it were, on a different planet from it. Nevertheless, it is possible to learn to intellectually understand in a general way the meaning that these elements once had and perhaps empathize them.

There is a third difficulty that lies specifically in the nature of dreams. Jung said, "a dream is too slender a hint to be understood until it is enriched by the stuff of association and analogy and thus amplified to the point of intelligibility" (*CW* 12 § 403). In dreams those mythological or "archetypal" elements usually appear in terribly abbreviated or fragmented, perhaps also a bit distorted form. It is rare that the full figure together with its complete story and the whole context and horizon are presented. To this we must add that the myths that have come down to us are in themselves late and not always reliable versions of them, written down at a time that was, to be sure, still closer to the time when the myths were "state of the art" truths, but, nevertheless, already definitely separated from them by a historical rupture, and thus separated from a deeper understanding (which would have required an initiation). Those who reported myths and fairy tales in their writings were often themselves at a loss with respect to the meaning of details and tried to make weird-sounding elements sound more plausible by providing motivations for their occurrence in the stories in terms of their own already post-ritualistic, post-mythological thinking. This is why there are quite different views today about how to understand the myths that we as psychologists have to rely on for our *amplifications*. For amplification is what Jung had in mind when in the above quote he spoke of "the stuff of association and analogy."

Amplification can only be used for "irrational data of the material, that is, of the fairytale, myth, or dream" (*CW* 9i § 436), for "images that can only be described as 'archaic' " (*CW* 16 § 246), for "contents which are difficult to understand, such as dream-images, manic ideas, and the like" (*CW* 17 § 162). It makes no sense whatsoever to try to amplify dream elements that belong to the first group of elements I mentioned, the ones that refer back to what is known by and familiar to consciousness and belong within the horizon of ordinary reality or the psychic (personalistic psychology). In fact, this would be a downright abuse of this method and of the actual dream images themselves, too.

This topic of abuse takes me to a second point to be noted concerning amplification. As we can see from Jung's above quote, the purpose of this method is solely that of "enriching," i.e., strengthening, increasing, what is contained in the "too slender" dream hint so as to bring it closer "to the point of intelligibility." The sense of "amplifying" that Jung had in mind is taken from electrical engineering, where it referred to the utilization of an input of voltage to obtain an output of greater magnitude through some technical device. Jung's method of amplification has the function of increasing "the magnitude" of intelligibility, while strictly leaving the specific content or meaning of the slender hint intact. Amplification is performed out of an intellectual interest, for nothing else but the "elucidation of the meaning" (*Sinndeutung*, *GW* 10 § 771), "so that it [*viz*. its symbolic language] may yield itself more easily to our understanding" (*CW* 11 § 788).

The abuse that the method of amplification has been widely put to in analytical psychology consists in using it for the purpose of inflating ordinary reality elements of the dream, what Jung called "impressions of the daily life," with mythic or archetypal meaning to gratify the ego's longing for a "higher meaning" of life. It then has become a purely cosmetic operation. The commonplace is dressed up with the deepest soul dignity, it is supplied with a sacred aura. Thought is replaced by subjective emotions, depth by a marshy swamp of personal feelings.

Amplification requires the ability to discriminate. It does not only need intelligence, it needs a "higher intelligence" or, as Jung also says, an *intelligence du cœur* (*CW* 8 § 543), as well as a highly developed, differentiated feeling function, that is, an organ capable of discerning differences of degree concerning such otherwise imperceptible qualities as depth, dignity, status, rank and value. This, in turn, presupposes that one's eyes have really been opened to the dimensions of "soul" in its fundamental otherness ("other side of the river," "the other picture that looms up"). "Naturally these things," Jung once pointed out, "can hardly be instilled into unintelligent people. An adequate capacity to understand is essential, for without a considerable degree of *subtler* intelligence they will only be misunderstood" (*Letters 2*, p. 410, to Dr. L. Kling, 14 January 1958, my emphasis).

Intelligence and good judgment are needed on two levels. On the level of the dream texts themselves, the ability to discriminate is required for determining which elements are slender hints capable and in need of amplification and which are not. On the level of the material used for the amplification of those slender hints in dreams it is needed for two different things. First, for choosing the deepest, most insightful, psychologically most illumining interpretations of the mythological or ritualistic material and rejecting the positivistic or simplistic (for example, "nothing but" type) readings. Second, it is absolutely crucial that a real analogy and correspondence between the dream image and the selected amplificatory material exists. A superficial, external similarity will, of course, not do. The inner essence has to be the same. *Similia similibus!* Without some depth of thought and soul feeling and without some real insight into "what the soul wants," what the soul concerns are, one will get nowhere here.

Narcissistic blow: "It has a say now, not you!"
Or: The patient as obstacle

In the chapter, "Whom does the therapist address when working on dreams with the patient?" we had already occasion to discuss the theme of free associations. Now we return to this topic, however no longer from the angle of what attitude the *therapist* needs to take but from the point of view what the *dream* needs. We know that Jung rejected free associations and other personal, extraneous patient comments (or, for that matter, subjective associations by the therapist) that are not necessitated by the dream content itself. His position is unambiguous. "I don't use free association at all" (*Letters 2*, p. 293, to Jolande Jacobi, 13 March 1956). Certain experience, Jung said somewhere else,

> taught me to mistrust free association. I no longer followed associations that led far afield and away from the manifest dream-statement. I concentrated rather on the actual dream-text as the thing which was intended by the unconscious, and I began to circumambulate the dream itself, never letting it out of my sight, or as one turns an unknown object round and round in one's hands to absorb every detail of it.
>
> (*CW* 18 § 430)

Jung's image shows that what he aimed at was a, as it were, tactile feeling and sensual awareness of the dream. He was solely concerned with the actual dream text. "It is chiefly and above all fear of the unexpected and unknown[22] that makes people eager to use free association as a means of escape" (*ibid.* § 434). This ("a means of escape") is a clear verdict![23]

Circumambulation means, as Jung put it, that one

> concentrates on the specific topics, on the dream itself, and disregards the frequent attempts of the dreamer to break away from it [the dream]. ...
> I do not know how many times in my professional work I have had to repeat the words: "Now let's get back to your dream. What does the *dream* say?"
>
> (*CW* 18 § 434)

Jung's moaning, "I do not know how many times" lets one think of an almost infinite number of times. This points to there being an enormously powerful spontaneous urge on the part of patients, when confronted with their dreams, to dwell on their own ideas and feelings. It seems to be the most natural thing for people to go off from the dream itself to what is in their own minds. Without being aware of it they thus tend to cover up what the dream says with their own associations. Their lack of awareness that what they are doing is a covering up is due to the fact that they innocently believe that their associations *are* what the dream is about, and they can believe this all the more since numerous analysts openly support this tendency. From a Jungian point of view, however, this tendency of patients is an enormous obstacle to dream interpretation. This is why Jung places the obligation on the therapist to circumambulate the dream and to *disregard* the patient's free associations. Jung does not want to spare the patient the narcissistic offense that the brushing aside the patient's ego comments causes.[24] As analysts we ultimately have to take sides for "the soul," i.e. the dream, and against the dreamer, i.e., the ego personality. And we have to do this because ultimately this is precisely in the interest of the dreamer, who has come to analysis only because he wants help in getting freed from his being stuck in his ego world.

The maxim for judging the value and legitimacy of these associations is best expressed in a statement in a letter by Jung about Socrates, parts of which I have quoted already earlier. Jung writes: Socrates "has shown us the one precious thing: 'To hell with the Ego-world! Listen to the voice of your *daimonion*. It has a say now, not you' " (*Letters 2*, p. 532, to Charteris, 9 January 1960). If we substitute "dream" for "daimonion," we could say that the dream must have a say now, not we (neither the patient nor the analyst). We can connect this with the other quote, also in a letter, introduced and discussed in the chapter "Actually working with dreams": "We have simply got to listen to what the psyche spontaneously says to us. What the dream, which is not manufactured by us, says is *just so*. Say it again as well as you can" (*Letters 2*, p. 591, to Herbert Read, 2 September 1960). We have got to *listen*, not talk, not associate, not freely fantasize, not immediately let out what momentarily pops into one's mind. The ego is condemned to silence. Jung's outburst, "To hell with the Ego-world!" speaks volumes. Listening means dwelling with the ununderstood as well as the readiness to accept the position of the one who is *being told* something by someone else (here the dream). A wonderful description of true listening is: "But Mary kept all these things, and pondered them in her heart" (Luke 2:19). Listening as receiving what is said as seeds and going pregnant with them, so that at their own time their meaning may emerge.[25]

Amplification, by contrast, is serious *work*. It needs professionality and shouldering the intellectual responsibility that comes with trying to comprehend dream images. It is a form of listening, not speaking. Amplification requires strict rejection of all ego comments, because, according to our alchemy-inspired golden rule of dream interpretation, we are not permitted to let anything from outside, that does not belong, get into the fantasy image.

The alchemical adage about the image having everything it needs within itself would be really simple if it demanded of us not to let in *anything at all* from outside. *That* would be a clear-cut commandment that we could apply just like that, mechanically, without further thought. But our dictum says: "Nothing from outside *that does not belong* should be allowed to enter." This entails an obvious contradiction. It does not flatly prohibit any external associations whatsoever. On the contrary, it confronts us with the idea that *certain* external material could, despite its externality, be internal to the image itself! Generally, our adage demands that what is outside of the dream image is *only* external and *must* be kept out; however, in some special cases, what is outside is also intrinsic to what is inside. And because it has, despite its factually emerging from outside as something external, nevertheless always already been inside psychologically (i.e., the inner property of the dream image), it is allowed also to *explicitly* enter.

This is an amazing idea. Here our thinking is needed. What can possibly be meant by this, at first glance, unlikely dictum? It is an open question that requires our concentrated effort to understand it, because the idea of something external that is, nevertheless, actually internal, and something internal that, in fact, appears only from outside, does not make any sense to our everyday commonsensical understanding. It cannot be imagined or represented (*vorgestellt*), it can only be thought. I will come back to this problem shortly.

Considering that Jung rejects associations from patients and demands that amplifications be restricted to "what belongs" to the dream itself, it is amazing that many Jungian analysts are, nevertheless, strongly convinced that (1) for dream interpretation they are absolutely in need of what the patient, as dreamer, has to say *about* his dream (his personal associations, ideas, imaginings[26]) and/or (2) that the cited golden rule for amplification cannot be followed because *who could decide* what belongs and what does not belong? An additional conviction (3), widespread among present-day Jungians, is that the primary access to dreams goes through our feelings and emotions.

I will start out with the second objection to Jung's position. "Who decides?" The implication is that there is no authority to objectively determine which analogies belong and which not. Nobody, even if he were Jung himself, could claim to legitimately function as this judge. And since there is no such expert judge in sight, and thus no possible objectivity, those who use this argument give up discrimination altogether and open the field for all and any subjective comments and other external material. The people who argue this way throw out the baby with the bath water. Since ultimate truth is impossible, they also reject *absolute truth* and say, in a way, "anything goes," as long as it comes from the person of the dreamer or is a phenomenon of the transference or counter-transference relationship. A real sellout. Any commitment to the dream itself is given up in favor of the contingencies of whatever happens to be going on in the mind of the dreamer at the moment of the dream discussion. There is no need to demonstrate that there is an inner, psychological connection between what the patient *says* and the dream image. The mere positive *fact* that *he* says it in this moment suffices. For indeed, who could decide whether there is an internal psychological connection *if*, after all, the point of this whole argument is that there is not and cannot be an authority that could decide? In other words, the dream has, with this stance, been thrown to the wolves: to the subjective psyche.

There *is*, however, a clear answer to the question, "Who decides?" It is (see above, chapter "My interpretation") that psychologist, that therapist, who happens to be working with this particular dream. He is called upon to come forward and show his colors. It is his *job* to decide what belongs and what not. This is what he has been trained for. He must not evade his responsibility. When I interpret a dream, it is, of course, not the ultimate interpretation. It is *my* interpretation and as such only absolute truth.

But then, I as dream interpreter am not totally alone and subjective in my *decision*. *Ultimately*, it is the dream itself that has to decide what belongs and what not. As Jung said,

> The dream is its own limitation. It is itself the criterion of what belongs to it and what leads away from it. All material that does not lie within the scope of the dream, or that oversteps the boundaries set by its individual form, leads astray and produces nothing but complexes.
>
> (*CW* 18 § 433)

"Only the material that is clearly and visibly indicated as belonging to the dream by the dream-images themselves should be used for interpretation" (§ 434). Again we see here that the dream is a self, an individual. *It* decides what belongs, not we, not our external ego mind. It, the dream, limits *itself*. Just as it is its own interpretation, so it is also its own self-limitation. It guards its borders, borders that the ego, however, can easily ignore and transgress, because qua ego it is not and has never been truly *inside* the dream.

Of course, this requires that we have abandoned ourselves to the dream. Because only when we are immersed in it, can its own self-limitation become actual for us in consciousness. *It* can only decide what belongs and what not, if *we* see it as a self and do not insist that we are the true self and the dream merely an expression of *our* self, *our* psyche (or the patient's psyche). In that case the dream would have something essential (*its own self*) outside of itself, namely in us. Here, I can come back to the question raised above about how what is outside can, nevertheless, be intrinsic to what is inside. When the dream has become fully real and present to us while we work with it in a therapy session and we have truly settled in it as in the imaginal world and the atmosphere that encloses us now, it not only tells us which amplifications from mythology belong, but it may even bring up memories of what we know about the childhood development of the patient, about details of his present real life or of what happened during a previous therapy session. In this case, *those* associations would not be external reflections, but the dream's *own* associations, reminiscences generated in us by the spirit of dream itself.—If the dream is a self and as a self also a whole world, *the* whole world (for the time of working with the dream), then the dream is wide enough so that anything, even my whole life can possibly have its place within it. It is potentially all-comprehensive.

But our discrimination is indispensable. "Believe not every spirit, but try the spirits whether they are of God" (1 John 4:1). We always have to ask: *Whose* memory is it, *who* has the association or amplification, I or the image? Does my amplification really come as *its*, the dream image's, self-interpretation, self-articulation, or is it my external reflection about it?

Now I turn to the other argument (#1). It states that we as therapists are dependent on this kind of input from the patient because *the patient knows best* what the dream refers to and means. It is *his* dream. How could *we* as analysts claim to be able to interpret dreams without his help? It would be presumptuous to assume that *we* could have a better, privileged access to dreams.

By way of a general diagnostic assessment we can say that what comes through in this belief is obviously a predilection for personalistic or ego-psychology.[27] The dream is supposed to be seen in terms of the patient, who becomes the center around which the therapy circles. The *dreamer* is the criterion for the dream. This is in direct opposition to Jung's circumambulation around the dream itself as the center, his "never letting it out of my sight," his approaching it "as one turns an unknown object round and round in one's hands to absorb every detail of it." Not the subject, the person of the dreamer, but the "object" is crucial. The view that the patient knows best what the dream is about shows that the naturalism of the *unio naturalis* has not been overcome; its rupture has not happened and the river that represents the gulf has not been crossed from the daily-life side to the soul side of it.

Before I come to my more detailed response to this argument, let me concede that it, of course, goes without saying that we need the dreamer to explain ambiguities, or what is unclear, in *his written description* of the dream. We need his input for further information about details contained in the dream experience but not specified in his text (the age and sex of a "child" in the dream, the size and form of particular objects, who were the persons in the dream known to him from real life, etc.), also perhaps for drawing a kind of map of the dream place of action, and so on. But apart from the case of details that are missing from the patient's dream report—what can and needs to be said in answer to this argument?

First of all, aren't we *professionals*? Have we not undergone years of training to become familiar with and understand the language of the soul, the soul's concerns (precisely in contrast to everyday ego concerns) and the dynamics of the soul's logical life, as well as its themes and interests, the horizon and perspective of soul, and, last but not least, its expressions in all sorts of phenomena: in symptoms, myths, fairy tales, religious dogmas, works of art, etc.? Can the ordinary patient compete with that? It is not merely a question of the *knowledge* of mythology and ethnology, the history of religions, etc. The issue at stake here is much rather the soul meaning of all that. What does the patient know about initiation, "the underworld," "fluidity," "transformation," "individuation," overcoming "the ego"? Can he answer the question: "what does the soul want?" Would it occur to a physician that he needs to hear from his patient what the latter thinks may be the best diagnosis of and the best medicine for his ailments, simply because, after all, it is the patient's own body and "he therefore must know best" what is wrong with it?

We must not castrate ourselves. And we must also not shove off onto the patient what is primarily *our* job as psychologists.

Second, it is simply an error to think that the patient is closer to the meaning of the dream than we are. Precisely not. He is too close to, too caught up in, his ego and his complexes, prejudices, pet ideas, etc., too impressed by the daily life impressions that the dream images evoke, and ipso facto not at all close to the dream itself. I know from myself that it is much easier to interpret other people's dreams than my own; in Jung's interpretations of his own dreams, too, we find some interpretations that are evidently untenable, tainted with ideological prejudices.[28] In fact, Jung himself stated that dreams "are always a little bit ahead of the dreamer's consciousness. I do not understand my own dreams any better than any of you, for they are always somewhat beyond my grasp and I have the same trouble with them as anyone who knows nothing about dream-interpretation. Knowledge is no advantage when it is a matter of one's own dreams" (CW 18 § 244). Dream interpretation needs a distance to the personal sphere and to the dream itself. It needs a shift, translocation (the crossing the river), and that is much more difficult to achieve with respect to one's own psychic material. Why do long-standing analysts at times consult a colleague when they had especially intriguing dreams? In general, the very reason for psychotherapy and thus also for dream analysis is that true self-reflection needs a real *other*.

Third, if this argument were correct, how could we dare to interpret psychologically fairy tales and myths, which have no "dreamers" (authors) to be asked about personal associations?

Fourth, Jung, too, criticized categorically the view that the patient is closer to the soul than the therapist: "It is as though everyone had the most direct access to what is going on inside him, was intimately acquainted with it and competent to pass an opinion on it" (CW 10 § 277). This concurs with what I remarked under the first point about psychologists as professionals. Hegel had already made much the same point for philosophy. He had said:

> In the case of all other sciences, arts, skill, and crafts, everyone is convinced that a complex and laborious programme of learning and practice is necessary for competence. Yet when it comes to philosophy, there seems to be a currently prevailing prejudice to the effect that, although not everyone who has eyes and fingers, and is given leather and last, is at once in a position to make shoes, everyone nevertheless immediately understands how to philosophize, and how to evaluate philosophy, since he possesses the criterion for doing so in his natural reason—as if he did not likewise possess the measure for a shoe in his own foot.[29]

Now I come to the last of the three convictions shared by many Jungians, but in obvious contrast to Jung's position. It is the belief that the main access to dreams goes through our emotions. Frequently, patients are asked by therapists in connection with dreams: "What do you feel about this image?" "What feelings does this image evoke in you?" They are encouraged to look (and feel) "into themselves" and to dwell on and savor their emotional reactions to images, all this in the belief that this is an essential part of working with dreams.

Not much needs to be said here after our lengthy previous discussions about Jung's own views about psychological dream interpretation. It does not need to be stressed that this is the opposite movement to a circumambulation *of the dream* and instead a circling about oneself, the ego-personality. Much the same arguments as the ones already raised against personal associations as a way to learn to understand a dream can also be raised against this type of procedure. But a different and additional objection is that Jung's strictly intellectual interest in making dreams intelligible (the "elucidation of the meaning," "so that it may yield itself more easily to our understanding") has been given up in favor of having feelings. Subjective feelings and emotions are strong psychic means to immure oneself in oneself.

Instead of "What do you feel about this image?" the psychological task would be to feel the *objective feeling* of the image. This would require a well differentiated feeling function, which is, as Jung stressed, a *rational* function like the thinking function, and it has nothing to do with personal *feelings*. Feelings are subjective *states*. Emotions are subjective *events*. The feeling function, by contrast, is really a *function*, something that is exercised, an act that is performed and that amounts to a value *judgment* or assessment about something real, in our context about a dream image. It means capturing a particular quality, the objective "feel" of it, and has nothing whatsoever to do with what *we* may feel. In interpreting dreams, we need to discern what the soul feels and which of *its* feelings are objectively embodied in the different dream images. Objective feeling is the equivalent of elucidating the meaning. Both serve the intellectual purpose of comprehending the dream.

The dream-I

Countless figures come up in all the various dreams that people have. But only one single figure, that of the dream-I, needs special attention.

It is to be assumed that the significance of the dream-I is far greater during the age of Modernity than it was in mediaeval or ancient and archaic times, simply because, well-prepared by the foregoing soul development manifested above all in philosophy with and after Descartes, modernity is the time when the subject, the I, became the center. This was a fundamental change, even a revolution, that alone was also responsible for the emergence of psychology, that is to say, of modern man's interest in himself, in his unconscious, his inner, his self-development, and of self-introspection. As Jung pointed out: "This distinguishes our time from all others" (*CW* 10 §161); "This situation is new. All ages before us still believed in gods in some form or other" (*GW* 9/I § 50, my transl.). Or take this statement:

I must, however, add at once that this is something peculiar, inasmuch as the soul is not always and everywhere on the inside. There are peoples and epochs where it is outside, peoples and epochs that are unpsychological, as, for example, all ancient cultures, and among them especially Egypt with its magnificent objectivity.

(CW 10 § 158)

It is to be assumed that for this reason the I did not play as important a role in dreams as it often does today. So it is not surprising that we find in ancient reports of dreams examples of dreams totally without a dream-I. Dreams may have been about the fortunes of a war that was going on, about sickness, economic necessities (such as Pharaoh's dreams about the seven well favored and fat-fleshed kine and the ill-favored and lean-fleshed ones).

Today this is different. Along with psychology, neurosis has been invented, and so numerous dreams particularly show the I dissociated from itself, something that would hardly have been possible in ancient days. In other dreams, the I can also simply be present as observer of dream events without being personally involved in what happens.

It is inherent in the appearance of the figure of the dream-I that it immediately makes the dreamer identify with it. In fact, the very meaning, function, *and achievement* of the word "I" is this identification. "I" is the existing concept: as concept it establishes its own existence, it brings about its own reality and presence. By saying "I," I have ipso facto *become* "I," a becoming that can be nicely observed when little children all of a sudden are able to refer to themselves as "I," something they could not do as babies. You can only meaningfully say "I" if you *are* "I," a self-conscious and self-relating subject.

Nevertheless, the dream-I is also a dream figure, a dream image—just one of the figures occurring in the dream. Of course, we tend to tacitly assume that because in the dream there is a figure that comes with the clear notion and felt sense of "I" it must also refer to me, the dreamer who had this dream. The sameness of the word "I" that is used both inside and outside the dream text seduces us into identifying the dream-I with the dreamer. But, as James Hillman has already insisted, the I in the dream is a symbol or image just as much as any other figure or motif in the same dream, that is, an imaginal figure, a fictional character, and it points *only* to *itself* and not away from itself to an external referent, not to the person outside the dream who had this dream.

Earlier, in the chapters about "Not knowing as methodological starting point" and about "Inner infinity," I pointed out that the dream and its images have to be seen as *fundamentally* unknown, that each dream and each image in it is like a person met for the first time, that each dream image has its own inner infinity. The same fundamental unknownness applies even to the dream-I. It is an imaginal, fictional character and can represent quite different things. What the dream-I is in each particular dream is determined by the internal specifics of the dream, (1) by the way the dream-I is, in fact, characterized (shown to behave) and (2) by the dream story as a whole. The dream-I is not a self that has its identity and substance a priori entirely within itself as its fixed possession. Rather, it only *gets* defined (and gets *defined*) in the course of the dream action, namely by what other figures it encounters, by what it sees, where it finds itself, and what befalls it. All this is the reflection of its nature, the unfolding of its definition. It receives its "definition" or character from the particular dream events rather than having it in itself as its fixed property (the way each real person has his or her nature as internal property).

The dream-I can be very different from the personality of the dreamer. And it may precisely be one function of dreams (the different dreams we have) to show that there is not one fixed identity for "I," but that "I" has a variety of possibilities of what and how it can be. It is not necessarily stuck in its habitual definition. It can theoretically also be otherwise. Therefore, the dream-I must not, in the sense of the object-level interpretation of dreams, be sight unseen confused with the dreamer. In fact, usually a dreamer sees and feels the dream-I as "different" and not "self," despite the word "I," just as the dream as a whole is in most cases felt to be strange and not ego-syntonic.

This non-identification with the dreamer is *therapeutically* important. One of the psychological problems of modern people is that they are often too rigidly identified with themselves and their sense of who and what they are is too narrowly defined and fixated. All the different dream-I's that may appear in the many dreams that a person has may open up a field of possibilities, and open the dreamer's eyes to other possible modes of being. It also teaches us to see that "I" is not an empirical fact, not a positively subsisting entity, but an idea, a concept and perhaps lets us understand that it is that concept that *qua* concept creates the—conceptual—identity of "I" with bodily existing "me."

So we have to treat the dream-I as an "it" (or "he" or "she," at any rate third person singular, not first person singular). As one of the dream elements we have to grant it the same objectivity that all the other figures receive. One figure in the dream may be called "my father" or "a doctor" or "a burglar," another one has the designation "I." They are basically all on the same level.

And yet this is not quite right. The dream-I is, to be sure, not identical with the dreamer, but nevertheless it is truly "I" and as such radically different from all the other figures in the dream, which are decidedly non-I. It is the dream itself that within itself characterizes the figure that we call the dream-I as a full-fledged I and thus necessarily establishes a connection to the dreaming person. This "I"-character is precisely part of its "character description," of how it is presented in and by the dream itself. The dream *within itself* creates the strong feeling of I, a feeling that is especially powerful and absolutely convincing in anxiety dreams or in dreams in which the dream-I desperately tries to get somewhere but is time and again frustrated.

Here we have to come back to our earlier insight on a higher level: even this intensive sense of I that seems *dream-internally* to naturally identify the dreamer with the dream-I, and through which the dream-I is singled out from among the ranks of all dream figures, is nevertheless part of the dream fiction. It is created within the dream as *its* internal component and does not imply any identity with the person of the dreamer *outside* the dream, in waking life.

The role of the dream-I can vary. Most of the time perhaps, the dream-I is central as the experiencing and acting person. In other dreams it may be *present*, so to speak, on the scene of the dream action without itself actively participating. It is merely a kind of witness or observer of what comes to pass. And sometimes the dream-I is not present in the dream at all, that is to say, does not appear as figure in it, but is I only as the external unembodied consciousness of the dream content. Pharaoh's dreams mentioned above could serve as an example.

In many dreams the dream-I shows a defensive attitude. It does not understand what is happening, what maybe wants to come to it and be integrated into its consciousness, or what, conversely, wants to initiate it into some soul truth. Because it has no access to the soul meaning of what is approaching it, it often needs to fight it or escape from it. Its style of consciousness is then that of the ego, and preserving (not so much itself, but) its *ego identity* is its highest goal. But the dream-I is not always in this position. There are, for example, dreams in which the dream-I behaves quite differently from the way it moves in most other dreams of the same person, in a decidedly non-ego fashion. In those cases the dream-I may even represent the authentic stance of the soul. It is then as if the soul itself had taken the guise of the dream-I to fulfill its, the soul's, needs. These two possibilities mentioned are just the two extremes. There are many in-between positions.

As therapists we should refrain from moral judgements. In cases where the dream-I shows a clearly defensive attitude and rejects or tries to run away from what the soul sent to it, thereby betraying its decided ego stance and opposition to soul, this is not "wrong." We should not think (or say) that the dream-I "should have" behaved differently, not tell the patient how it would have been appropriate to have reacted in the dream, intimating that maybe next time, in a similar dream situation, "he" perhaps might be able to behave more "psychologically correct." With such an inner attitude, and even more so with such an explicit reaction, we would ourselves be stuck in "the ego," despite ostensibly advocating the interests of soul. Through our own unspoken feeling or our expressed words we would appeal precisely to the ego in the patient. Semantically, we would, of course, try to advance the soul work, while syntactically doing the opposite, namely confirming the ego, its moralizing, its "shoulds" and "oughts," and evoking ego will and ego efforts. We must not enter with our ego judgements and therapeutic ideas and desires.

This is also why I think the following statement of Hillman's problematic: "everything in the dream is right, except the ego [i.e., what I call the dream-I]. Everything in the dream is doing what it must, following psychic necessity along the wandering course of its purposes, except the ego."[30] Hillman has with this sentence fallen into the trap of early Jung, the idea of "The Relations Between the Ego and the Unconscious." I would here remind Hillman of his own other dictum in the same book (p. 105), "that *the ego too is a soul*," and of mature Jung's dictum: "What the dream, which is not manufactured by us, says is *just so*. Say it again as well as you can." Tautologically! No wish for correction or improvement. The dream is the way it is. And it is the *whole* dream, *including* the ego. Just as I had occasion to point out above that the dream-I "only *gets* defined (and gets *defined*) in the course of the dream action, namely by what other figures it encounters, by what it sees, where it finds itself, and what befalls it," so we must here not treat the dream-I as a self-identical, a priori given entity, as a self-enclosed self, that stands vis-à-vis the soul. The dream-I is itself a product of the soul. It is just as much a dream-internal invention by the soul as are all the other characters. It is unpsychological to treat the dream-I as if it had been thrown into the dream from external reality. We must not dissociate the dream and put the dream-I on one side as "bad," "wrong," inimical to soul and all the rest of the dream figures to the other side as the authentic expression of soul. We have to stick to the image the way it is and think "tautologically." How could the behavior of the dream-I be wrong? It, too, "is doing what it must," it, too, follows its psychic necessity along the wandering course of its purposes. The dream with all its figures (including the dream-I) shows one soul situation, one possible moment and constellation in the soul's life, and as such it is perfect. "And [there is] nothing of all this that is not Zeus," we might, *mutatis mutandis*, say with Sophocles (*Trachinian Women*, last line). What it needs is our hatching it out, our warming it with our own body heat.

On the other hand, this does, of course not mean that we should be blind to the *internal* problems and tensions in the dream as well as to the possible sadness or tragedy of the situation displayed in it. On the contrary, all this needs to be clearly seen and "said again"!

A certain blindness to a behavior of the dream-I that is shown to be wrong in and by the dream itself (although, after what I just explained, the dream-I too "is doing what it must"!) is revealed by Jung's interpretative comments on a dream of his own (the one already referred to, the dream with his father as custodian of sarcophagi who led the dream-I, Jung, "into the highest presence").

> I had to submit to this fate, and ought really to have touched my forehead to the floor, so that my submission would be complete. But something prevented me from doing so entirely, and kept me just a millimeter away. Something in me was saying, 'All very well, but not entirely.' Something in me was defiant and determined not to be the dumb fish: and if there were not something of the sort in free man, no Book of Job would have been written several hundred years before the birth of Christ. Man always has some mental reservation, even in the face of divine decrees. Otherwise, where would be his freedom? And what would be the use of that freedom if it could not threaten Him who threatens it?
>
> (*MDR* p. 220)

Outside the dream, Jung was clearly aware of the faulty behavior of the dream-I, but he justified it with rationalizations. This justification is just as egoic as the moral condemnation of the dream-I that I criticized before.

The dream-I and the other

Jung thought that many dreams have a formal structure not unlike that of a drama, with several distinct phases or parts (*CW* 8 §§ 561 ff.). Such dreams begin with an introductory statement of PLACE and a statement about the PROTAGONISTS (and perhaps about a PURPOSE, GOAL, or TASK to be performed). Second, we get the DEVELOPMENT of the plot ("*Verwicklung*," complication). "The third phase brings the CULMINATION or *peripeteia* (a turning of the action). Here something decisive happens or something changes completely." The fourth and last phase is the *lysis*, the SOLUTION or RESULT produced by the internal dream-work.

One can indeed find elements corresponding to these phases in many dreams. But it would, of course, be totally wrong to use this as a rigid schematic approach, an abstract formal principle, and to apply it routinely to dreams in order to divide a living dream into separate sections. Furthermore, in many cases it would be quite forced to try to find such a structure in actual dreams. It is simply not there. It may be better to take this idea of Jung's about the *dramatic formal* structure of dreams as a hint that can help us to become aware of something else that is no longer merely formal: the living internal tension and dynamics and movement that are so characteristic of many dreams. Instead of a structure, which contains separate parts expressing a development (complication) of the plot and a *peripeteia* (the turning of the action, we could almost say, with a psychoanalytic term: a reversal into the opposite), I prefer to stress the internal oppositional logic of many dreams as the real drama that happens in those dreams.

We have already touched on the possibility of a veritable conflict between the attitude of the dream-I and what it is confronted with in a dream. Although frequent, this is, of course, only one possibility. There are many dreams that are without any such oppositional structure, e.g., dreams that merely show some more or less static scene, or a process that happens, or the manifestation of something before the eyes of the dream-I. But because the tension between the dream-I and some Other is so common a theme I will devote some reflections to it. Before, I discussed the importance of the interpreting subject and of its circumambulating, thereafter I had focused on the dream itself as the object of interpretation and its general character as a self, and then I turned to the stance that we need to take towards individual images. Finally, with the topic of the dream-I, only one of many dream images or figures was singled out. Now we turn to a new aspect, the *action* or *story* of dreams, what takes place in them, the *relation* between different sides in them, but only in those dreams that betray a dramatic tension between two sides, an opposition of two tendencies, two interests, two stances or views.

1. Necessary distinctions and decisions

Before we devote ourselves to this topic, I need to introduce two distinctions that become relevant for the assessment of the oppositional structure in dreams and the interpretation of dreams in general. The first distinction concerns two fundamentally different types of soul story according to the role that the sequence of the narrated events plays in them. The second distinction has to do with opposite intentionalities or aims that a dream might pursue.

1. Two types of narration: the difference in the nature and meaning of the temporal sequence of events presented in stories or dreams.

In order to explain this difference I will use as an example the two well-known ancient, but structurally quite different types of story, fairy tale and myth.

Genuine fairy tales, i.e., the ones designated as "tales of magic" beginning with no. 300 in Antti Aarne's and Stith Thompson's classification of folktales,[31] describe a soul movement or soul journey (to the beyond) as the story of the initiation of the protagonist. It is a movement from an initial situation of predicament to a final solution through the acquisition on the part of the protagonist of "the great treasure of the soul" (represented either by gold, as the symbol of the metaphysical light substance, or the "water of life," or the "princess/prince" from the beyond). The action has a clear direction and leads to a final goal.

Myths, on the other hand, show an action that only seemingly leads from here to there, but in reality merely unfolds the internal complex logic of one "archetypal" soul moment or soul truth. There is not really any change. "Myths, if they truly are to be myths," Plotinus pointed out, "are forced to divide what they talk about according to a temporal sequence and to separate many things from one another that actually belong together and can only be distinguished according to their logical position and functions" (*Enn.* III 5 [50] 9, 24–29). In the case of myths it is the *narrative genre* that forces "to represent in sequence what actually is a permanent simultaneity of becoming and being" (*Enn.* IV 8 [6] 4, 40–42).

In other words, in fairy tales the sequence of events is inherent in the story itself, the progression of the action being the very content and subject matter of the story told. The progressing time is the *story's* time. Fairy tales are about a progressive development from an initial situation, such as a predicament, toward a final goal, the solution, that the story was heading for from the outset. By contrast, in myths the sequence of events that may perhaps look in principle much like those in fairy tales, is, nevertheless, in truth merely due to the narrative form. In them the story itself (with all the many events and changes occurring in it) does not have a temporal process as its subject-matter. What myths are about is rather one single, "momentary" reality, one unchanging "archetypal" situation, and the time sequence of the action narrated in a myth is the *narrator's* time, the time he needs to describe the different aspects and logical "moments" of this one "archetypal" reality. It is similar to how any description of an object (a house, a violin, an elephant) takes time because each part of it, each view of it (front, back, sides, etc.) need to be stated one after the other. The difference to ordinary descriptions is that myths do not *come* as descriptions, but *translate* the different aspects into a story, making them appear as if they were consecutive events (which makes them more interesting and vivid than an abstract description). At any rate, myths do not present events in time. They present the inner logic, the syntax, the internal logical complexity of one respective soul truth. They require what I have called (and discussed) elsewhere "the 'tautological' presupposition" of myth interpretation.[32]

Fairy tales are, so to speak, told from the perspective of the biographer or historian, myths from that of the anatomist or physiologist. The narrator of fairy tales *travels* with his car. The narrator of myths takes the car apart like a car mechanic in his garage or explains the internal construction of this car like an engineer.

Dreams may be like fairy tales and have the purpose of portraying a progressive sequence of events, different happenings, a course of action. A task may be set by the dream in the beginning, and then we hear about attempts of the protagonist (usually the dream-I) to achieve this task, and also maybe about his being hindered time and again by obstacles. Or a dream may show a movement that is comparable to initiation processes as we know them from reports from ancient cultures or more recent ethnological findings. The truth of the "other" that appears in dreams of this type is really an *other* in the full sense for the protagonist, a reality to encounter and come to terms with one way or another.

But dreams can also be like myths, the narrative unfolding of the different moments of *one soul truth*, one soul situation. Here we would have (1) the *simultaneity* of all events in the dream[33] and (2) the sameness of the seeming "other." By this I mean that all the different figures depict one *constellation* of different aspects, sides, or elements that make up this one truth. There is not really the dream-I's meeting some other person (even if the dream may narratively present it as such). But what happens *between* the two in reality shows the internal relation, possibly tension, between different aspects of the in-itself *complex* SAME. What happens to the dream-I is not a new event that befalls the dream-I, but a reflection of who or what the dream-I in truth *is*. All the figures and the events are *reflections* of each other, rather than separate, independent realities.[34] There is a mutual dependence of their natures, of their characteristics.

Thus the dream-I's running away is not only due to his being pursued by a dangerous man, but it is also the other way around: his being pursued is the consequence of the dream-I's running away. The attacker and the flight imply and "cause" each other: they are two sides of one and the same coin. It is as if the fear *produced* the aggressor (much like even in empirical reality it can often be observed that dogs respond with particularly aggressive behavior to people who have great fear of them). Even more than that, timidness itself needs, requires, an aggressor or some danger in order to be what it is. So the timid dream-I meets in the aggressor only *its own* presupposition and requirement. (Again, there is a parallel in reality: school-children who become victims of mobbing meet in their aggressors the external objectification of the inherent counterpart of their own internal timidness, and the aggressors' aggression is, at least to some extent, provoked by the pupil's timidness.) In general, the degree of the danger, maliciousness, or monstrosity of "the other" that appears to the dream-I reveals the degree of the hostility, defensiveness, or innocence of the latter, just as conversely a very bossy, aggressive, overpowering dream-I may be confronted with a very timid, gentle, helpless "other."

With Jung one might want to think here in terms of compensation. But it is better to understand that what seems to appear as a real other is not an other at all, not something to be added or included, but rather its *own* other half. The dream-I and "the other" are not two. They are one single reality. One always gets a psychic reality as the whole reality, with a "+" AND with a "–" sign, as light AND as darkness or shadow at once, even if only the one side may *appear* on the surface. "The other" in dreams is not really a new *discovery*: it has been present all along, only perhaps not seen. It is present from the outset in and as the *logic* of this reality.

As far as dream interpretation is concerned, we need to determine each time with respect to each dream or dream scene and each appearance of an oppositional structure in it, whether we need to identify it as a story of genuine progressive movement or as the self-display of the internal dialectic of one and the same soul truth or moment in the soul's logical life. Does the dream or a particular scene follow the fairy tale type of narration or the myth type? We have to determine this: it is something we as interpreters have to *decide* according to our best judgment.

2. The second important distinction can be illustrated with the following brief dreams.

Dream 1

A woman, in real life a medical doctor, dreams that a very big, fat woman advances towards her, hurls her to the ground and throws herself upon the dream-I so that the latter is completely immobilized.

Dream 2

The same woman dreams that when she comes to her practice there are incredibly many people in the waiting room. She feels completely overwhelmed and has no idea how to manage this situation.

In some way the two dreams are similar. Both show the dream-I being confronted with a new reality and completely overwhelmed by it. But the soul's interest in each dream seems to be very different. In dream 1 something approaches her very actively. It is a substantial reality: a certain form of the feminine, physically very impressive, corporeal, massive. This reality imposes itself quite physically on the dream-I, seeking total body-contact and impressing its weight and body volume upon the dream-I so that the latter deeply senses with her own body its presence and solid reality. Whatever else the dream might be aiming for, one thing is obvious, namely, that it is interested in exposing the dream-I to the very personal, immediate physical experience of "body" as weight and mass. By bringing to the dream-I a non-ego as that which is to have a healing effect, that is, a new awareness, we could call the tendency of this dream a *therapeutic intentionality*.

The dream-I is completely put out of action. It is, so to speak, silenced, which means that here we have a literal case of the dream-internal "It (the other, the big, fat woman sent by the soul, the non-ego) has a say now, not you (the dream-I)." The dream-I is, we might say, taught a lesson.

The second dream is very different. Nothing different and new, no substantial reality as a real other (subjectively for the dream-I), is sent to the dream-I. Even if there is an excess compared to the usual work situation because of the incredible number of waiting patients, this is only a quantitative change. Qualitatively, everything in the dream remains within the horizon of the daily world, the ordinary ego-experience. Instead of being silenced or threatened or exposed to an authentic soul-sent reality, here it is precisely the ego that is called for and put in the center, the ego's coping with a problem, its organizational talent, management qualities, and its hard work. The patients are merely passively waiting. They do not have "a say now," they are silent and "immobile." The whole action in the dream happens in the dream-I's own mind: as its frustration and worry. The dream-I immures itself in itself. It has no eyes for the patients *as others*, as people who need help from the dream-I, but only eyes for them as *its own*, the ego's, *problem*. Here we might speak of the dream's *neurotic interest*, by which I do not mean a neuroticizing tendency, but the interest to simply show the dream-I's neurotic egocentric frame of mind. Precisely the feeling of being overwhelmed is indulged in and celebrated, and by indulging in its own worries and delightfully making a fuss over its being overtaxed, "the ego" neurotically celebrates itself. The excessively many patients in the waiting room are merely the externalization and visual objective representation of the dream-I's own inner stance of feeling as a victim, as being unfairly treated, of being expected to do what is too much. (The first dream, by contrast, showed a situation of a real being overwhelmed by a real other.)

These two tendencies or interests need to be clearly kept apart. With each dream or dream part, we need to decide whether the "other" *brings* something to the dream-I or dream protagonist (therapeutic tendency) or whether it merely *reveals* something neurotic or problematic about the dream-I. It needs a psychological understanding of the dream scene as a whole and often a differentiated feeling function to make this decision in a concrete case of dream work.

After discussing these preliminary topics we can now turn to the actual theme of this chapter, the dream-I and the Other.

2. The antagonists

In dreams with an oppositional structure, that is, with a clash or conflict between the dream-I and "the other," we have to see this conflict not so much as between two persons, but as between two interests, views, tendencies, or stances embodied by the dream persons, the interest of the experiencing dream-I, on the one hand, and that of what Jung called the non-ego and often the unconscious, and what I call "the soul," on the other hand. Sometimes the two opposite tendencies stand clearly vis-à-vis and interact or clash, most notably in dreams where the dream-I is persecuted or attacked by enemies, murderers, shadow figures, or animals. Here there is a clear separation. The interest of the dream-I is to escape, to get out, to *survive* (which psychologically means: to rescue its old *form* of consciousness, its present orientation and mind-set, itself *as ego*, and to prevent any necessary change), whereas the persecuting figures want to get into contact with the dream-I, to enter its structure of consciousness and become integrated into it, which would amount to a logical revolution of the present consciousness of the dream-I. Much of the dream action in such dreams is the interplay between these two tendencies, where, e.g., the dream-I escapes for the moment, but only to find out that the enemy all of a sudden comes from some other unexpected side and that it has to find a new way out, and so on. It is like a play of cat and mouse.

There are many other ways in which the dream-I's Other may appear. The other, non-ego tendency does not have to be expressed by figures. It can also have the form of events or developments. For example, a car that the dream-I is driving gets out of control and rolls towards a terrible abyss; or the dream-I is on a frozen lake and discovers the ice is all of a sudden melting under him; or it is on a high scaffold and the railings are breaking away. The dream-I just wants to light a candle, but all of a sudden the whole house catches fire. There are innumerable dream situations of quite different character that follow the same pattern.

3. *The soul's* via negativa

The soul tendency in all such cases is to do something to the dream-I that the dream-I absolutely fears or rejects. The soul wants the ice to melt under the feet of the dream-I to make it fall into the icy water; the soul sends a snake so that it might bite the dream-I and the thereby injected "poison"/medicine start an internal "alchemical" process of fermenting corruption in the person of the dream-I, etc. This type of intention is always a sign that the soul works via negation. In order to produce a necessary change for the better it does not use instruction, moral lectures, preaching. Nor does it use introspection and insight. It does not want to persuade, nor to entice the dream-I through promises of a better future or by advertising the advantages and desirability of the necessary change. In fact, it does not present the goal to be achieved at all. No hope. No growth. Nothing is grafted on. On the contrary, in such dreams the soul wants nothing else but to undermine and decompose the old ego structure from within. Any new possibility that might emerge (after and outside the dream) would have to be *this decomposition's* own result, so that it is definitely not an imposed or demanded change ("you ought!"), but truly the internal alchemical transformation of the prevailing logic.

In all such cases of the oppositional logic, the dream follows the idea expressed in the proverbial phrase, "to reckon without one's host." Already before Freud the psychological question had emerged whether the ego is the master in its own house, and both Freud and Jung repeatedly stressed the point that it is not. The oppositional logic of the dream is a portrayal of this tension. The dream-I feels as the master of his house, but is exposed in the dream, and by the dream action, to the experience that this is an illusion. There is an Other, and this Other is the host, although the dream-I tries its best to be saved from having to acknowledge the host as the host and master in its house.

What from the point of view of the dream-I (in its *ego* position) is a catastrophe to be avoided at all cost, is from the point of view of the soul necessary. It represents indeed the dream's prospective, therapeutic tendency.

Another example.

> There is a fire in the city. A part of the city is already aflame. Oil is being poured into the other part of the city. People try to keep the fire away because otherwise there would be an inferno. I am helping in a store to move articles of clothing away, as a precaution.

This dream shows an obvious ambivalence. There are two intentionalities, two "wills." The one will is apparently that the whole city turn into an inferno, that this already imagined inferno become actually real, be made true. Otherwise oil would not, according to the proverbial "adding fuel to the flames," be poured into the not yet burning part of the city. The second will wants to prevent the fire from spreading to the rest of the city and to rescue the articles of clothing.

4. How to view the ego defenses in dreams

Here it is important not to intrude with our subjective value judgments. We could, of course, think that, fortunately, the inferno will probably be prevented because its actual happening in the dream would amount to a psychic catastrophe; that in general the appearance of this danger in a dream is an alarming sign. Conversely, we could also say: the fact that there is a fire is the actual intention of the unconscious, of the soul; the soul will not make do with half measures; it wants a "holocaust" (from Greek *hólos* = whole and *kaustón* = burnt offering), a "sacrifice or offering entirely consumed by fire." As the alchemists said, *omnes superfluitates igne consumuntur*, everything superfluous is [and is supposed to be] consumed by the flames, to be exposed to the purifying, spiritualizing fire. We can think of Nietzsche: "Yes, I know whence I have sprung!/Insatiable as a flame/I burn and consume myself!/Whatever I seize hold on becomes light,/whatever I leave, ashes:/certainly, flame I am."[35] But the dream-I resists such a change in the sense of an ego defense. It wants above all to rescue what belongs to the sphere of the persona, as the fact shows that what the dream-I wants to save is articles of clothing.

But no matter which side we would take, in either case the two intentionalities would offset one against the other. This is not the way psychology deals with oppositional tendencies or wills. We must not choose one side and dismiss the other as inessential or inauthentic. To be sure, *phenomenologically*, descriptively, we can speak of a defense on the part of the dream-I, and of course "defense" in the psychoanalytical sense amounts objectively to a decidedly *negative* stance towards the soul tendency, in other words, to a psychological verdict. It is clear that as the patient's *psychotherapists* it is our job to side with the soul tendency. So we have landed up with a dilemma: how can we, as psychologists, deal with the defensive tendencies in dreams, if we are not permitted to condemn them despite our siding with the soul tendency?

We can moderate the dilemma a bit by realizing that we must not regard the psychologically negative term "defense" as a *value judgment*, and that our siding with the soul dynamic should not be emotional and moralistic, but a logical and objective siding with it, inspired by our knowledge of the soul and by our professional and therapeutic commitment to the soul. But the problem itself still remains.

What is wrong with any such partisan responses to the dream is that the opposites would be set up as existing on one and the same level. This way of thinking has only one level at its disposal. It is not aware of a difference of levels, as it is expressed in the dictum: "Render unto Caesar the things which are Caesar's, and unto God the things that are God's." This sentence opens up the psychological difference. There are two concerns or wills, but they are located on two different levels. Despite their mutual exclusion, they must not be played one against the other. Both have claims on us. It is the interest of the soul in the presented dream that there *be* fire, everywhere, without exception. But because this is the interest *of the soul*, we must not view this with the eyes of the ordinary ego (i.e., positive-factually, empirically). It is a soul *mysterium* and as such not to be equated with a literal inferno in practical reality. Conversely, it is also the legitimate interest of humans (of the I), to rescue themselves from the fire and also to protect the clothes.

But this still does not resolve our dilemma. We have to go one step further, namely back to our earlier insight that the dream is a self, closed within itself, and as such the soul's speaking about itself. The dilemma we found betrays that so far, we have not taken our stand fully within the dream itself, have not allowed ourselves to be interiorized into it, but have instead taken the stand of external arbiter. Once we take the idea of the soul's speaking about itself absolutely seriously, it becomes clear that everything in the dream is "soul." The dream-I with its defense is not the opposite of soul. The defense against the soul is the soul's own defense against itself. To be true psychologists, we therefore cannot play the soul tendency against the dream-I's ego defense. As I pointed out earlier, we must not think that "everything in the dream is right, *except the ego*." We must not fall into the trap of viewing the dream as an expression of "The Relations Between the Ego and the Unconscious," which is an approach to the soul's life from a decidedly *external* standpoint and itself creates the very dilemma between two fixed, totally dissociated opposites that it wants to overcome therapeutically. No, the ego in the dream, i.e., the dream-I, is "right," too, for it is a dream reality, not an external ego-personality; it is *with its resistance* invented and posited by the soul, just as much as is the representation of the other specifically soulful tendency. Only the whole truth of the dream is the soul's truth. *We must not psychologically, on the syntactical level, isolate one half of the dream-internal opposition as "soul" and dismiss the other as anti-soul,* despite their, on the semantic, descriptive level, indeed being "soul" and "anti-soul"! That is, we must not literalize the semantic truth, not ourselves repeat and condone the dissociation. The dream as the soul's speaking about itself is in cases of dreams with an oppositional structure the representation of the soul-internal tension between the opposite soul tendencies. Such dreams are probably dreams that display the soul situation in the *modern* world.

This way of seeing it is also therapeutically important. Our siding with the soul tendency, while absolutely necessary for a truly psychological stance, should never degenerate into moralistic or emotional pressure, i.e., an egoic reaction. The dream-I *has every right to his or her resistance* to the imposition by "the soul" as its host or master. The analyst's task is not to be against the dream-I's resistance or fight the patient's resistance. The resistance *is* part of the dream as a self, part of the whole picture, and the whole picture is just right, right as it is.[36] *We* must not wish for any changes. If we did, we would intrude with *our* ego intentions into the objective reality of the dream! *We* would ourselves portray an ego resistance against the soul as expressed in the dream. No, it is the other way around. We have to learn to *release* the dream *into its own reality and truth* (even a threatening or catastrophic dream, and even a dream that does not find any kind of solution because of the strong resistance on the part of the dream-I). *We* don't have to solve what is problematic in the dream; it is the dream, the soul, that has to take care of its own problems. All *we* have to do is to attend, as honestly and carefully and with as much psychological *comprehension* and human *feeling* as we can muster, to all aspects of the dream and highlight both the ego's resistance attitude and the soul tendency, so that they can be clearly seen for what they really are. *Both* have to be released into what they are; we have to grant both of them the right to be what and how they are. They have to have free play. We do not have to change anything (and not the dreamer either). If anything in the dream has to change, it has to change of its own accord, in the soul itself.

If what is represented in dreams with an oppositional structure is a soul-internal tension, we could say that the soul makes a proposal or offer *to itself,* and that it is again the soul that within the dream either accepts or tries to refuse its own offer to itself. If, by contrast, we were following the logic of "the relations between the ego and the unconscious," we would tacitly construe this offer as coming from the unconscious or soul to the *patient* in external reality, to the ego-personality, thus confounding the dream-I with the dream-external real dreamer. This in turn would mean that we would at least implicitly *blame* the patient for his own defensive attitude and burden him with the obligation (the "should" and "ought") to work on overcoming this resistance and become able to accept the soul's offer. This moralism and superego stance is sheer ego-psychology.

It is psychologically essential to *release* the patient completely from the only too likely identification with the dream-I into his own, and ipso facto also release the soul (including the dream-I) into its being-so and into its freedom. We must not meddle with our judgments, agendas, and emotions in the soul's life or its self-presentation. What we must do as psychologists is objectively, dispassionately perceive what the dreams indeed show (no matter what it may be that they show) and thus also, with all the *intelligence* and *feeling power* that we can muster, perceive, admit to ourselves, and unsparingly articulate for ourselves, whatever problematic, painful, pathological, possibly dangerous, alarming features there may be. This would be *therapeía* of the soul: one's simple serving the soul, attending and dedication to the soul. Or as Jung put it: it would be simply *saying again* as well as we can what the soul has said.

Will the soul become able to reach itself? Will it succeed in making itself heard and understood by itself and in softening its own heart? Or will it close its mind to its own offer to itself? Will it perhaps *not* penetrate itself, remaining untouched and unmoved, self-enclosed, indurate towards itself?

These questions would indicate the prevailing presence of the spirit of true psychology. To see things this way, namely from within the soul itself, and see them as its, the soul's, business, would have an enormous freeing effect for therapy. It would unburden the patient (and, for that matter, also the therapist) of responsibilities that are not his from the outset. It, the soul, has the sole responsibility for the soul's life. (By this, I hasten to add, I do not wish to imply that the patient should be relieved of all responsibility. On the contrary, I believe that therapy has to give the patient full responsibility for how he leads, and in the past has led, his life in actuality. No excuses by blaming parents or external circumstances for *his own psychological reactions* to his parents and to the maybe bad circumstances that he was exposed to. But responsibility for his behavior and reactions is one thing. Responsibility for soul processes quite another. The psychological difference!)

Now I want to discuss four *special* ways how the internal oppositional tension within many dreams can present itself.

5. Opposition as obvious conflict between Two and the dialectic of successful flight

The first form to be reviewed is that of a clear confrontation or conflict between the dream-I and an aggressor or pursuer and the dream-I's defensive reaction. Let us suppose that the dream-I is running away in panic from "the Other," for example, from a bull, which, as *we* know, is in reality its own internal Other and the very content that the soul wants to bring home to consciousness. The bull might be the imaginal form of the dream-I's avoided and feared wild, powerful masculine instincts. In working with such a dream, there could be two possible problematic reactions to such a dream situation. The one is, that one is happy if the dream-I's safe escape is successful. Of course, the patient, the dreamer, usually identifies with the emotions and interests of the dream-I and therefore wants it ("himself") to escape and thinks that the threatening animal (or whatever, in other dreams, the danger may be) absolutely needs to be avoided inasmuch as being reached by the bull would amount to a catastrophe. But we know that psychologically the two psychic "structures" (the dream-I here and the bull there) are supposed to come together (furthermore, that they represent from the outset nothing but the two [perhaps neurotically] dissociated halves of the whole). The very aim of such a dream is the union of opposites.

Having spoken of "dissociated halves of the whole," I want to expand this point a bit. Both structures, the dream-I and the Other (the non-I, here the bull), are soul. The soul is, in general, the unity of itself and its Other. It *is* this living tension. Within itself it posits itself and its own Other; it unfolds itself into the opposition of itself and its opposite and then lets these two loose upon each other. This is the soul drama produced by it and depicted as the dream action. As such "the soul" is also the unity of itself and the (ego-) resistance to itself. It is in itself different, in itself contradictory. Or: It is Contradiction.

Now the other problematic and mistaken reaction to such a dream would be to think that the dream-I's defensive reaction, his flight from the bull, would be bad because in this way the deeper purpose that the soul has with this dream would be frustrated. If the dreamer escapes, the intended and necessary union would not take place.

But the dialectic of the dream-I's flight from the threatening Other is such that the flight is—against appearances—the very way the persecuting Other in fact reaches, and comes home to, the dream-I. The successful flight from the danger *is* the success of the endangering Other in getting to the ego!

How so? Here we need to remember that with dreams we are in the land of the soul and thus in the realm of logical negativity and not in empirical reality, which is the realm of positivity. In empirical reality the persecutor only catches up with the person running away if he can factually grasp him, i.e., if the catching up is itself a *positive* catching up. In the "crazy" land of the soul, however, its own Other can take hold of the dream-I even if it does not literally, positively "get" it. The psyche does not need physical violence to reach its goal of taking hold of someone. It can reach this goal through the very opposite of this goal; the persecution can be successful precisely if, and when, it fails. We spoke already about the soul's *via negativa*.

How is this to be understood in our case? The answer is that in the dream-I's panic and its running away in utter anxiety, the very content that it runs away from makes itself present in its mind with utmost intensity and reality (power of conviction). The more the dream-I runs in terror and tries to escape, the more the *reality* of "bull" inscribes itself into its consciousness. So the result is that whereas in the beginning the consciousness of the dream-I was an innocent one, completely ignorant of "the bull" and what it stands for, because the bull reality had systematically been excluded from consciousness, now consciousness has indeed experienced the bull and knows from its own prolonged penetrating experience at least this much, that it is a pressing reality.

It is psychologically crucial that this knowledge is not a merely intellectual, theoretical one. Through the intensive affect of fear and through the prolonged flight in absolute fear it went under his skin, into his guts.

Here again it is also important to realize that it is not so much the dream-I that needs to integrate the "bull" reality. It is much more essential that, conversely, the "bull" reality or, generally speaking, the Other, interiorizes *itself*, inscribes *itself* into the dream-I, of its own accord. No egoic "ought-to" or "should." It is the soul's business to impress itself upon consciousness, not our business to realize soul needs in ourselves, and not the patient's business to "open himself to the bull reality." Plotinus is supposed to have said when asked why he did not go to the sacrifices: "They (the gods) have to come to me, not I to them."

There are some therapists who ask the patient to imagine better dream endings or better alternatives to the dream-I's behavior in the dream. I think this is not at all a good idea. The dream is a self. We should not prescribe to it how it should be. What counts psychologically is the real self-movement, the actual self-development of the images, the real process, not our ideas and ideals of how it should be. No manipulative actions. Even one's silent mere *wishing* for a more hopeful ending would have a manipulative character. What had Jung said? "What the dream, which is not manufactured by us, says is *just so*. Say it again as well as you can" (*Letters 2*, p. 591, to Herbert Read, 2 September 1960).

Patients who have read some psychology books sometimes say, when in therapy a dream is being discussed in which the dream-I ran away from the persecutor: "The dream-I should have turned around and talked with the aggressor." This is not a good idea. The dreamer or patient, too, should learn to let the dream be exactly the way it was. There should not be any "shoulds." The dreamer should *see* what is problematic in the dream, maybe feel the pain that seeing it causes, but he should not react with a moralistic or correctional attitude. The dream-I "*should not*" have behaved better. We must not wish that anything "should" be different in the dream, because then we would detract from and depotentiate the *reality*, *integrity* (wholeness) and *perfection* (!) of the dream. We would prevent *it* from continuing the soul's own movement. We would, through our moralistic and egoic interference, arrest the self-movement, self-transformation of the images in the soul.

As I explained earlier, our ego wishes for improvement or correction of, e.g., painful images are therapeutically completely inappropriate. Our job is to release the dream into its being-so, into its indeed having been so and precisely into its being perfect the way it is, *including* all the possible faults in it (the anxiety and pain causing images, the defenses of the dream-I, the wretched ending without solution, etc.). This releasing the dream into its actual having been so is the release of the dream into its truth.

At any rate, we have seen that we have to respect the defensive reaction in a dream not only because it is part of the dream, but also because it is not always what it seems to be: thwarting the dream purpose can at times precisely be one possible way the dream purpose finds its fulfillment. The union of opposites does in such a case take place; however, not on the superficial *imaginal* (or content) level, but on the fundamentally deeper level of *thought*. To be able to *see* a union in the dream, the imagination would need an image that actually portrays the successful happening of the union. The union would have to happen explicitly, spelled out, as literal *semantic content* of the dream; the imagination cannot possibly see failure of union as the very form of the realization of union, in other words, as something that occurs invisibly in the background, "behind the impressions" created by the semantic content, "behind the scenes," "behind the thin veil of actual facts" shown on the imaginal level in the dream. It cannot see this because it has no eyes for the *syntax* or *logical form* of the dream.

Only with the syntax or logical form have we entered the home territory of soul. What the present discussion of dreams about the dream-I's successful escape from a persecuting force taught us is one example for the general insight that in psychology we must not get stuck in the imagining/imaginal mode. The latter is too crude, too literal.[37] In itself the soul is much more subtle. If psychology in the strict sense means crossing over (or *having* crossed over) to the other side of the river separating the ego's ordinary day-world and the land of soul, then it also means our crossing over from the semantic to the syntactical: to the dimension of (on principle unimaginable) logical form or relation. It can only be *thought*, *comprehended*, not depicted or *vorgestellt*, represented. That is to say, it is no longer object or content of consciousness, no longer somehow still "out there," in front of consciousness, but happens exclusively in the interiority of the mind itself. And it no longer has the form of substance, of a "something," but it *is* only to the extent that it is as consciousness's actual own *performance* of the act of thinking the respective thought inherent in, e.g., a dream image. A doing, a process.[38] Pure actuosity.

6. Opposition as the dream-I's malgré lui doing the other's bidding

The second special aspect of how the internal oppositional tension within many dreams can present itself is that the other, non-ego tendency makes itself felt through the actions of the dream-I itself. Sometimes, the dream-I does something unwittingly, innocently, which is actually counter to the dream-I's own tendency. Without need it opens, e.g., a forbidden chamber and thereby is confronted with what it most fears or wants to avoid. Here, the Other that is behind the closed door to the hidden chamber *is already working within* the ego that stands before the door and is driving it to open it. In this way the dream-I brings about something that is the opposite of what it wants. It does voluntarily, but unwittingly, "the soul's" bidding. Unawares, it is already "the soul's" instrument for advancing the purposes of the ego's Other. There are many examples for this possibility. The dream-I accidentally knocks against a wall with the result that it collapses and gives the view free to some horrible thing, etc.

Whereas in the first type of cases (persecution) the dream-I and the Other were logically radically separated as opponents and the dream-I wanted to escape, here the dialectic has come much closer to the dream-I, inasmuch as the Other has already indirectly taken hold of it and forces it from within itself, yet without its own knowing, to do something that brings about the confrontation with the Other. Instead of a running away, we have here an unwitting move on the part of the dream-I precisely in the direction of the Other. Although not about contra-intentional effects of actions performed by the dream-I itself, all dreams in which the dream-I discovers in some unlikely place a lonely neglected or wounded or dying baby, vagrant, or animal could perhaps also be grouped under this heading, as attenuated examples of this category. There would be no attack or persecution, no literal threat; the oppositional tension would only appear as a shocking sight.

The unmitigated version of the dream motif of the dream-I's bringing about the opposite of what is intended is a bit similar to what we hear about how in ancient times oracles worked in Greece. In most, maybe all, reports about oracles the person who received the oracle faithfully obeyed what the oracle said needed to be done in order to avoid a calamity or to reach a desired goal; but precisely through this faithful behavior he brought about the very calamity that he wanted to avoid. It is not the same as what I just explained about the innocent actions on the part of the dream-I, but the one aspect that is similar is that the fulfillment of the psychic Other comes about through the ego's own action, an action that was precisely intended to work in the opposite direction.

Another phenomenon to be mentioned here is what Freud called *Fehlleistung*, Freudian slips. Here, too, something is done by the person himself that is contrary to his intentions. The difference is, however, that the *Fehlleistung* is not intended by the ego, whereas the dream-I fully wants to open the forbidden chamber or to obey the oracle.

7. Opposition as antithetical meaning of one and the same

The third special possibility of the interaction between the two opposite tendencies to be found in many dreams is what I call the *Gegensinn* (antithetical or oppositional meaning) of dream motifs, a wording that I modeled after the *title* (not the ideational content) of Freud's paper "Über den Gegensinn der Urworte" (1910, "The Antithetical Meaning of Primal Words"), based on an 1884 essay with the same title by the philologist Carl Abel. I will explain what I mean with the help of a dream.

> I am one of the workers in an experimental laboratory where remedies or repellents (*Abwehrmittel*) against poison gas are being developed. We, the workers, agree to test the substance. We are locked into the laboratory and the gas is discharged into it. We have a bit of an uneasy feeling; however, it is routine, we continue with our work. When the time for opening the door comes, it continues to remain closed. Nervousness. I become restless because I want to respond to an invitation. There is a rumor that there have been alterations in some people. But there is no clear information. A mood of anxiety. But then the door opened.

The motif of poison gas in this dream can serve as an illustration of the *Gegensinn* of a dream motif. In this motif, one and the same motif, two opposite, enantiodromic tendencies come together. In contrast to what we mean by enantiodromia in Jung's sense or what Hegel's statement that everything moves into its opposite is about, I do not have here in mind a movement from a first direction into the opposite direction. Rather, the one motif of poison gas has both meanings at once, it expresses both tendencies simultaneously. And the difference between the two is merely one of *interpretation*. The first meaning or tendency is the result of how the dream-I interprets the phenomenon or what happens, while the other tendency is the result of the soul view.

- There are, first of all, the point of view and the interests of the dream-I (as well as of the everyday mind, our pragmatic orientation and our will for survival). The dream-I is usually interested in preserving itself, which psychologically means preserving or rescuing and conserving its old habitual *form* of consciousness or attitude or sense of identity (self-definition). From this point of view the substance that is discharged into the laboratory is poisonous, something absolutely terrible. The *name* "poison gas" for this substance comes from the perspective of the dream-I. Because this substance is so terrible there has to be a prophylactic or repellent against it, and the fact that the dream-I works in a laboratory whose only purpose is to develop such a pharmaceutical against the effects of this substance, shows that the dream-I is here totally enwrapped in a defensive stance against a danger that is vaguely expected as a possibility, but not yet acute. The consciousness of the dream-I is very innocent. This shows in two features. Although it already has the clear notion of "poison" and "poison gas," it does not seem to realize *what* it is that it has let itself in for. It agrees to the test voluntarily and treats it as mere routine. The work at this laboratory is not done with any sense of impending threat or urgency. It is just a job like one in the post office or some other bureau. The second feature displaying an amazing innocence is that after all that happened, the idea is still that the dream-I should go to an evening appointment. Totally harmless.
- Whereas from the point of view of the ego the substance at stake here is poison gas, we can suspect behind this façade and from the soul perspective that actually what is meant is an active substance that is supposed to bring about a psychological transformation, hinted at later in the dream by the phrase "alterations in some people." It is not just something destructive, absolutely evil, but something that aims for a psychological change and a kind of alchemical process of, let's say *putrefactio, mortificatio, fermentatio, corruptio*.

Similarly, the dream-I interprets the purpose of the laboratory as the development of an *Abwehrmittel*, lit. "means of defense." It is not able to understand that from the point of view of "the soul" what is called laboratory is in truth a place of initiation or transformation, a kind of alchemical retort.

The point that I want to make here is that often one and the same dream motif has one meaning from the point of view of the ego and this point of view determines the choice of words and the description of the phenomenon, while underneath this obvious description and naming the psychological mind can sense the opposite meaning. Here: Poison vs. medicine (something to promote healing and transformation). This is a place where we can repeat again the statement that was made by Jung in the context of the topic of dream and transference, but applies to our present context just as well:

> we see that behind the impressions of the daily life—behind the scenes—another picture looms up, covered by a thin veil of actual facts. In order to understand dreams, we must learn to think like that. We should not judge dreams from realities because in the long run that leads nowhere.

Another time Jung said in another context something that may also be relevant here. Having talked about one's having at times to make certain statements "without objective reasons" that are nevertheless justified psychodynamically, and about the usual dismissal of such statements as merely "subjective" and a "purely personal matter," he says:

> But that is to commit the mistake of failing to distinguish [NB the psychological difference!] whether the statement really proceeds only from an isolated subject, and is prompted by exclusively personal motives, or whether it occurs generally and springs from a collectively present dynamic pattern. … [I]t is not the personal human being who is making the statement, but the archetype speaking through him.
>
> (*MDR* p. 352)

We should not sight unseen take over the (dream-internal!) interpretation of the dream-I. Often patients say in such a situation: "but the dream says poison gas. So it *is* bad." But to stick to the image does not mean to stick to (and thus fall for) the surface and egoic version of it, the literal aspect of the semantic image.

8. Opposition as impugning the known truth

To really stick to the image means to penetrate to its truth, i.e., to the *Concept* that it embodies and that "looms up, covered behind a thin veil of actual facts." Again, I want to illustrate this point with a dream example. The first sentence of a dream is: "During a therapy session I am sitting there, wrapped in a woollen blanket." I will not quote and go into the whole dream, since I want to demonstrate only one single point. In my dream seminars we usually begin discussing the dreams by starting with the first few words of the first sentence and thinking about them alone, before going on to the second phrase. When this first sentence was discussed in a dream seminar, one of the participants said that maybe the patient still *needed* such a protection. Maybe the female patient still feels without protection, helpless, is not yet strong enough to open herself to the therapist. She still needs to enclose herself in a blanket and to stay on her own. Maybe it would be expecting too much of her that she could already open herself to the analyst ...

This suggestion is again a perfect example of the fallacy of "fake (or fictitious) possibilities" discussed earlier. It talks about possibilities that might, of course, indeed exist outside the dream, in external reality, namely in the dreamer, in the patient as factually existing human being. But they do not exist in the dream and for the dream-I. The dream-I is a fantasy figure, and what is possible for a fantasy figure is strictly limited by what is *real* and *explicit* in the fantasy story, that is, in our case in the dream. As far as psychological dream interpretation is concerned, the confounding of the dream-I with the real patient is a fatal flaw. It is not only that with this view one leaves the dream while at the same time pretending to interpret the dream; one also *fraternizes with the patient's neurosis*, falls for the patient's neurotic way of thinking. One's arguing this way is motivated by the ego wish (in the psychologist) to excuse the dream-I and thus shows that one has not yet arrived in soul country, in psychology, but is still dwelling in the realm of the human-all-too-human.

So let's leave the patient or dreamer aside and go back into the dream and stick to the image. The first sentence begins with the idea, "during a therapy session." We have to take this phrase at its word. What it says and implies—namely, its *Begriff* (concept, notion), see the chapter "Concepts cloaked in sensible shapes"—must be binding for us as psychologists. In its interpretations, psychology inevitably subscribes to a *methodological* (not ontological, metaphysical) "concept realism" in the sense of the medieval universals controversy, to an essentialism. This means it must not be nominalistic. In this sense, the first phrase of this dream must not be taken as a superficial statement, as it might be in empirical reality. In empirical reality "during my therapy session" could mean no more than the time of my factual, physical presence there. My factual presence there would be compatible just as well with my eager participation in the therapeutic process as with my refusal to it, or with my having fallen asleep on the therapeutic couch, etc. But as a dream image, "during the therapy session" means that I am truly *in* my therapy, that the reality of what therapy is has taken hold of me and that I therefore fully behave and feel accordingly. To truly *be* in therapy means to feel as patient and in need of and wanting analysis, therapy, help; it means to have accepted the therapeutic setting and the therapist as that person with whom I want to work, to whom I want to entrust myself and reveal myself; it means to let myself in for the therapeutic relationship. It means further to know that to be in therapy in itself means to be in a *temenos*, a safe and protected space, where one precisely does not need an additional literal blanket that warms and protects one; to know that there is no need to encapsulate or cocoon oneself and to shield oneself from the analyst, simply because the analytical situation and the therapeutic relationship *are* in themselves psychic warmth and security. The true, i.e., *psychic* "woollen blanket" (in contrast to it as a mere name, a nominalistic word[39]) consists in nothing else but in one's releasing oneself and abandoning oneself into the consulting room and the therapeutic relationship.

If all this is not true for me, then I am not really in my therapy session at all. So the first sentence of this dream shows a neurotic self-contradiction. What in the first few words is asserted ("during my therapy session") is denied by the rest of the sentence. By feeling the need to enwrap and cocoon herself in a blanket the dream-I shows that she has not really, namely psychologically, entered the therapy room. She is still outside, alone with herself and keeps the analyst outside of herself. The threshold to the therapy room has not really been crossed by the dream-I, although the first three words indicate that it has been crossed.

So we have to *think* what the words and images in the dream really say. We must not confuse dream images with references to external empirical realities of daily life, where "during the therapy session" would just be an indication of a time period and a location where the most diverse conditions might prevail. The dream image has to be taken as the Concept that it represents. If the dream speaks of the therapy session, then this is the image of therapy that is posited within the dream, *within psychic reality,* and therefore the image of its concept, of what therapy in truth *is as* the soul's own process! It does not refer to the banality of external life or empirical facts.

Reality is characterized by the fact that name (or title) and true nature of the person or thing so named are two different things. They *may* more or less coincide, but always differ, at least somewhat and often very much so. But in dreams and poetic works or novels name and truth are identical because they are Concepts, essences, and reveal what the elements in truth *are*. They are not mere *names* as for nominalistic understanding.

To excuse the dream-I's cocooning herself in the blanket by saying she may still have too weak an ego, is therefore therapeutically completely wrong. A dream-external condition or possibility is *smuggled* into the dream. She could not dream the idea of "During my therapy session" if she were not already truly in therapy. Her psyche is already ready to be in therapy. This is her truth. But the dream-I reserves itself for neurotic reasons. The dream-I contra-factually *plays* the weak ego that *cannot* trust, the ego that *demonstrates* helplessness and being poor and in need of a blanket, and thus pampers itself. She neurotically indulges in the simulation of being in need. If she really were too weak and cold to psychologically enter the therapeutic relationship, the dream would not put her into a therapeutic situation. The dream would show the dream-I in a lonely, cold, helpless situation. This is one aspect. A second aspect is that if she really were cold and afraid, she would not be wrapped in, indeed would not even *have* a woolen blanket. A psychic *need* never shows in *having* what satisfies the need. The blanket shows that she wants to, and has the means, to take care of herself and does not *want* to enter the therapeutic relationship, and that she only pretends to be in therapy but, sadly, is *incapable* of opening herself to her therapist. If we as analysts fall for this self-presentation of the dream-I, we become accomplices of a neurotic idea and behavior.

The most important point here is that all dream images have to be taken as psychic images, as poetic inventions of the dream and we must not resort to the trick of taking *some* problematic images of the dream as factual empirical conditions while *others* are supposed to be dream symbols. Remember: the dream has nothing outside of itself. The psychological difference!

I called this type of oppositional structure "impugning the known truth." This phrase (originally Latin: *impugnatio veritatis agnitae*) comes from the Church Fathers (and later Christian theology) and refers to one form of the "sin against the Holy Ghost," the eternal or unforgivable sin. For us as psychologists, the phrase and idea needs to be wrested from the religious context and from all sense of "sin" so that it can be taken simply in its literal meaning as a description of a structure. As such, it can accurately describe the core of what makes neurosis neurotic. Neurosis is at bottom the obstinate refusal to let a truth that has already become real *be* true and to replace it by another alleged or fake truth. Only this last of our four types of oppositional structures is neurotic. The defensive reaction to "the Other," the flight from it, although psychologically definitively problematic, has nothing neurotic about it, maybe even not anything pathological, since it is a quite normal, indeed, "healthy" reaction. Why should one not seek protection from an attack? The second and the third types betray merely different forms of unconsciousness, which is also nothing neurotic. But the last form shows that the actually prevailing truth is actively denied.

Psychic and biological processes in dreams

A boy in his late teens dreamed:

> When I wanted to go down a descending escalator, I got caught up in it. First my feet got entangled in it and then one part of my body after the other was swallowed by it until finally only my head still stuck out. There was no feeling of pain. I woke up and felt sick.

At first glance we might think that this dream is another example of "the dream-I and the Other," here represented by the escalator. But on second thought we realize that this is by no means the case. There is no encounter of or confrontation with an Other, no vis-à-vis. The escalator is not like an enemy who wants to attack or like a tiger or dragon ready to devour the dream-I. This dream does not have the purpose of making the dream-I or the dreamer aware of hitherto repressed or unconscious aspects of psychological reality or of the dreamer's own personality, thereby aiming at an expansion of consciousness and ultimately at an integration of what appeared as the Other into the structure of consciousness. Normally, the experience of the Other in a dream, as frightful as it may appear to the dream-I, is nevertheless therapeutic. Here, the escalator is not an active agent at all. It is not approaching the dream-I from outside, not trying to get at it. Rather, it is clearly the dream-I itself that gets itself entangled in it. So we see ourselves forced to leave any idea of a relation between two (the dream-I and its own Other) behind and comprehend this dream as depicting exclusively a process within the self of the dream-I. There is only one single dream figure, the dream-I, and nobody or nothing else. The whole action in the dream remains dream-I-*internal*.

The escalator, a *descending* escalator at that, visualizes the dream-I's own descent, its going-under, its disappearance within itself. Again, when we hear "descent" we might at first glance be inclined to view this theme along the habitual patterns of psychological interpretation such as in terms of the mythological motif of a descent into the underworld, and when we hear of its "going-under" perhaps in terms of the alchemical processes of nigredo and fermenting corruption, decomposition, *mortificatio*. But again we have to leave such ideas behind. Both the mythological and the alchemical motifs refer in different ways to the psychological necessity of the dissolution of the *unio naturalis*, to the "death of the ego." These images and topics are, it is true, concerned with the negation or destruction of the ego-personality, the habitual "civilian man." The "crucifixion of the ego" (*CW* 9ii § 79), "the passion of the ego: the ordinary, empirical man," the "violence done to him by the self" (*CW* 11 § 233) and "the defeat for the ego" (*CW* 14 § 778) are indispensable for the entrance into the land of soul. Soul *is* absolute negativity; it has, as Hillman insisted, a "special *relation with death*."[40] But in all such cases this negation is *psychological* negation, the negation of the ego is its *logical* death, a *mortificatio* of the logical *form* or *structure* of conventional consciousness. It is in the service of soul-making, of the alchemical *opus*, of initiation (or, in Jung's terms, of individuation, the becoming of self).

The negation that happens in the present dream through the dream-I's being piece by piece absorbed by the escalator seems, by contrast, to wish to express the literal extinction of the personality. It is not a dream of a psychological event or change, but of a *psychic* disintegration.[41] The personality is completely disintegrated into the escalator, with only the head remaining, as a rest-consciousness just enough to still be *aware*[42] of the loss it suffered. It is a *descent from the psychological to the psychic level*, a reduction to a merely functional plane. The escalator does not lead the dream-I downwards, into the depth of soul. Inasmuch as the dream-I gets stuck in the escalator, it is not taken anywhere, but has become part of the instrument itself that was supposed to lead to some goal in the depth. The escalator as machine does not move anywhere. Its movement is one that forever stays on the spot. It is the endless mechanical repetition of a circular movement simultaneously down in the front and up again in the back, an eternal recurrence like in biological life that of inhaling and exhaling, eating and excreting or like the daily routines of getting dressed in the morning and getting undressed at night. As long as the escalator or the routines mentioned are used by someone for a higher purpose, they are meaningful. The moment the escalator ceases to be a means to an end and becomes something in its own right, it is utterly meaningless.

This dream image presents the threat of a possible malignant development. The very personhood of the personality of the dreamer is shown to be endangered. In this dream the soul does not try to invite, lure, seduce the dreamer into itself, nor does it wish to confront the consciousness of the dreamer with itself as his own inner Other, or expose and subject it to some psychologically necessary ordeal. On the contrary, this dream is not the soul's speaking about itself at all. What is expressed in the dream is much rather a precarious condition of the biological organism on the verge of ceasing to be the support system of *human* existence as consciousness and soul and instead turning into its own end.

It makes sense that there is no feeling of pain in the dream. The loss of personality or consciousness, as terrible as it is, is in itself not painful. It is just a reduction. But for the consciousness of the dreamer outside the dream, for the still existing personality, the threat of this loss is sickening. That the dreamer upon waking reacts to this dream with feeling sick is the only prospective sign in this dream report.

The dream, I said, shows a possible malignant development. The possibility must not turn into a reality. But such a dream serves as warning to the therapist that a psychiatric problem is involved.

I leave now the discussion of the dream presented, by means of which I introduced the idea that certain dreams may not be psychological but are indications of purely psychic dangers, and will only touch briefly on a related problem. Jung was of the opinion that in some cases dreams, far from representing the soul's speaking, even depict organic, physical disorders and not only psychic conditions. We must expect, he said (*CW* 18 § 136), "to find dreams which are more on the physiological side than on the psychological..." A particular dream was for him even "very clearly a representation of an organic disorder. ... I have had other cases, for instance a very doubtful case of progressive muscular atrophy in a young girl." Whereas a colleague thought this case might be one of hysteria, Jung was solely on the basis of dreams convinced that it was an organic disease, a diagnosis that was finally proved correct.

Jung did not give any reasons for his judgment, explaining that the criteria by which he judges such dreams are too special and too difficult and obscure to explain.

> I should have to give you a course of about four semesters about symbology first so that you could appreciate what I said. / That is the great trouble: there is such a gap between what is usually known of these things and what I have worked on all these years.
>
> (*ibid.* § 138 f.)

I find the idea that it might be possible to see from certain dream images that an organic illness (and possibly even what specific type of illness) is reflected in them very interesting. Unfortunately, Jung leaves us in the lurch concerning the basis for his judgement. I would still need the course of four semesters about symbology from him. I do have criteria for deciding whether certain dream images are indicative of psychic problems (as in the case of the dream discussed in this chapter). But I do not have criteria that would allow me to determine that dream symbols such as the draining of a pond and the appearance of an extinct animal, a mastadon—these are the ones in the dream referred to in the referenced discussion of Jung's 2nd *Tavistock Lecture*[43]—definitely represent a physical illness and should not be given a psychological interpretation. And so I mention this possibility only without further comment.

Semantic content versus syntactic structure

In the previous chapter we were dealing with the topic of dream images or symbols that amount to a clear indication of psychic (in contrast to psychological) problems or possibly even of organic diseases. In these dreams it was the semantic content, the dream image itself, that revealed the threatening condition. But there are sometimes dreams that seem to indicate either a fundamental structural problem of the personality such as the absence of a unity and firmness of personality (a generally reliable ego-structure) or the danger, for an existing personality, of being overwhelmed by unconscious contents, in other words, of a prevailing or impending psychosis, where this judgment does not suggest itself on basis of the *content* of the particular dream symbols. In order to approach that topic, I first need to introduce an extremely important, but often neglected general distinction, the form distinction between the *semantic* and the *syntactic* or structural aspects of dreams.

Most dreams seem to focus on the semantic, or substantial contents, i.e., on figures, actions, events, things, relations between the dream-I and the "other," etc. This includes dreams with powerful symbolism and with archetypal or mythological motifs. All the things and persons and happenings appear in or take place in a given, but only implicit "world," ordered sphere, spatial realm. The "world" is only implicit because the dream is concerned with *what* is to be seen in this world, not with wherein all this takes place. "The world" is tacitly presupposed.

In other dreams there are no personal figures or things, but only abstract structures, maybe geometric forms such as a triangle, a square, a circle, a pyramid, etc., or more concrete forms, such as a building, but not a building as a place of action or as the home of people, but only as a complex architectural structure. The interest of the dream seems to be exclusively in the design, the number of stories, halls, and rooms, the layout of different wings. Or the points of the compass, the basic orientation in the universe (north, south, east, west) may be the topic of the dream. What is emphasized in such cases is a definite order, a framework, the rational plan, arrangement, pattern. These are dreams whose *semantic* content is the *syntactic* form or *structural* order, or the other way around: dreams *about* syntactic form, in which, however, this *form* is presented as semantic content.

What is psychologically most important, especially with respect to the question of whether a dream shows an impending psychosis or a serious structural deficit of personality, a lack of so-called ego-formation, is the reverse: the *syntactic form* of the semantic content of a dream. A dream with overwhelming archetypal, numinous content does not have to point to the danger of psychosis. Of course, archetypal ideas, numinous experience, may always invite an inflation of consciousness. This is a possibility. But the overwhelming power of an archetypal motif does not by itself mean that an inflation will happen. Its inflating effect is dependent on other factors outside the dream (just as conversely consciousness can become inflated by ideas that come from outside, collective ideas in society of a philosophical, political, or religious nature). Dream images may *semantically* be utterly weird, showing something totally unrealistic and even, compared with ordinary world experience, impossible, they may be bizarre, disturbing, threatening, and yet these images may in themselves have clear contours and in their form an inner stability and consistency. In literature we find similar examples; I mention only Franz Kafka's *The Metamorphosis*, which tells an absolutely bizarre and unrealistic story in a very realistic, rational style of presentation. The semantic contents are absolutely weird, appear to be delusional, but the logical framework, the "order of the world" *in which* they appear, is preserved undamaged. When this is the case in dreams, one need not worry about a coming psychosis. The mind that sees these dream images, that is to say, the syntax or logical form *of the mind*, is not shattered. It is fully oriented, still possesses the strength to assemble what it perceives into one consistent order, no matter how odd and counternatural, indeed "crazy" it may be. It has a center point that organizes the *logical field* into which its experienced contents are placed.

There may also be the opposite case. This case does not even need particularly weird contents. The things and events seen in the dream could also be relatively ordinary. But what is at any rate not ordinary is that what is seen is seen as if in a shattered mirror. The individual images are in themselves refracted; their internal unity and coherence has disappeared. Their syntactic form thus strikes one as really uncanny, very disconcerting. Instead of one organizing center for the whole experience, the framework has fallen apart into so many bits, each with its own point of origin and direction. I need to add that the "shattered framework" quality does not only apply to the sequence of images or scenes in a dream, but may also already appear in each individual dream image. The mind has no longer the power to perceive an image as an in-itself consistent whole. It no longer exists as the one stable center point, a firm organizing center that stays the same even if it should in the course of time move around to new locations in space, which makes such a dream atmospherically eerie (even in cases where the individual contents seem to be ordinary and familiar).

An impending psychosis must not always and exclusively reveal itself through the syntax of dream. A latent psychosis may, of course, also show in *semantic* dream images. Jung reports an example in his *Memories* (p. 135). It is a long dream. The most conclusive element in it is the final scene where the dreamer discovered in the middle of a large, empty room "an idiot child of about two years old. It was sitting on a chamber pot and had smeared itself with feces." Not only the dreamer awoke at that moment "with a cry, in a state of panic," but Jung, too, became scared when he heard this dream. "I must say I sweated as I tried to lead him out of that dream. I had to represent it to him as something quite innocuous, and gloss over all the perilous details."

Dreams showing an existing psychosis or the threat of a latent psychosis (and thus of the possibility of a *dissolution* of the ego-personality) must be distinguished from dreams in the case of serious structural personality disorders where there does not seem to be a coherent ego-personality from the outset. In dreams of the latter type, dreams of "persons who are incapable of neurosis" (*MDR* p. 352), the syntactic incoherence, as the reflection of *the general, "normal" structure of the dreamer's personality* (i.e., the *absence* of a unified ego-personality), may feel a bit weird, but generally not uncanny. These dreams rather strike one as boring, empty, pointless. Nothing really develops and makes sense. Maybe important things happen in the dream, but without leading anywhere, let alone to any resolution, or the dream-figures do not at all interact with each other, the dream-I does not react to what happens nor feel involved in it or addressed by it. Complete disconnection.[44] Such dreams are not likely to cause the therapist acutely to get into a sweat, as in the case of a latent psychosis, because the pathological condition is not threatening to break out, but is the "normal" state. They rather make the therapist feel helpless.

In the case of dreams in which the syntax is the crucial aspect, it often requires a certain amount of special psychological sensibility and *intelligence du cœur* to prevent the Jungian therapist interested in images and symbols from being lured into the semantic contents of the dreams, as if *they* needed his attention, and instead to enable him to become fully aware of the psychological significance of the syntactic dimension.

Notes

1. I mention only "An Inquiry into Image" (in *Spring 1977* and *Spring 1978*) and "Image-Sense" (in *Spring 1979*). In addition, his book on dreams, *The Dream and the Underworld*, New York et al. (Harper & Row) 1979, is, of course, highly relevant.
2. In a letter Jung once spelled out the demands he made on an analyst in training. "Above all, I demand knowledge of clinical psychiatry and of organic nervous diseases. Secondly a training analysis, 3. a certain amount of philosophical education, 4. study of primitive psychology, 5. of comparative religion, 6. of mythology, 7. of analytical psychology, beginning with knowledge of the diagnostic association technique, the technique of interpreting dreams and fantasies, 8. training of one's own personality, i.e., development and differentiation of functions which are in need of education. These are the demands I put to a pupil. Naturally there are only a few people who can fulfil them, but I have long ago given up producing manufactured articles. Above all, I don't want to evoke the impression that I think psychotherapy is intellectual child's play, and I always take pains to make it clear to people that real knowledge of the human psyche requires not only a vast amount of learning but a differentiated personality. In the last resort the psyche cannot be handled with any one technique, and in psychotherapy it is

just the psyche we are dealing with and not with any old mechanism that can be got at with equally mechanistic methods. One should therefore avoid giving the impression that psychotherapy is an easy technique" (*Letters 1*, p. 188, 22 March 1935, to Otto Körner). Some of the demands still betray the early "scientific" Jung for whom psychology had not yet really come home to itself. Nevertheless, the emphasis on substantial knowledge (I highlight: philosophical education, the study of ethnology, comparative religion, and mythology) and his rejection of the idea of psychotherapy as "intellectual child's play" are all too clear, as is his unabashed insistence that psychology is only for the few.

3. Of course, the example of the violinist I used is in some points not fully comparable to the situation in psychotherapy. In the case of the musician there are two systems or levels, the mental and the physical (muscular and nervous) systems. The knowledge about where and how to place and move the fingers becomes a *habit* through unending physical practice; it is now located "in the fingers" and no longer in the mind, which thereby is freed to concentrate on the non-technical aspect of the musicality of the music piece. The knowledge of the therapist has no fundamentally other system to disappear in. The freeing of consciousness of its psychological knowledge must take place in the same system, in consciousness itself. Here the situation is more like the following: If we are full of an experience or idea and want to share it with a friend, we usually do not need to think of how to express it in words and are pretty much oblivious of our sentences. We are completely given over to *what* we want to tell the friend, and the words and sentences take simply care of themselves underneath "the radar" of our conscious involvement. "For of the abundance of the heart his mouth speaketh."

4. The English *Letters* translate, "in a circumambulatory fashion," thereby losing the decisive active *verbal* sense of Jung's "*zirkumambulierend*" (lit., "circumambulatingly").

5. Lothar Schäfer, *Das Bacon-Projekt. Von der Erkenntnis, Nutzung und Schonung der Natur*, Frankfurt am Main (Suhrkamp) 1993.

6. The Latin word from which "aggressive" is derived has the basic etymological meaning "to step, walk toward," "to approach." Aggression with an inimical or violent intent is not necessarily implied. The Baconian epistemic approach nevertheless happens in the spirit of conquest.

7. For the patient, the dream is psychically his own dream. But even by circumambulating it the patient's dream will of course *not psychically* become the therapist's own.

8. The same applies to "alchemical retort" and veritable *prima materia*: it is the alchemical vessel that turns substances into a true prime matter, and only if the matter in the vessel is truly a *prima materia* can the vessel become an alchemical one.

9. "Personal relation" must not be misunderstood in terms of the modern romantic sentimental attitude to nature, which is only the technical apprehension's own counterpart and just as thoroughly egoic. The personal relation to nature in the sense of alchemy was completely sober, matter-of-fact. It was psychological, i.e., a logical truth, not a psychic feeling.

10. James Hillman, *The Dream and the Underworld*, New York et al. (Harper & Row) 1979, p. 80.

11. Pirmin Stekeler, *Hegels Phänomenologie des Geistes. Ein dialogischer Kommentar*, vol. 1, Hamburg (Meiner) 2014, p. 502.

12. A thorough critique of the concept of compensation as interpretative key to dreams was presented by James Hillman in his book *The Dream and the Underworld*, New York et al. (Harper & Row) 1979, pp. 77 ff.

13. Just compare: "That is why the *lapis*, as *prima materia*, stands at the beginning of the process as well as at the end" (*CW* 9ii § 418).

14. Here we are reminded of Hegel's dictum, "Quite generally, the familiar, just because it is familiar, is not cognitively understood" ["*Das Bekannte überhaupt ist darum, weil es* bekannt *ist, nicht* erkannt."]. Hegel's *Phenomenology of Spirit*, transl. A.V. Miller, Oxford et al. (Oxford Univ. Press) 1977, p. 18. The familiar, the already known (in this sense) is psychologically a trap, make-believe.

15. The word "tautegorical" means "saying the same" in contrast to "allegorical" "saying other." It was introduced by Coleridge as well as by Schelling to indicate that the mythological gods do not mean something else, are not allegories (imaginal representations of concepts), but mean only what they themselves in fact are. They *are* their meaning.

16. The *logic* of consciousness in contrast to the personality.

17. I use the word "tautegorical" here in a different sense from the one above and from Schelling's and Coleridge's usage, namely, for the sameness of what we "say again" concerning dream images, on the one hand, and what the dream images themselves say, on the other.

18. Here again, with Jung's insisting on "tautology," on "saying it again," we see that the logic of sameness and center is what determines Jung's psychological thinking, his attitude to the soul.

19. Joh. W. von Goethe, "Ernst Stiedenroth, Psychologie zur Erklärung der Seelenerscheinungen," in: *Goethes Werke*, Hamb. Ausg. 13, p. 42.

20. James Hillman, *The Dream and the Underworld*, New York et al. (Harper & Row) 1979, pp. 131 f.

21. But even if the doctor in this dream had lived at the lake of Zürich, indeed, even if he had been expressly called "Dr. Jung"—from the standpoint of "the soul" we would nevertheless not be allowed to identify the dream Dr. Jung with the person by the same name in outer reality. The dream Dr. Jung receives his identity and meaning from the characteristics of this dream motif and from the dream as a whole, not the other way around (as if this dream motif were an element inserted into the dream from external factual reality and identical with that Dr. Jung who outside the dream is *familiar* to the dreamer). The same applies to all elements of the first group of dream figures or objects. Although they doubtlessly refer back to daily life as their horizon, what they mean and who they are in the dream has to be learned from how they appear and behave in the dream. They are and remain *dream* figures, the psyche's own property. This whole caution possibly also applies to the dream elements mentioned in the first paragraph of this chapter. Maybe what appears to be only psychic is psychological, after all!

22. I would put the emphasis not so much on a *fear* of the *unexpected and unknown* as rather on a lack of strength, endurance, and courage to keep *persevering* at the unknown and not-understood in order to attempt to, so to speak, hatch it out. What we find here is a *horror vacui*, similar to how people frequently are not able to endure a sudden hush and times of silence. It is so much easier to quickly fill the vacuum of one's not understanding and of the silence with one's own *speaking*, and so satisfying to hear oneself speaking, twittering and tweeting. It is a fear of simply *listening*, a refusal to bear the narcissistic offence of having to shut up.

23. By using free association (or even other not totally free, but subjective associations), one does not only formally move away from the dream images at hand; one also changes the subject or topic of discussion and thereby deserts the dream. Naturally

so, because subjective associations circle around the (human) subject and his personal feeling-toned complexes. One stays within the scope of ego-psychology. Jung: "[…] in the soul the entire content of a life could ultimately be disclosed from any single starting point […]" (*CW* 8 § 454). We can start from any dream motif, indeed, as Jung repeatedly points out, even from any external phenomenon like a sign in a train and begin associating. We would ultimately always end at our own complexes. As far afield as our associations might go, they would center around the ego personality. Free association "always leads back eventually to the emotional thoughts or complexes that are unconsciously captivating the mind. *To get there, we have no need of dreams*" (*CW* 18 § 432, my emphasis).

24. Of course, we must distinguish between the logical, psychological meaning of this "brushing away" and the actual style in which it is performed in the empirical situation in the consulting room. It goes without saying that it requires a tactful way of handling such comments so as not to hurt the feelings of the patient. But in effect such comments need to be depreciated, devalued as irrelevant and ultimately dismissed. The point is to win him over to the non-ego approach to dreams, to make him see its validity and its merits. This is why Jung himself reports his way of showing this disregard having taken the mild form of, "Now let's get back to your dream. What does the *dream* say?" But this softer form of the expression of the therapeutic disregard for the patient's own associations in no way reduces the fact that it amounts to a rejection, dismissal.

25. Here I can refer back to my earlier statement that a psychotherapy in the spirit of Jung is not a "talking cure," not the patient's "chattering on," but a *listening cure* in the sense of both the therapist's and the patient's learning to receive and open themselves up to the soul's speaking. As the quote about Mary as well as the story of the Annunciation to the Blessed Virgin show us, listening as to *receive* in the full sense of the word means in itself to conceive.

26. A few distinctions concerning the types of associations: A frequent type (1) of comments by the patient, e.g., about persons occurring in a dream is what I call *relationship comments*. "He is very nice." "He often insulted me." Here the patient talks about how he or she feels about the other person or the object, or vice versa. Then we have (2) so-called *Tagesreste*, remnants of memories of what happened the day or days before the dream. (3) There is purely factual, *descriptive information*, (a) more precise explanations of how things looked or were in the dream, more details, information about how precisely persons or things looked in the dream, about the atmosphere going along with persons, situations, events. In other words, these are comments about things experienced *in* the dream itself, but not mentioned in the written text. And (b) identifications and descriptions of persons and things that occur in the dream and that the patient knows or has information about, but are not given in the dream text. For example, "the table that we sat at in the dream was exactly like the one that stood in my grandmother's house," "my mother (who occurred in the dream) was always very nervous, full of worries, afraid of conflicts." And finally (4) there are *free associations*. The difference between the three other categories and free associations is that while the former were still intrinsically connected to the particular dream motifs, free associations are not substantially connected, but *only* connected "by association," i.e., by the irrational fact of the contingent *event* of a momentary idea that pops into the mind and randomly goes off to all sorts of other contents.

27. Since such a verdict as "this belief shows a predilection for personalistic psychology" refers to the logic or syntax of a type of thinking it does by no means exclude the

possibility that the critiqued thinking *semantically* makes use of mythological material, the idea of archetypes, of symbols, and that it talks about Jung's idea of the self, etc. Or to put it the other way around: the use of and interest in such material and ideas does not by itself disprove that a given psychological position is an exponent of a thoroughly personalistic stance.

28. I demonstrated this with respect to his already mentioned dream of his father as custodian of sarcophagi and distinguished scholar who led Jung "into the highest presence" (*MDR* pp. 217 ff.). See my "Jung's Millimeter: Feigned Submission – Clandestine Defiance: Jung's Religious Psychology," in: W.G., *"Dreaming the Myth Onwards": C.G. Jung on Christianity and on Hegel. Part 2 of The Flight Into the Unconscious* (= W.G., *Collected English Papers*, vol. 6), New Orleans, LA (Spring Journal Books) 2013, now London and New York (Routledge) 2020, pp. 3–46. I also showed it with respect to a spontaneous fantasy (not a dream) of his, the Basel Cathedral vision (*MDR* pp. 36 ff.), in my "Psychology as Anti-Philosophy: C.G. Jung," in: W.G.: *"The Flight Into The Unconscious. An Analysis of C.G. Jung's Psychology Project* (= W.G., *Collected English Papers*, vol. 5) New Orleans, LA (Spring Journal Books) 2013, pp. 21–65.

29. G.W.F. Hegel, *Phenomenology of Spirit*, tr. by A.V. Miller, Oxford University Press, 1977, p. 41.

30. James Hillman, *The Dream and the Underworld*, New York et al. (Harper & Row) 1979, p. 117.

31. *The Types of the Folktale. A Classification and Bibliography*, by Stith Thompson, Helsinki (FF Communications No. 184), Second edition, 1981, based on Antti Aarne's *Verzeichnis der Märchentypen* (FF Communications No. 3) of 1910 (revised 1928).

32. *The Soul's Logical Life: Towards a Rigorous Notion of Psychology*, Frankfurt am Main, Berlin, Bern, New York, Paris, Wien (Peter Lang) 1998, 5th edition 2019, pp. 119–123.

33. This was nicely discussed by Patricia Berry in her highly recommendable essay, "An Approach to the Dream," in her: *Echo's Subtle Body*, Dallas, Texas (Spring Publications) 1982, pp. 53–79, here esp. p. 59 f.

34. See also P. Berry, *op. cit.*

35. Friedrich Nietzsche, *Die fröhliche Wissenschaft*, Vorspiel "Scherz, List und Rache," # 62 ("Ecce homo"), my translation.

36. This follows indirectly from the point made in Hillman's *The Dream and the Underworld* where he states (p. 80), "… nothing has to be introduced by anyone from anywhere, because the opposite is already present. Each dream has its own fulcrum and balance, compensates itself, is complete as it is."

37. This statement may be surprising since in Hillman's archetypal psychology "imaginal" is precisely the opposite of "literal," which on a first level or as a first preliminary step certainly makes sense, but takes one only into the forecourt of soul. By saying this, I do not attack images as such. I advocate on the contrary a true appreciation of "image," above all the "poetic image" and the dream images, by demanding that it/they be "seen through," i.e., be thought. The merely semantic aspect of the image is not sufficient. Psychology needs to move beyond it to the syntax of the dream image, and only then does it do justice to the image.

38. This also means: something temporal. Remember: The rose "blooms *while (as long as)* it blooms." When the process of actually thinking the dream image is over, we have instantaneously left the land of soul and dropped back into the world of everyday life.

39. In contrast to the antithetical sense of dream motifs, we must speak here of the *equivocation* inherent in dream words or phrases, depending on whether they are understood from the point of view of the ego or that of the soul, from a standpoint on this side of the river or on the other side of the river, the river that is the metaphorical image for the psychological difference.

40. James Hillman, *Re-Visioning Psychology*, New York et al. (Harper & Row) 1975, p. x, and *The Dream and the Underworld*, New York et al. (Harper & Row) 1979.

41. Of course, we could also call it a *psychological* dream event inasmuch as, or to the extent that, the dream image shows the impending *disappearance* of the psychological level as such. The psychological level is, in other words, still present in this dream.

42. On the important distinction between psychic awareness and psychological consciousness see the very last chapter (in Part X) and, above all, Chapter 4 of my *The Historical Emergence of the I*, London, Ontario (Dusk Owl Books) 2020.

43. See *CW* 18 § 135 fn. 15.

44. Syntactic disconnection in contrast to neurotic dissociation.

Part VI

By way of one example

A dream and its *psychological* interpretation

In this book I have used actual dream examples quite sparingly, and only for the purpose of illustrating one particular point in each case, rather than studying them for their own sake and in their intactness. Now I want to present at least one dream and show what a close reading of a dream strictly from the point of view of soul and its interiorization into itself might look like.

It should not come as a surprise to the reader who has read up to this point that I will not say anything about the person of the dreamer, but solely concentrate on the dream *as a self*. I refer to Jung who in a similar situation said: "I omit personal details intentionally, because they matter so little to me."[1] Personal details would not contribute anything to a deeper understanding. In fact, they would be that "thin veil of actual facts" that tends to cover and obscure the *psychology* depicted in the dream.

The text of the dream reads:

> I relocated. It was a move to another place within Switzerland. Before I knew what I was doing, I said to someone, "The air is warm in the southern part of the country." My cat found a place to lie down in the house and slept there. I remembered the house before I moved in. There was a crack in one of the windowpanes in the house. At the time of moving, I wanted to tell the owner that I did not cause this crack, it had already been there before. But I couldn't tell him that because I couldn't see the owner then, so this kept worrying me.

I relocated. The first sentence gives the theme of the dream as a whole: it is about a move, relocation. The soul wants to live somewhere else and for this reason makes the dream-I relocate. A move is psychologically a fundamental shift to a new standpoint or new level or new logical constitution of consciousness. The wording of the first sentence presents the move not as a plan, but as either already accomplished or as underway. Such a relocation also implies a departure from the former place, the old status of consciousness. It must have been left behind for good. A rupture with a whole previous "epoch" in the soul's life has taken place.

I said that with the first sentence the theme of the dream is given. The scene is set, a task is given. Instead of "theme" and "task" it might be better to say that the first sentence introduces a *concept*, the concept of relocation. What follows in the dream has two functions.

- On the one hand, it has to present the unfolding of this concept, the description of what it involves, the details of its internal logic.
- On the other hand, since the notion of "moving to another place" (*together* with its internal logic) *qua concept* belongs to the sphere of ideas, of ideality, the rest of the dream has to show whether the concept is proved true, "veri-fied," fulfilled. Will the dream action measure up to this concept? Does the move to the new location in fact take place in this dream and take place in its full sense?

It was a move to another place within Switzerland. The move stays within the dream-I's home country. It does not lead abroad, into a completely foreign world. Otherness (new place) and sameness (same country, home country) coincide. If the concept set for the dream is removal, it would not be necessary to mention that it is one "within Switzerland." Where it goes makes no difference for the *concept* of "move" as such. The fact that the dream specifically provides this additional information must have a purpose. It could perhaps be a hint that the intended change is expressly supposed to be understood as an *internal* one ("within the same"). The dream stays, of course, in a spatial fantasy (change of location); this is a consequence of its being presented in imaginal, narrative form. Maybe what on the image level appears as a change of location is actually meant as a psychological transformation: a *form* change, the change of the logical constitution of consciousness, not of a place.

Before I knew what I was doing, I said to someone... The dream-I says something without reflection and without conscious intention. It follows an autonomous impulse coming spontaneously from within it, Jung might have said: coming "from the unconscious." We could also say: from the dream-I's bodily being. At any rate, it is not an ego that is speaking.

The person to whom the dream-I says what it says does not appear as *person*, as a thou, a face. "Someone" is just an anonymous placeholder to indicate that the dream-I's speaking is not a soliloquy, but its sharing a feeling it has with another.

"The air is warm in the southern part of the country." The dream-I is now in the southern part of the country. This must be where it moved to. The body sensation of the warmth there is so strong, so pleasant and surprising that the dream-I cannot help giving voice to it. The dream-I's remark about the warmth of the south suggests that it probably comes from the north, which is so much colder. In the warmth one does not need to protectively bundle up in order to keep one's body warmth within. One can let go, feel free, open up towards the outside. One can feel at ease, relaxed. The south is also associated with sunshine and thus with light. People there are often more outgoing and emotional than in the north, where people are said to be more reserved.

On the body, vital, or instinctual level the dream-I has arrived in the new place, has opened itself up to it.

My cat found a place to lie down in the house and slept there. The cat is nothing but the visualization of the dream-I's body or instinctual side as a separate dream figure, and what the cat is said to be doing is accordingly its full-fledged acceptance of the new house *as* real home. No hesitation, no reserve, and no watchfulness. No need for the cat to get first acquainted with and accustomed to the new place. Its falling asleep shows a total sense of trust and security as well as feeling perfectly at one with its surroundings, so that it can let itself unreservedly sink into the abyssal depth of its own being, forgetting itself and the world. The cat has truly moved into the new home, has, as it were, taken root in it.

I remembered the house before I moved in. But the dream-I itself remains distinct. It does not follow the cat (as its own vital side). It cannot let itself fall into the new situation in total trust and a feeling of oneness with its new surroundings. It can also not give itself over to the Now and, in its dedication to the Now, forget itself and the move: it "remembers." Just as the cat and the "I" remain separate, so with remembering the sense of time is severed into the Now and a "before." We must not literalize this "before" as an actual past in an historical sense. Memory is always an event in the present. It is the appearance *now* of images in the mind. The "before" signifies that what is remembered is not part of present (visible, tangible) reality. As a dream invention, this "before" probably refers to a logical "a priori," in which case the remembering is something like the Platonic *anámnêsis* (the recollection of things known before birth), since we do not learn from the dream that the dream-I had actually seen the new house before. It would be a "fake (or fictitious) possibility," as explained earlier, if we assumed that the dream-I had seen the house during an earlier visit.

Be that as it may, the temporal fantasy of a "former time" is just as due to the imaginal form of the dream as is the spatial fantasy of a change of "location." In reality, what is remembered in the dream does not have its immediate origin or referent in the past. Memory images do not come from sense perception. They have their place in and are produced by the reflecting mind. "I remembered" means that the dream-I has moved to a higher, supra-empirical level of reflection or, the other way around, it means that reflecting consciousness has intruded into the dream-I's unreflected presence in the now of the sensation of the warmth of the south.

The world of memories is a completely inner, subjective world in contrast to external reality. By remembering, the dream-I *dwells in its own self* (whereas in feeling the warmth of the south it was in contact with the real world around it). This staying enclosed within itself makes it impossible for the dream-I to wholeheartedly enter the house out there, to move into it as the cat did by absolutely abandoning itself to sleep, to unconsciousness and just *being*. The dream-I is, as it were, "condemned" to consciousness, to that consciousness that inevitably brings with it the split from "the cat," from simple, unreflected being. This consciousness is what we call self-consciousness.

There was a crack in one of the windowpanes in the house. On the surface of it, this sentence simply tells us what the content of the dream-I's memory is. The crack is not presently seen in the house. It is, as a memory content, an internal image. Again, we must not take this "crack" literally as an empirical fact. Rather, the image of the crack is the separate objectification of the split that comes with self-consciousness. The crack is therefore not a new piece of information or add-itional detail in the dream, but tautologically merely the explication in imaginal form of what self-consciousness amounts to.

In connection with this crack inherent in self-consciousness we may think above all of the time in personal development, approximately at age 10–12, when the innocence of childhood existence is ended through the sudden intrusion of an awareness of oneself. Jung, who experienced it very vividly and consciously, probably more consciously than most people, described his experience as follows.

> Once there was a moment when I had the overwhelming feeling of having just stepped out of a dense fog, with the conscious awareness: now *I* am. At my back it was as if there was a wall of fog behind which I had not yet been. But at this moment, I *happened to myself*. Previously I had existed, too, but everything had merely taken place. Now I knew: now *I* am, now *I* exist. Previously things went on with me, but now *I* willed (*MDR* pp. 32 f., transl. modif.).

There is in Jung's experience also the sense of a rupture (stepping out of a dense fog, having the previous state "at my back," and the absolute difference between "I had not yet been" and "now *I* am"), but in contrast to the dream-I Jung did not seem to experience it as a "crack," i.e., a fault, but rather hailed it as a boon. It is important to know that this radical change does not have to be seen nega-tively. It can also be seen as beneficial. Conversely, what in our dream is the cat's total sense of perfect oneness with itself and its surroundings appears in Jung's description in rather derogative terms as "wall of dense fog" and not yet having existed. Whether the change is appreciated as boon or feared as fault seems to depend one's standpoint. From the standpoint of the earlier position (the innocence of childhood existence, the old house) it is something terribly wrong; from the standpoint of the *accomplished* change it is a boon, one's having been transported to a higher status. In other words, it depends on whether the move into the new house, which is what this dream is about, has unreservedly been completed or whether one pauses at the door of the new house, uncertain whether one should also *logically* enter or not, relocate one's very *identity*, one's sense of self. (The cat's entering the new house merely meant that the dream-I has *positive-factually*, as physical body, moved to the new place.) By "remembering from before," the dream-I shows itself clinging to the standpoint of the old, now obsolete situation.

Jung's satisfaction with this change and his hailing the appearance of the emphatic sense of "I" let us see in retrospect why the move took the dream-I to the *southern* part of Switzerland and its warmth. If the south is connected with sunlight, rather than referring to a literal geographic region, it can, psychologically, be symbolic of the region where light (the light of consciousness, of enlightenment) shines, that light of reason that also brings the autonomy and self-responsibility of the full-fledged I ("now *I* willed"). We can say in this sense that the move intended by the soul is not into a literal new house, but from the dense fog of unreflected existence (of one's drifting through life, being moved by one's desires, emotions, fantasies and by circumstances) to self-consciousness, to reflection.

Descriptively, i.e., apart from any value judgment (boon vs. fault), we can say that over against that existence in which "everything had merely taken place," had happened merely as a natural process without reflection and without *I*, reflection (or reflecting consciousness) *is in itself* what is experienced in this dream as a "crack" in one of the window panes. The pane is the medium through which the I can see and experience what is outside of itself (of the house, its own "inner").

The concept of relocation intended by the dream involves precisely the move into the *house with the crack*. This means that the "crack" or rupture is not only the gulf between "north" and "south," old place and new home, not only one's having the previous home or the innocence of childhood irrevocably "at one's back." The distancing that happened through the move from the previous place imparts itself also to and permeates the logical form of the new place of existence itself, because this new place is not an indifferently "other" in spatial terms, another place on the same map. As a psychological reality it is the *result* and *product* of one's having moved, having left, having negated the old place. Without the move this new place would not exist at all. Therefore, even for him who uncompromisingly moves into the new house and welcomes the boon of having become "I" in this totally new sense, everything that he experiences of the world and life will from now on inevitably be perceived through the pane with the crack. The form of the subject's entire experience will a priori have a logical negation in it, be a reflected, logically "broken" one. That is to say, it will be an experience of *self-consciousness*, of an I that as seeing consciousness is irrevocably vis-à-vis, and thus logically fundamentally separate from what it sees. And it is irrevocably vis-à-vis because in its seeing what it sees it is at the same time *conscious of itself* as the seeing subject. A crack in the pane cannot be healed, not be made undone. The primordial wholeness of the pane, that is, the fundamental *immediacy* that characterizes one's experiencing during the innocence of childhood, is irretrievably lost.

At the time of moving, I wanted to tell the owner... That the dream-I is concerned with "the time of moving" shows that it has still not once and for all settled in the new house and made it its own. *Before* really moving in, so it thinks, something must first be settled with the owner.

We, for our part, realize that the notion of the crack ipso facto brings up the awareness of the true owner of the house and along with it a division in the self between self-conscious I and this "owner." This is completely different for the cat or for a child. A child may be aware of parents and teachers as authorities, but as far as its own house, its selfhood, is concerned, it feels totally in possession of its house, so much so that this issue does not even appear for it (which is also the condition of the possibility of the frequent feelings of omnipotence and all-importance of children). We have previously already come across the idea, much-cited in depth-psychology, that the ego is not the master in its own house. For the child, any idea of this division between itself and the owner or master in its own house is simply out of the question. This division and the notion of the true master or owner of the house comes into existence only through self-consciousness, on the basis of the emergence of the pronounced I. It is the gift of the crack.

One might, of course, think that it is normal that a house into which one moves is owned by someone else. After all, houses or apartments are often offered for rent. But this idea belongs to the dream-external world of daily reality (Jung's "impressions of the daily life"), and to toy with it here would again be working with a "fake possibility." In a dream, the new house could just as well be set up as being the dream-I's own house, or the question of ownership might simply not be raised, not be of interest for a given dream. If, however, the notion of "the owner" explicitly appears, then the distinction between I and "the owner," the larger personality, the Self in Jung's sense, has happened. The former total at-one-ness with oneself is over. The "crack" also goes through the new I itself. It is the emergence of the idea of the crack that produces the dream-internal idea of an "owner."

I did not cause this crack, it had already been there before. Now we hear what the issue is that needs to be settled with the owner. The dream-I feels the need to protest its innocence. It can only wish to do this if (1) the crack is interpreted as a fault or flaw, as something wrong, for which somebody must be held responsible and if (2) the dream-I thinks that it, the dream-I, might be accused. But since in the dream nobody else is concerned about the crack, and nobody accuses the dream-I, the latter must unconsciously accuse itself, find itself guilty. *Consciously* feeling the need to protest one's innocence although nobody questioned it and *unconsciously* accusing oneself are the two sides of one and the same coin.

Now it goes without saying that the dream-I did not cause the crack. As the house (the new status) of self-consciousness or reflecting consciousness, the crack had indeed "already been there before," namely, *a priori*, as the inherent characteristic of this new house. This house necessarily comes with, is built with, a crack in the pane from the outset; this is what it is all about. Without the crack, the whole move would not make sense and could not take place, since any move to a house without crack would psychologically simply be the old house once more (which it is for the cat). In this regard, the dream-I is indeed not responsible. It *is* innocent. This is the one side. The other side is that "the crack" that inevitably comes with the presence of self-consciousness is nevertheless accompanied by the notion of guilt, sin—see the Biblical story of the Fall and original sin, the Greek mytho-logical idea of the loss of the Golden Age, or the Indian idea of our now living in the worst age, the Kali Yuga. This is inherent in the logic of self-consciousness inasmuch as it is a kind of departure from and thus "betrayal" of the state of ori-ginal absolute oneness with oneself and with one's surroundings. Reflecting con-sciousness is fathered by a fundamental negation, a "destruction," almost an act of psychological "killing," which, however, is not a literal act, an actual happening in time, but the pictorial representation of its a priori logical character.

At this juncture there is a parting of ways. The I can *adopt* this "guilt," accept it as an integral and constitutive part of "the new house," its own new objective-psychological truth. In this case the crack becomes nothing but the inevitable (logical, not emotional) alienation and self-division that goes along with con-scious existence, with being a self-conscious I. To go this way, the dream-I would have to relentlessly move into the new house-with-this-crack, to cross over the threshold and to make it its real home. Then it could be experienced as a decisive boon, as it obviously was in Jung's case.

Or the I can, as in our dream, insist on "the crack" being something terribly wrong and thus interpret and reject it as *guilt*, so that somebody must be guilty. This harping on guilt inevitably produces guilt feelings. The I's "main business"[2] will from now on have to be to prove its own innocence, which, however, means that it wants to indulge and settle in its own subjective *feelings*. In general, dwelling with one's feelings is a substitute for simply seeing, and submitting to, the soul's objective *truth*. By indulging in guilt feelings in particular you do not have to *bear* your guilt. While on the behavioral level indeed feeling (= confessing) your *empirical* guilt, you try at the same time to restore or pre-serve your *logical, psychological* innocence and unbroken wholeness, because by *feeling* guilty you demonstrate for yourself that you condemn the bad and thus are *in truth* on the side of the good. *Feeling* guilty is always a defense mechanism.

In addition, guilt feelings are one marvelous way of cocooning oneself in the ego, of erecting and solidifying oneself (the I) as *self-identical* (logically unbroken, uniform, self-consistent, "whole") ego. By going the way of feeling, our dream-I settles *in itself* as ego *instead* of settling in the new house, in the objective status of reflecting consciousness.

However, despite settling in its subjectivity as ego, which keeps itself alive through its constant dwelling on its own *feelings*, the dream-I is nevertheless already irrevocably in the new place. The move has in fact taken place (which is also why it could appreciate the warmth of the south); the dream-I is already bothered by the tell-tale mark of the new place, the crack, the notion of which it "remembers" (*erinnert*), that is, comes from its own innermost self. The old place has once and for all been left behind, and there is no way back to the former innocence and oneness prior to the move. The I can only define itself as ego if at bottom it has already become self-conscious I; a child—the soul that is still in the old house—cannot be "ego." But the I's defining itself as ego also means refusing to unreservedly enter the new house and make the "crack" its own form of experiencing the world as self-conscious I or reflecting consciousness.

"I did not cause the crack" has psychologically a double function. On the one hand, it has to reduce the crack for the dream-I from being the character of a form of consciousness as a whole to nothing but a particular phenomenon, one single thing within the experience of consciousness, furthermore, to reduce its origin from a logical necessity of consciousness and a timeless soul truth to one special happening in the course of time, and responsibility for the crack from a development in the soul's logical life to something on the behavioral level, a one-time empirical human act, a misdeed or mistake. On the other hand, as the dream-I's protesting its innocence concerning this one particular event, "I did not cause the crack" also has the opposite function of covertly—symbolically and pars pro toto—representing the restoration (already *known* to be counterfactual and illusory) of the former innocence as an entire logical status of consciousness and mode of being-in-the-world. The urgently defended innocence in this one single point is psychologically supposed to carry the immense weight of the fictitious rescue of the already lost status of childhood innocence.

But I couldn't tell him that because I couldn't see the owner then... The owner does not appear because "who done it" is simply not an issue. Nobody has done it. The crack is not a fault. It is an inherent necessity and absolutely right. It is in fact the very essence of the new place to which the owner, the soul, made the dream-I relocate. It is the very goal of the move, namely, self-consciousness.

... so this kept worrying me. The dream-I's worrying is a way to establish itself permanently in "the ego" instead of in the house with the crack. In this worrying the I circles around itself as possibly falsely accused, immuring itself within itself, and, since this issue cannot be resolved, permanently halts before an unflinching entrance into the new house that is actually assigned to it: it halts before the *accomplished* move.

This helps us to realize that the owner not only did not but also *must not* appear. Because "the show must go on": the *ego* wants, needs, to keep worrying. To worry about this problem is so to speak its, the ego's, life insurance. Worrying is not one of the things the dream-I as ego happens to do, but is rather its very mode of existence. From the point of view of the owner the goal set for the dream-I is self-consciousness, but for the ego the goal is worrying. It is an end in itself, as much as the dream-I, if confronted with this assertion, would naturally deny it. It is at this surreptitiously *substituted* goal that the dream-I has indeed arrived.

The more the dream-I worries as its subjective emotional state, the more the "crack" itself is depotentiated as the objectively simply prevailing, self-consciousness-constituting soul truth. This worrying is a good example of what Freud, following Abraham, called "appropriation with the intention of destruction."

The state of constant worrying is, of course, also a form of disunity with oneself. As such, it is a way, namely the bad way, of how the "crack" is in fact *lived*.

The good way would be looking from inside the house through the pane, *not minding* that crack that goes through it and inevitably comes with existence as self-conscious I. In analogy to the old dictum that Jung had inscribed above the entrance of his house, *Vocatus atque non vocatus deus aderit*, we could say: whether in the good way or in the bad way, whether welcomed or defended against, the "crack" will prevail. Constant worrying is the price that has to be paid for the fictitious restoration of an innocent wholeness that is already known to be obsolete.[3]

By first remembering (reflecting), then worrying, the I *dissociates* itself from the dream-I's deeper bodily self that could appreciate the warm air in the new surroundings and, represented by the cat, has no problem, not even the least hesitation, feeling absolutely at home in the new house. It is only the in this way split-off I, the I as ego, that makes such a fuss. But the cat's having whole-heartedly entered the new house does not represent the completed, accomplished move. As cat, as bodily self, it does not know about "the crack." It stays in the original innocence of being. For it, the new house is by no means the house of *self-consciousness* that alone makes the house a *new* house and worth moving to in the first place. It is simply another *house*. Since for the split-off I the new house is already the house with the crack, the house of self-consciousness, the I is in this sense *psychologically* already more and deeper *in* this house than is the sleeping cat. But *psychically* the I remains outside. Conversely, the cat is psychically fully inside the house, but logically, psychologically outside, since for it the house is just another ordinary house on the same level with the old house.

This is a state of dissociation, and dissociation is the *perverted*, literalized, acted-out form of "the crack." Split-off I and "bodily self" have physically and logically parted company, have lost contact with each other; the dream-I has ceased being *homo totus*.

More than that. The *logic*, namely the very concepts of "inside" and "outside," have *in themselves* become dissociated, self-contradictory.

It is not the crack that splits the *homo totus* apart. The crack is not incompatible with one's being *homo totus*. The dissociation is the result of the refusal of *homo totus* to move or be transformed from the status of innocent wholeness to the state of reflected, in-itself "broken" ("cracked") being.

The dream, as a whole, does not show any development, any progression of action, any change from an initial situation to a final situation. Rather, it is the self-display of the internal logic of one single moment in the soul's life, one single "archetypal situation," that of "relocation," with its inner complexity and contradictions. All parts of the dream that I discussed separately must be understood as being simultaneous. In this way the present dream can be considered a good example of the one narrative type concerning the temporal sequence of events that I distinguished above at the very beginning of the chapter "The dream-I and the Other," namely that represented best by myth (in contrast to fairy tale).

This is *my* interpretation of the dream in the sense of "my" explained in an earlier chapter. Now I let this interpretation disappear in the pure "standing there" of the dream.

> I relocated. It was a move to another place within Switzerland. Before I knew what I was doing, I said to someone, "The air is warm in the southern part of the country." My cat found a place to lie down in the house and slept there. I remembered the house before I moved in. There was a crack in one of the windowpanes in the house. At the time of moving, I wanted to tell the owner that I did not cause this crack, it had already been there before. But I couldn't tell him that because I couldn't see the owner then, so this kept worrying me.

Notes

1. C.G. Jung, *The Visions Seminar*, From the Complete Notes of Mary Foot, Book One, Zürich (Spring Publications) 1976, p. 2.
2. Jung citing Goethe, *MDR* p. 206.
3. Jung spoke in a somewhat similar sense of the "Regressive Restoration of the Persona" (*CW* 7 p. 163).

Part VII

The dream and the patient

With this new topic we leave our "circumambulation of the dream" and look at it from outside.

The therapy situation as impairment of dream interpretation

In the two previous parts the actual "working with dreams" in this book has come to an end. Now I come to an entirely new topic: the dream and the dreamer; the dream in therapy. What I said so far mostly referred to the dream as such, the dream in isolation, as it would be in an *ideal* interpretation situation, sort of under "laboratory conditions," such as in a dream seminar. But usually we encounter dreams in very real, empirical therapeutic situations where we are confronted with the dream as well as with the dreamer, the patient as human being and ego-personality.

Jung was well aware of this difference. For example, he stated after a theoretical discussion of symbols (such as the phallus) and his attributing "an as it were indefinite content to these relatively fixed symbols," that

> [p]ractical necessity may call for something quite different. Of course, if we had to interpret a dream theoretically, i.e., give an exhaustive scientific interpretation of it, then we would have to refer such symbols to archetypes. But in practice that can be a positive mistake, for the patient's psychological state at the moment may require anything but a digression into dream theory.
>
> (*CW* 16 § 340 and 342, transl. modif.)

The difference is that between the theoretical demands and the practical demands of dream interpretation. The theoretical demands call on us to take the dream in isolation as the self that it is, while the practical necessities may require us to see the dream also in the context of this therapeutic process and in the light of what this patient now needs, is able to understand and to digest. Now all of a sudden we have to weigh up the interiority of the dream against external considerations, due to the fact that one aspect of therapy is that it not only takes place

in the interiority of the soul, in a strictly inner space, but also in the positivity of
an empirical consulting room where there are two empirical human beings. So, in
reality, the therapeutic situation *is* itself the whole psychological difference, the
two sides of the river, and not just the soul part of it. This is why we need to follow
the adage, "Render unto Caesar the things which are Caesar's, and unto God the
things that are God's."

The positive-factual, empirical conditions work as a restraint. One cannot
always simply take the dream as a self in therapy, because a patient maybe has
no, or only very little, psychological insight, no or only little access to what we
call soul. One main purpose of therapy is of course to slowly teach the patient in
the course of all the therapy sessions to get a better inner access to the realm of
soul and thus also to dreams, so that the latter can be understood in the therapy
session as individuals, selves. And, of course, even as long as a patient is not or
only minutely able to approach dreams psychologically, *we ourselves* as therapists
should nevertheless try for ourselves to see the dream as a self, even if in such a
situation we cannot share with the patient what we see and feel in the patient's
dream. The reason for our own having to view the dream psychologically is not
only that we may thus get some insight into the psychology of the patient. There
is also a therapeutic reason: our own unspoken soulful understanding of the dream
may surreptitiously, subliminally even have some actual helpful effect on the
patient, inasmuch as therapy does not merely work on the level of explicit communication between therapist and patient, but also as a deeper nonverbal, atmos-
pheric influence of the real *being* and *presence* of the therapist.

I also notice, conversely, in my own practice that for dream interpretation *I am*
to some extent dependent on what spirit the *patient* brings into therapy, what the
atmosphere in the particular session is, and how ready and capable the patient is
to enter the space of the interiority of soul. I say I am dependent on this, because
I sometimes am objectively inhibited in my psychological capacity. With certain
difficult patients with a strong one-sided leaning towards the practical-technical
side of reality and a narrow-minded positivistic outlook, or with patients with a
very defensive attitude and ego-resistance, it may be that I simply get hardly any
good ideas about the dream they presented, and the deeper dream meaning does
not reveal itself by working with them. (The same is true for dream seminars with
training candidates or colleagues. If their orientation is firmly personalistic so
that they cannot abstract from the dreamer and the case history, if, furthermore,
they come rashly up with their own free associations and are quick to stick psychological labels on dream images, subsuming them under the stereotypical theoretical constructs [Jung spoke of "premature understanding"], if they are driven
by the wish to speak and develop their own opinions *about* the dreams, then they
bring with them and to the dream the bright daylight of the ego and ordinary
life, so that one can no longer see the dream's own dim light (and not see *it* in its
own light). This prevents consciousness from having the opportunity to become
in its own constitution slowly attuned to the dream's dim light and in turn from
becoming enabled to let itself—as it were "sleepwalkingly"—be guided by the

hints of the dream's images.) With other patients (or colleagues), who are psychologically much more open, more willing to listen to the dream's speaking, even
difficult dreams may in the process of our immersing ourselves into the dream
freely incite illumining insights and allow the dream discussion to get more and
more interiorized into its unexpected depths.

The dependence on the spirit and basic atmosphere prevailing in the therapy
situation (or in the seminar group) shows that the work under such conditions is
basically a communal one, *even if* it may be the analyst who contributes most to
the dream discussion.

Having mentioned a possible serious obstacle to the working with dreams in
the process of therapy I might as well add a brief comment about two other not
so common forms of defensive attitudes against dreams. The first one may at first
sight not even appear as a defense. It is that one starts brooding what a dream or
a particular image in it might mean. In a way this is a mode of taking the dream
seriously and getting involved in it. Nevertheless, what it ultimately amounts to
is that consciousness takes its position outside and vis-à-vis the dream or dream
image. It wants to "unpuzzle," as its own achievement, the strange images, and
thus implicitly claims to be the one who has to decide what they mean. It is the
opposite of Jung's "It has a say now, not you." It amounts to a denial that the
dream *has* already spoken, that the meaning is already there in the images, so
that they are not in need of being unpuzzled. What they need is our listening,
our going under, our letting the *images* be, and letting them *be* their already present meaning—a meaning that can take hold of us of its own accord from within
ourselves.

The second problematic attitude I have in mind is a kind of blasé reaction to
a patient's personal problem that is exposed by a dream, namely the patient's
response: "But that is nothing new to me! I have known that all along!" What is
wrong with this reaction is that it pooh-poohs the dream images as old hat and
thus relegates them to the bygone past. One deprives *them* of their potential nov-
elty and potentiality, instead of *oneself* getting with verve onto the Pegasus of the
dream image in order to let *it* take one's consciousness to where it might lead. Nor
does one relate to the dream image like children take colorful glass balls into their
hand with curiosity, simply enjoying looking at them without wanting anything
or feeling under the pressure of any "ought." The blasé reaction is the opposite of
that of Molière's bourgeois gentilhomme, who rejoices when he learns that what
he is speaking is "prose" (which it had been all along).

As much as the situation in the consulting room limits the possibility of a more
thorough-going dream-interpretation (not only for the reason just given, but also
simply due to the limited time frame in a session), our goal should be to do justice
to the dream as a self as much as possible and at any rate not call something
dream interpretation that is merely the employment of the dream material for
other personal-therapeutic purposes. We have to *know what* it is that we are doing
in each situation.

Absolute-negative interiorization of the patient into the dream

Ideally, even in therapy when it is a matter of working with dreams we should be devoted to the dream, not the dreamer, to the dream as a self. But what about the dreamer, the patient? What function does dream work have for him? If the dream is closed in itself, and if we are supposed to relentlessly enter it, isn't the patient left outside? So it seems, but this is not so. Dream interpretation has, on the most general level, the purpose for the patient precisely to lose himself in the dream, to forget himself. The point of dream work for the patient is to learn to see himself and his reality, and his life history, *from within* the dream: *to receive himself as a gift* given to him by the dream. Just as one should not *apply* any knowledge from outside the dream, knowledge that has not been logically melted down and absorbed by the dream world as *its* property and creatively reborn, returned to us by the dream, so the dreamer should, as far as dream work is concerned, not remain outside the dream. The dreamer, too, has to go under and learn to experience himself as a sublated moment within the movement of the *dream*. His going under is the therapeutic potential of dream work. No doubt: a lofty goal! And a distant goal.

It means his being "baptized" by the dream, being reached by it from within. An illustration of this "being reached from within" may be a passage in Kafka's *The Judgment*. The protagonist has spent some time writing a letter to his friend living under rather miserable conditions in St. Petersburg, but writing it, without being aware of it, in a rather condescending tone, bragging about his own successes. He then goes to his old father to tell him about his letter before posting it. His father surprisingly denies point-blank that the protagonist *has* any friends in St. Petersburg, which the son takes as a sign of his old father's loss of his mental faculties. But then his father accuses him of having all these years been playing the person in St. Petersburg false and that the latter would have been a son after his own heart! Only then, all of a sudden, "His friend in St. Petersburg, whom his father suddenly knew too well, touched his [the son's] imagination as never before."

This being touched and "baptized" into new awareness in therapy does not have to be a literal *felt experience*, an explicit emotional event, as it is in this Kafka story. It can also be a hidden background process that tacitly and unconsciously affects the *inner logic* of consciousness. It may then someday surprise the patient that, all of a sudden, he feels and behaves in a new way: the altered consciousness has imperceptibly become his new truth! Having pointed out that "A great work of art is like a dream," Jung says, "To grasp its meaning, one must allow oneself to be shaped by it, the way it has shaped the poet" (*CW* 15 § 161, transl. modif.).

A psychiatrist dreams that:

> he is in his practice where things are completely chaotic. He is extremely busy. Very many people. In his practice, a clothes horse with his private

laundry is standing around. All of a sudden, paramedics bring a patient with diabetes into his practice whose blood sugar level needs to be checked every hour. The dream-I thinks, I cannot possibly manage all that, and on top of it I am a psychiatrist and my practice is not equipped for such treatment.

Once this dream has been interpreted by circumambulating it and the interpretation has been concluded then we re-emerge from our immersion in the dream and, now *outside the dream*, can raise the question: Why does *this* patient dream this? Why does he dream *this*? What does the dream want to tell the patient or do to the patient? What effect does it want to bring about? To what experience does it want to expose the patient? What does it want him to live through in the dream?

One way to think about all this might be the following. "The diabetic" is no-one else but he himself. He is unbeknownst to himself a really sick person. He *is* his illness. But he does not want to take responsibility for it, being unaware of the fact that he himself is sick and needs constant attention. The patient and his sickness are completely alien to him, very, very far away. He only sees them as an annoying disturbance and imposition, and reacts somewhat indignantly. This also corresponds to his self-relation in actual life.

Now a new question arises, the question of what consequences such an insight into the dream idea should have. Frequently, patients ask the question (and it seems to be the most natural patient reaction to an in-depth dream exploration in analysis), "So the dream shows me *that*. And now?" or

This is all well enough, I see that all this is the truth contained in the dream and that the dream clearly shows what the soul wants and needs; but how does what is displayed in the dream become relevant in my life, what can I, what should I do so that it becomes real in me? How can I develop my masculinity/ my feeling function/the self (or whatever may have been the particular need shown in the dream)? How can I attain wholeness?

We will turn to these questions in the next chapter.

"So the dream shows me *that*. And now?"

It is psychologically crucial that the consequence to be drawn from such a dream must not be that the patient should try hard to take himself more seriously as the really sick person that he is, the diabetic, and to pay more attention to him. All such conscious effort would be wrong. As ego-consciousness the patient *is simply not in a position* to take himself more seriously. Any such attempt would be artificial machinations, merely ego work—and as such precisely a defense against what is actually needed. The actual necessity is to simply comprehend that "the soul" has already sent the paramedics and that they have taken the sick person to his practice, to the *dream*-I. The dream reality is what counts. He as ego-personality or consciousness does not need to do anything. *It is the dream or the soul that has to do its own work*, the really important therapeutic work. We just give our dedication to the dream to bring living warmth to the cold corpse. That is all. Nothing needs to be *done* in external reality.

The rest is the dream's or the soul's business! Not ours. No ego effort! (Ego effort is important only on the behavioral level of pragmatic ego matters, matters which are really within my sphere of jurisdiction, my responsibility, and my competence. For example, a lazy person can pull himself together and study harder. I can learn to give up bad habits. One can learn to behave socially more properly, etc. This is self-education, not psychology.) The whole idea of implementing in practice the insights gained from the dream, to put its "lessons" into practice, is mistaken. *I* must not integrate my shadow, not "work on myself," must not "develop my inferior function," "give up my defenses." This would only be ego-psychology.

The dream reality must *reach me* from within, *it* must shape me. All I can really *do* is to take the dream reality seriously, live with the dream images (but again: casually, without much ado), let them do their thing. In addition, dreams may *start me thinking* about the issues raised.

Ultimately it is our *releasing the image into its truth* and thus also into its freedom, its free play, which in turn makes us free from it ("the truth shall make you free," John 8:32); truth is the home of "the soul"; by releasing any soul phenomenon into its truth we release it from ourselves, from the empirical human being, from the ego and *its* interests and wishes, its cherished values, its fears, and return it to its home; this would be the true *epistrophê* (James Hillman after Proclus[1]) and true soul-making; it would be the psychological difference in action. The home of "the soul" is not the mythological underworld, nor the semi-metaphysical realm of the archetypal or imaginal. These are still too literal places. Still undistilled and still *vorgestellt* (pictorially represented). No, the home of "the soul" is *truth*. Releasing the dream image into its truth and letting the spirit out of the bottle is what is needed. It means unreservedly allowing *it* to *be*, and us to expose *ourselves* to it so that it can do with us and with the world what it wants or needs to do. This would also mean exposing ourselves without reserve even to the pain it may possibly cause.

Earlier, in the chapter "The dream as corpse," I said that in the pain or sorrow we feel in view of a sad dream situation or dream ending we release the dream into its being-so, into its having been so *and* into its being perfect the way it is, while at the same time connecting our conscious knowing and feeling with it. By simply being pained or sad or disappointed without wanting the misery or a clearly defensive ego reaction in this particular dream to be any different, we give this dream event a place of honor in our consciousness; we appreciate it; much like the Furies (Erinnyes) were given a place of honor in Aeschylus' *Oresteia* as the 'Semnai' (Venerable Ones), or in Euripides' *Orestes* as 'Eumenides' (Gracious or Well-Meaning Ones). To be given such a place in our consciousness is what the image, what "the soul" needs in order to have full reality. This is also what might enable the psychological situation expressed in the dream to change of its own accord. It is *all* that the soul needs; and it is also the way we can "feed" the dream with new energy, nourish it with "blood." Only a change that happens of its own accord, only the self-change of the prime matter, is a real change. Any change brought about deliberately by us is—psychologically—artificial and inauthentic. It is manipulation. As paradoxically as it may sound, we have to let the dream be the way it is so that *it* (or the psychological problem it is about) can possibly change by presenting us, e.g., later with *another dream* in which the relation of the dream-I to the forces of the soul are less characterized by defensiveness, hostility, or a wish to escape.

In the desire for practical action in response to dreams we clearly detect the dissociating ego at work: "The dream is just an image, just an idea, representing a possible insight. But it is not *real*. Truly real is only objective reality, the ego world of literal deed and positive fact." This view is expressive of a programmatic hands-on mindset. The ego is not capable of conceiving the idea of the *reality* of "the soul," of absolute negativity.

For any psychology that has actually comprehended the reality of "the soul" and therefore understands that the dream *is* itself the *reality* that it is about and has everything it needs within itself, any such desired activity by the ego for the purpose of implementing the dream idea in "real life" would precisely *detract* from the dream itself and prevent or defer the dream's *own possible further development* into a future new dream situation. It would be an acting out, where instead an *Er-innerung* (interiorization, inwardization) into the dream would be needed. Here we can think back to the Aeschylean Erinnyes whose will was precisely not allowed to be acted out in practice (as Goddesses of the archaic tribal, "blood"-based ethical life, they were acknowledged to be obsolete), but who received, under the new name of Semnai and Eumenides, a place of honor only in memory. The ego would take things into its own hands, when actually it is the ego's "host" who needs to change the conditions. *It* would carry out a process in the ego's day-world that would only make sense in the night-world of the soul, and it would thus replace, or try to replace, by an egoic activity what could only happen underneath the surface, in the negativity of the soul's logical life.[2]

Nothing needs to be *done*. No implementation in practical reality. On the contrary, the psychological art consists precisely in leaving the dream to its own devices and actually understanding that it is in itself "perfect." Even if it shows precisely what, as the soul feels, is *lacking* and urgently *needed*, it, i.e., the very dream that reveals this soul need, nevertheless *has* everything it needs. All that the dream indeed needs from us is that it is fully understood to *be* that very reality that the ego deludedly thinks needs to be established through ego effort. The dream needs to be left alone.

Terrible dream images, unbearable for the patient?

Therapists sometimes think that their patients have dreams with too terrible images, images that consciousness cannot endure. The ego of these patients is said to be too vulnerable. What can we say about this view? I want to offer three different arguments.

1. It is to be questioned whether this fear that dream images are unbearable for the consciousness of the patient may not to some extent be the therapist's problem, a twofold problem. On the one hand, the therapist's consciousness may be a very timid, innocent one that insists on harmony and unwoundedness so that it is easily shocked, maybe even paralyzed, by cruel images and therefore also easily fears that the patient cannot endure his or her own cruel dream images. Is perhaps the therapist's own need unconsciously projected upon the patient? We might contrast this view and personal attitude with Jung's, who said: "As a medical psychologist I do not merely assume, but I am thoroughly convinced that *nil humanum a me alienum esse* is even my duty" (*Letters* 2, p. 589, to Read 2 Sept. 1960). As a therapist one needs to know the facts of life and not make a fuss about them. And one also needs to be familiar and feel at home with the brutal or cruel images that the soul has come up with in history, images of brutal castration, flaying, dismemberment, crucifixion, rituals of human sacrifices, headhunting, etc.

    On the other hand, there may be in the therapist a too innocent idea of therapy as an undertaking the purpose of which is to protect patients from all pain and wounds and to see them like small children or babies.

    If the therapist in his own soul has difficulties with brutal images and wants to retain his or her psychological harmlessness and oversensitiveness, then images that by themselves may be quite endurable to the patient despite their brutality or cruelty might, via the unconscious deep connectedness of patient and therapist, also in the patient create the feeling that such images *are* unbearable. We must here remember that young children usually have no problem hearing fairy tales with quite brutal images. If they find them too terrible this is usually induced by their parents' attitude, their wish to protect the child from such images. Likewise, therapists can see their patients as (and even *make* them) oversensitive, feel easily hurt, wounded by brutal dream images. The fact that children seem to have no problem with cruel images is due to their being closer to the soul. Conversely, the fact that adults think that such images might be unbearable for their children is a result of their being "in the ego" and literalizing these images.

    Patients, as patients, need to be wounded by their own truth. This is what they are in therapy for. And truth hurts. Therapy is about truth; about patients' finding out *the truth about themselves*. By saying as therapist that the ego is vulnerable, one makes excuses for the patient's not confronting himself or herself with their own truth.—No doubt, very often we also have to reckon with and deal with the patient's narcissism. We nevertheless have to try to approach them, but carefully. We have to slowly make them see that they have to confront themselves also with things that hurt. Of course, not suddenly. We have to slowly, consistently prepare the ground so that they gradually can become ready to accept something that they really don't want to hear or, if it comes in the form of dream images, see.

2.   The soul, I think, probably does not generally produce images in a dreamer's own dreams that the consciousness of this dreamer cannot endure. This is because the same soul that *produces* the images produces them *for this person*, for this consciousness. In the dream images the soul speaks to itself, itself as represented by the consciousness of the dreaming person. A "terrible" image is not coming from outside (from external reality, from other people) to patients. It comes from their own psyche and is invented solely for the one person which dreams this terrible image! What is in the image is the soul, their own soul's speaking to them, *only to them*, to nobody else. And so I think it is unlikely that an image could really be too much for a patient, too difficult, too hard to endure. For the *ego attitude* of consciousness, a particular image may seem to be too terrible. But that does not mean that it truly *is* too terrible for consciousness.

3.   The phrase, "the patient's ego is too vulnerable" does not make sense. There is no such thing as "the ego." The *patient*, he or she as really existing person, may be vulnerable, oversensitive, etc. But he does not *have* an ego, even if the logical form or style of his consciousness may be that of "ego." One must not turn "ego" into a subject, an organ or agent, an entity. No hypostatizing!

Notes

1. J. Hillman, *Loose Ends*, Zurich 1975, p. 50. Also, e.g., *idem, The Dream and the Underworld*, p. 4. My speaking of "the true *epistrophē*" indicates that I am not fully in agreement with *his* sense of the term (return to the Gods through likeness).
2. Jung would say: in the unconscious, whereas Hillman would perhaps prefer: in the underworld.

Part VIII

Miscellaneous questions

In this part I want to comment only briefly on a few questions of very different nature that are sometimes raised relating to dreams.

The types and topics of dreams

It is impossible and would be presumptuous to wish to provide a list of all the different themes and types of dreams that can appear to people, or to give a systematic account of their basic categories. The soul is creative, inventive, and people and life situations (both collective or historical and personal) in which dreams appear are so different that the variety of dreams is endless. Even after 40 years of working with patient dreams, one is time and again surprised by totally new, astounding dream contents, dream inventions. Nevertheless, in dreams we will certainly many times also discover well-known symbols and mythological motifs, which is one observation that gave rise to Jung's developing his notion of archetypes. On the other hand, many modern dreams are free of specifically mythological reminiscences or obvious symbols, and seem to be situated in our modern world, which, however, does not exclude the possibility that even in them very strange, unexpected, weird or mysterious, even realistically impossible things take place.

Despite the open-ended variety of possible dream images, in one's therapeutic practice one nevertheless also encounters a certain number of dreams that can be grouped together into types according to their content or theme. I mention a few examples: dreams of an intruder, of finding oneself confronted with a dangerous animal, dreams of being persecuted and trying to escape, dreams of air raids or the approach of an enemy army, dreams of erring through a kind of labyrinthine building, dreams of being prevented again and again by ever new obstacles from getting to where one wants to go, toilet dreams (e.g., dreams of the urgent need to use a public toilet, but finding that it is disgustingly messy or without privacy), anxiety dreams, dreams of flying, of falling (or being about to fall) off a cliff, of a sexual union, of having given birth to a baby or child, etc. There are dreams in which the dream-I has the opposite sex from the dreamer, or it appears as a hermaphrodite. Sometimes the dream-I is confronted with or discovers a dead or dying person (or animal). There are dreams in which there is no real action, but just a landscape, or an object (e.g., an altar or crucifix), or a certain person is seen. Occasionally, nothing is *seen* in the dream at all, but the only thing that happens is that one hears a voice saying something.

Interesting, even if not so common, are pathognomonic dreams, dreams in which the particular psychological symptoms occur in the course of the dream itself.

In popular usage, the term nightmare is used for anxiety dreams in general. But there are also nightmares *sensu strictiori*, dreams in which the dream-I feels the oppressing heavy weight of an *incubus*, an evil demon (the "nightmare" himself), lying on the dream-I and causing the very real bodily fear of suffocating. For this form of dream I refer to the essential study, *Pan and the Nightmare. Two Essays*, by Wilhelm Heinrich Roscher and James Hillman.[1] When such dreams occur they *happen* usually *to* a consciousness that is cut off from the body and the physical world, from sensuality, instinct and sexuality, from the reality of things, a consciousness too much up in the air, too light, fluffy, silly, innocent. In such dreams the soul wants to brutally force the experience of the reality of the sense of touch and body upon the dream-I.

From a soul point of view especially important are dreams that seem to intend the dream-I's going to and undergoing an initiation. Sometimes there is another dream figure that serves as soul guide, a psychopomp. In other dreams the dream-I moves into a lonely forest, into a cave or to an underground location, or is taken by a boat across a river to a grotto in which "an event" is supposed to take place. In our *modern* Western world, such dreams are mostly concerned only with the *approach* to a place of initiation, whereas according to my experience the actual performance and conclusion of the initiation ceremony itself is rarely dreamed. There are also dreams of dismemberment or of being bitten by a presumably poisonous snake, which have an actual initiation aspect.

Individual persons from non-Western cultures rarely, but occasionally, report clearly shamanistic dreams or at least dreams with shamanistic motifs. It seems that in Japan this happens especially to persons who come from families with a shamanistic tradition, that is, whose forebears used to exercise an actual shamanistic function in society. This gift of a closeness to that "other" reality seems to be inherited even to certain present-day members of these families, often to their dismay, because it is a burden and hard to integrate into the demands of modern life. At any rate, such dreams are in character far removed from the ordinary social reality in which we now live, and the dream-I is from the outset removed from the status of an ego-personality.

Jung introduced the idea of the *Initialtraum* ("initial dream"), that is, a dream dreamt very early in a therapy that is different from other dreams in that it seems to foreshadow what the soul process is heading toward.

As such anticipation it is a bit similar to and yet different from what is called "prophetic dreams." Therapeutically, the problem with prophetic dreams is that they do not come with "a label" attached saying "I am a prophetic dream." This means, we can know only much later, in retrospect, whether it is a prophetic dream or not, after what the dream showed has indeed happened in reality. So in our therapeutic practice, the idea of prophetic dreams is rather useless. Since we cannot possibly know that they are about something that is *factually* going to happen in the future, we must interpret them in the same *psychological* way as all other dreams. Later experience may then show that such a psychological interpretation was mistaken because the dream really presented future factual events. It is important to realize that "prophetic" and "psychological" are incompatible, the former being concerned with positive-factual happenings in the day-world, the latter with psychic or psychological meanings, insights. Sometimes patients come with the idea that dreams are prophetic, foretelling the future, and in most cases this is a superstition.

There is one more issue that I want to at least mention in this chapter on the types of dreams. It concerns the difference between dreams that are more or less concise, on the one hand, and endless run-on dreams on the other. It is only the former type that can be considered as a self, as discussed above. Should one say that the second type consists of numerous selves, as if it were, composed of many separate units, each of which would correspond to a concise dream and as such represent a self? I rather tend to think that such run-on dreams are more likely to be "self-less." And I must admit that in therapy I did not really know what to do with them. I felt that it would not make sense to take them seriously the way I said in this book that dreams should be taken seriously. They would for practical reasons force one to pick out a few of the many individual images or scenes, which would make the whole procedure of working with dreams completely arbitrary. I suspect that there is also a kind of defense (against a direct and specific "confrontation with the unconscious," to use Jung's phrase) behind such long dreams. They amount to a kind of psychological diarrhea, if you excuse this expression. And my hunch was that it is best to explicitly ignore them in therapy and instead to turn to the patient's conscious issues.

Does the dream have a message for us?

In Jungian literature one often finds examples where somebody thinks that he or she should not do what they actually intended to do because the latest dream (allegedly) "said no." In such cases the dream is taken as if it were an authoritative oracle to be obeyed. For this stance, the dream has a clear message: this is good or right and that is bad. And so, the dream turns into the decision-maker for the human person. Of course, it must not always be so crude that one believes that one's dream said directly "no" (or "yes"). It can also be that one merely thinks that the dreams points into a certain direction and that one should take this into consideration in one's decision making. I also remember study groups of Jungians that had formed for the purpose of collecting dreams from their various patients to seek guidance "from the unconscious" concerning collective developments or themes. This happened once after all the public excitement caused by the Club of Rome's report on *The Limits of Growth,* later once when the "no-nukes" and peace-movement was virulent, and once still later concerning dreams about the earth's ecological problems. The hope was that the dreams of numerous individuals would show a way out of the collective troubles experienced by the members of those groups (but, in truth, probably to back up their own ideological and political positions).

Although things Jung said sometimes might also be interpreted in this direction, we have clear statements of his that contradict this oracular use of the dream, a use that ultimately amounts to an abdication of human consciousness and our own responsibility. Jung states,

> one would do well not to overestimate this [viz., the prospective] function, for one might easily be led to suppose that the dream is a kind of psychopomp which, out of a superior knowledge, is capable of giving life the infallibly right direction.
>
> (*CW* 8 § 494, transl. modif.)

guide of souls

The dream is not a psychopomp. It does not give us the right answers to our questions, does not tell us what would be right to do.

Again:

> Many people who know something, but not enough, about dreams and their meaning, and who are impressed by their subtle and apparently intentional compensation, are liable to succumb to the prejudice that the dream actually has a moral purpose, that it warns, rebukes, comforts, foretells the future, etc. By thinking that the unconscious always knows best, people can easily be tempted into passing the responsibility for necessary decisions and resolutions to the dreams [...]. The unconscious functions satisfactorily only when the conscious mind fulfils its tasks to the very limit.
>
> (§ 568)

Dreams do not know best, and above all the responsibility for our decisions is solely our own, consciousness's own! It is our own job to find the right direction.

"No dream says 'you ought' or 'this is the truth'; it presents us with an image, just as nature makes a plant grow, and it is entirely up to us to draw conclusions from it" (*CW* 15 § 161, transl. modif.). The conclusions are then our own! It is we who have to make up our mind as to what to do. And we have to accept responsibility for our decision. The dream must not be used as a crutch, nor as a possibility to hide behind some *other,* allegedly superior, authority. And it must not be abused as a means to an end.

All this means that from a Jungian point of view the dream does not have a *message.* And our dream work is thus also not about finding out "its message." Dream work is about one's absolute-negative interiorization into the dream as a self (a self that, as we know, includes the concrete situation and persons interpreting the dream). But when we emerge from this having gone under and when we are back in reality from this journey into the land of "the soul," then we have to fend for ourselves (all the more so as our working with the dream, our "saying it again as well as we can," is already only *our own* interpretation!). We have to make our own decisions, on our own responsibility. Making our decisions is *our* job, the job precisely of the *conscious* mind (*outside* and *after* our absolute-negative interiorization into the dream, i.e., after our return from the immersion into the dream!). However, having come back from our immersion into the dream we may have come back with a somewhat expanded consciousness on account of the dream experience, so that we may also look at things a bit differently from before, and this might influence the decisions we make.

By the same token, we should not think that the dream has a meaning to be applied to the patient or that the patient should apply it to himself. This would be a technological approach. The meaning for, and the effect on the patient have to be *dream-internal*. No cause/effect relation. To the extent that the patient, the dreamer, is truly *in* the dream, the dream naturally affects and transforms him. And to get into the dream is not an ego-achievement and a conscious act. Nobody knows if and to what extent the dreamer (or oneself as dreamer) is in the dream or not. There are patients who seem to have no access to the dream, but deep down and unbeknownst to themselves they may nevertheless be in it and reached by it. And with other patients one seems to be able to do excellent dream work in analysis; they seem to be with it and in it, but since they are not really in it nothing changes. Interiority cannot be positivized.

Archetypal dream motifs. Numinous, religious dreams?

We just had to accept the insight that dreams do not have a message for us, and we also know that they do not have a fixed, clear-cut meaning. But we could ask: what about mythological motifs, about archetypal patterns in dreams? Do they not have relatively fixed meanings that exist long prior to and thus outside the dream and merely reoccur in it? Yes and no. It is like with language.

The words we use are not invented by us. They exist and have a meaning prior to our using them in our specific speech. In normal speaking or writing situations the meaning of each particular statement is originally created by the idea to be conveyed. It is not the other way around: words as fixed building blocks are not assembled together and do not, through this combination of separate elements, create the meaning of the sentence. Normal words are not like technical terms and cannot be mechanically inserted into a sentence. No, the idea to be conveyed re-collects *within itself* the words provided by one's language and necessary to express this meaning, spontaneously fetching them from the reservoir of one's linguistic memory. In normal, natural speech the idea to be expressed does not use words as ready-mades. It rather melts down the words it finds as givens and recreates them from within the living meaning of the idea to be expressed. "For of the abundance of the heart his mouth speaketh." The "assembly" conception concerning our speaking does not work, or does so only in special technical situations. The message to be conveyed in each case appropriates and interiorizes into itself the words delivered to us by tradition, so that the words used in a statement have become *the message's own* words, its own property. The message is the mother and source of the words used in the sentence.

In a similar way a dream makes use of both traditional archetypal motifs and memories from one's biography or experiences from the previous day, but only after having appropriated and integrated them into itself. The internal depth of the dream message or meaning is the ultimate and only reality that creatively gives birth to all the particular images and symbols that make up the dream. So if dream motifs come with a rich cultural and mythological echo, or with a personal-biographical echo, this richness is not inserted into the dream from outside, in the way that in former ages in Europe people used stones from Roman ruins as building material for their own houses or churches. The dream, as it were, within itself—within the depth of its own inner meaning—remembers, and alludes to, archetypal and mythological (or biographical) reminiscences.

What I am trying to suggest is that we should not think of archetypes as existing (*vorhanden*) powers that sometimes forcefully intrude into our dreams. The dream has nothing behind it; like a poem it creates its own meaning from out of its own center. This corresponds to what we heard Jung say about the dream as itself deciding within itself what belongs and what does not. "The dream is its own limitation. It is itself the criterion of what belongs to it and of what leads away from it" (*CW* 18 § 433). So here, too, the dream remembers and recreates traditional meanings within itself.

Just as Jung hypostatized *the* self as a quasi-metaphysical entity by abstracting and isolating the self character of psychic phenomena as a separate psychic entity, so he also hypostatized the archetypes by extracting the quality of *mythological depth* that some soul phenomena have and assigning an independent existence to them above psychic phenomenology. He criticized that even people who admit the existence of archetypes nevertheless "usually treat them as if they were mere images and forget that they are living entities" (*CW* 18 § 596). He operates here with the binary opposition of mere images here and archetypes as living entities there. This disjunction needs to be overcome.

There are only the images themselves with nothing behind them. However, the images *are* not "mere" images. The moment that they come alive in us or that we become interiorized into them, they are themselves "living entities" with—at times—archetypal depth and numinosity; if this be so, the "archetype" exists only within the images and *by virtue, by the grace of*, the images, not outside them. With this view, the hypostatization still prevailing in Jung is overcome. The image *creates* its archetypal nature within itself. It is not the other way around, that an archetype comes down from heaven and reveals itself to a human in a dream. In Jung it sounds different: he posits existing archetypes-in-themselves of which images are the expression or manifestation.

Despite all my objections to Jung's view presented here there is, nevertheless, some justification in Jung's above-mentioned criticism of people's treating archetypes as mere images. But it lies in the fact that people reduce the *images* to "mere" images and do not see and acknowledge *them* as selves, as "living entities," as having their archetypal, their own abyssal depth within themselves. The fault is not that people treat *archetypes* as mere images. We have to move from "archetype" as noun to "archetypal" as an adjective, an adjective that refers to a certain depth and transpersonal meaning quality that images (or other psychic phenomena) may or may not have.

Dream images do not come with objective semantic distinguishing marks that would allow us to ascertain their mythic or archetypal nature. A particular dream motif may from an abstract-formal point of view quite obviously have a mytho-logical or archetypal content and yet as a whole be only a content of the ego and an ego experience, part of the dreamer's private *opus parvum*. In fact, this is the normal situation in modernity. What Jung called the individuation process as part of modern psychology (and psychotherapy), *if* it occurs at all, belongs to the sphere of the ego and this sphere's internal complexity. The sphere that erst-while was represented by myth is inaccessible to *born* man. What is mythic in a semantic sense and as such is experienced in dreams is syntactically already the psychologized ready-made props from the property room of the psychic. It is what Jung once referred to as the fallen stars,[2] i.e., sunken, sedimented cultural heritage. Psychologically and syntactically (even if not always psychically and semantic-ally) all this has been subjected to the ego.

Such insights meet, of course, with the emphatic resistance of many modern people, Jungians or New-Age-inspired persons as well as others who crave for some kind of "high" through the belief in a "higher meaning" to be found in archetypal, numinous dreams. For them dreams *must* have archetypal meaning, must provide the aura of numinosity or the sense of "the sacred." It is clear that it is paradoxically an ego desire that is here the driving force. The desire is a wish for self-gratification. One wants to have something to look up to, to idolize, to gape at in wonder. Dream images with mythological character are exploited for ego purposes.

It goes without saying that Jung put his psychological hope in the experience of archetypes, of the numinous (just think of his statement, "The main interest of my work is not concerned with the treatment of neurosis but rather with the approach to the numinous," *Letters 1*, p.377, to Martin, 20.VIII.45). But this is only one side. There is a crucial other side. Late Jung warned against abandoning oneself to the emotional impression (*Gefühlseindruck*) of motifs that sound "so solemn," "so religious, so splendidly religious" and against a state of mind "in which we do not think anything any more and just succumb to absolute suggestion. One becomes suggestible when one does not have conscious thoughts, but only unconscious ones."[3] Another time Jung stated:

> What is above all important is the distinction between consciousness and the contents of the unconscious. ... Only in this way can one deprive them [viz., the contents of the unconscious] of their power that they otherwise exercise over consciousness.
>
> (*Erinn.* p. 190, my transl., cf. *MDR* p. 187)

"In the final analysis the decisive factor is always consciousness, which understands the manifestations of the unconscious and takes up a position toward them" (*MDR* p. 187, transl. modif.). "In order to free oneself from the tyranny of unconscious presupposition both are needed: fulfillment of the intellectual as well as the ethical obligation" (*Erinn.* p. 192, my transl., omitted in *MDR*). "The aim of individuation is nothing less than to divest the self of the false wrappings of the persona on the one hand, and the suggestive power of primordial images on the other" (*CW* 7 § 269).

What is decisive for Jung is that instead of one's simply allowing oneself to be seduced by the intensive emotional impression of the numinosity of dream images, and giving oneself over to this emotionally powerful experience, thereby becoming unconscious, one starts on a process of *conscious thought*. For mature Jung, soul-making happens in *consciousness* and requires intellect, comprehension. The contents of the unconscious need to be deprived of their (emotional, seductive) power. Emotion has to give way to understanding: "The whole energy of these emotions was transformed into interest in and curiosity about the image," Jung said about a development in himself (*MDR* p. 187).

This is the one objection to dedication to the numinous. There is a second objection. The moment that numinous images do not simply factually occur to a dreamer as unexpected events and that at the same time there is a consciousness that from the outset *longs for* numinous experiences and systematically cultivates so-called "numinosity" by using mythological images and dream reports by others about their numinous images for working itself up into the state of feeling "so solemn, so splendidly religious," we have to diagnose the presence of a (not even hidden) agenda, a program. Such an agenda has nothing to do with psychology, it is an ideological ego-trip. Where this program prevails, there will be a surreptitious tendency to inflate dream images that have a mythological quality with "numinosity" and to seek for "imaginal likenesses" to dream images in order to use them for the production of simulated numinosity. Self-indulgence! And all that for the sole purpose of bringing about "consciousness's becoming unconscious" (*GW* 12 § 563, my transl.).[4] The poet Gottfried Benn once nicely poked fun at such deep phony desires in modern man when he wrote the lines: "O daß wir unsere Urahnen wären. / Ein Klümpchen Schleim in einem warmen Meer" ("O that we were our own primordial ancestors. / A little clot of slime in a warm sea").

In connection with the topic of phony numinosity I also want to at least mention one other surprising possibility. A dream reported in a book review[5] reads:

> My beloved and I are partners in a creativity contest to see who can make the most original object. Playfully, board by board, we build a small, sturdy boat. "What shall we use for a sail?" he asks. "It has to be silk," I say. "We talk and kiss and try to think of a sail. I lie in the boat with my head by the mast. Suddenly, I've got it. So has he. He kneels beside me and weaves my long blonde hair into a golden sail. A quick gust fills it. My beloved grabs the rudder and we are carried into a sunlit sea. I don't know if we win the contest.

Nothing matters except that I love him and he loves me and we both love the water and the wind. I am the sail, he is the rudder. In our little craft we are borne by the Holy Spirit over the eternal sea."

In case that this is an authentic dream and not "made up," we are forced to learn from it that "the unconscious" or "the soul" can also produce kitsch, psycho-kitsch, decidedly corny dreams. It would mean that the sentimentality of the consciousness of the dreamer can even shape the spontaneously appearing dream images! A somewhat shocking insight. Dreams would not only and always be the voice of the soul's truth, not always really come "from the other side."

Or is this dream perhaps not innocent and straightforward at all, but produced by the soul much rather as a deliberate spoof to confront consciousness with its kitschy sentimentality?

I want to give one additional example for this type of dream. In his "Letter to the Editor" of the *Journal of Jungian Theory and Practice* (Vol. 6, No. 2, 2004, pp. 61f.), Julian David once cited a dream that he said Roberto Gambini shared with the Zentrum in Switzerland and possibly with the Cambridge IAAP Congress. As David wrote,

> It figured a group of scholars sitting around and discussing Jung. Enter a poor man, dressed in ragged clothes. He is not recognized by the scholars. It is Jung. He winks at the dreamer, and starts picking up nuggets of gold from the earth.

Again this is obviously psycho-kitsch. Even if it is of a different, not sentimental type, it is, nonetheless, embarrassing. Again the question is: does in such a dream the unconscious soul do the ego's bidding, the bidding of a naive ego that has become identical with a simplistic and clichéd version of Jungian psychology and the salvatory promise that it projects upon it, the bidding of an ego for which the psychic gold openly lies around, all ready to be just like that picked up by whomever is humble enough (no lengthy, laborious *opus* being needed to transform the *vilis* and *exilis* prime matter found *in stercore* into the *aurum nostrum*)—or does the soul conversely try to show the dreamer, as if in a mirror, what silly idolizing and idealizing frame of mind is prevailing in him? At any rate, the preachy tenor of this dream story reminds one of medieval legends of Christian saints.

Both dreams were used by the authors who reported them in their writings to confirm their *beliefs*. It apparently needs a developed and differentiated feeling function to be able to distinguish between what is soul and what is ego and to be shocked by the kitsch and gain critical distance towards these dreams.

So much for the topic of kitsch in dreams. I now attach to this chapter on archetypal dream motifs and the question of numinous dreams a few comments in which I return to the question of "initiations in dreams" briefly touched on earlier. It is clear that in modern reality initiations no longer exist as a social institution and that the form of modern culture is in a fundamental way adverse to initiations. We have replaced initiation a long time ago by education, and now by "information," the media, and propaganda. As Jung has said, in the modern world the "stars have fallen from heaven." Along with it, "heaven" as such, indeed, the very distinction between the earthly, sublunar and the celestial spheres, has disappeared. We have lost our myth, our authentic religion, and any authentic "metaphysic." We live in a *closed*, irrevocably positive-factual or positivistic world. Modern man is *born* man (born out of the soul) and has become an ego-personality psychologically completely alone, himself responsible for himself.

Nevertheless, occasionally there are nowadays dreams with motifs that remind one of initiations. Could it be that the psyche may in them *reenact* initiations during the person's sleep? On a first level, I would think that this is so. Such dream experiences may be important for curing the psychological illnesses of the dreamer and also for the dreamer's general psychological development.

What is important to see is the difference between initiation motifs in dreams today and real initiations in the past (ritually performed initiations in traditional societies, on a much earlier level of consciousness). Real initiations were initiations of the *person*. The whole person was initiated, and initiated on an existential level. Furthermore, this initiation was supported and authenticated by the whole lived truth of the respective ancient society. It happened within a culture with myths, gods, and "metaphysical" truths.

Now, however, an initiation experience in a dream is from the outset a sublated (*aufgehoben*) initiation, merely a private, personal experience in the sleeping soul and a fundamentally alien body in psychic life. As such, it also does not refer and belong anymore to the real person, it just *happens in* the person. It doesn't affect the *person* as a whole, does not transform his logical constitution or identity; it is also cut off from the logic of the world and thus it is, in the last analysis, without *truth*. Only what is in accordance with the logic of the world at each particular locus in the soul's history has truth. It is only a *psychic* event in the "inner museum" of the person. Before, the person as a whole used to be transformed and initiated into the tribe's actual truth.

Above all, there *is* nothing valid any more into which such a dream initiation could initiate. What is preserved in such dream motifs is merely the outer *form* (schema) of initiation without real content, substance, truth. The empty shell.

However, as I suggested, a modern dream initiation motif could possibly also bring about a certain helpful change for the person. But this change would be a *methodological* shift, in the sense of what we discussed earlier about one's logically "crossing a river" from the one side to the other. It would be an intellectual methodological shift, the opening of the eyes of the person to "the soul" as a reality in its own right (of course, not a literally existing or even a metaphysical reality, but the reality of another logical point of view). It would be the event of a "Then, suddenly, friend! One was changed to Two."[6] In this sense initiation dreams can maybe bring it about that a modern dreamer all of a sudden becomes able to make this intellectual shift. Nevertheless, a methodological change has nothing to do with the person as a whole and with an existential transformation.

Having declared that full-fledged initiations are not possible in modernity I now have to qualify this statement a bit. There is the problem of the simultaneity of the non-simultaneous. Jung taught that people factually living today may nevertheless psychologically belong to the nineteenth century, to the Middle Ages, or even further back in history to prehistoric times.[7] Heino Gehrts also showed in his analysis of a concrete example that a man living in the first half of the nineteenth century in a German town, namely Jacob Dürr (1777–1840), a tailor in Kirchheim/Teck, had been an authentic shaman (without posing as such).[8] Taking such possibilities into account, we also have to allow for the possibility that in people living in present-day reality true initiations might occasionally, even if rarely, occur. But of course, they would nevertheless be totally out of context, isolated events and as such not fully comparable to initiations in archaic cultures.

Whose dream is it?

At first glance this question seems to be pointless because dreams are, of course, always the dreamer's dreams. But the question of "ownership," of "mine" or "yours," is in psychology not so simple as it seems to be. We just need to remember Jung's discussion of the question of the "mine-ness" of the unconscious. He said:

> But I am not at all convinced that the unconscious is in fact only *my* psyche, for the concept "unconscious material" means that I am not even conscious of it. As a matter of fact, the concept of the unconscious is merely an assumption for the sake of convenience. In reality I am *unconscious* of it—in other words, I do not know at all where the voice comes from. ... Under such conditions it would be presumptuous to refer to the factor that produces the voice as *my* unconscious or *my* mind. ... / There is only one condition under which you might legitimately call the voice your *own*, and that is when you assume the conscious personality to be a part of a whole or to be a smaller circle contained in a bigger one. A little bank-clerk, showing a friend around town, who points to the bank building with the words, "And this is *my* bank," is making use of the same privilege.
>
> (*CW* 11 § 64 f.)

This point of Jung's, as well taken as it is, is not what I want to discuss in this chapter. I have another insight of Jung's in mind that comes out in an occasional comment in a letter. It is at one and the same time more concrete or specific and transcends the relation between "the bank-clerk and *his* bank" altogether. The passage I have in mind reads, "As soon as certain patients come to me for treatment, the type of dream changes. In the deepest sense we all dream *not out of ourselves* but out of what *lies between us and the other*" (*Letters 1*, p. 172, to James Kirsch, 29.IX.1934).

We see immediately that the relation between "me and my unconscious" or between "the employee and the company he works at" is exploded because a Third is introduced in addition to the subjective Two ("me" and "my unconscious"), namely the totally other person in objective reality, the analyst. This Third is more concrete than Jung's bigger circle containing a smaller one inasmuch as the analyst is a real-life person, visible, sitting over there in the consulting room across from the patient and being an object of the patient's consciousness. What "lies between us and the other" refers to an *interpersonal relation* in empirical reality and "the other" therefore to a real other human being, whereas the relation between me and the unconscious (the bigger circle) is (a) an intra-psychic relation (it excludes other persons) and (b) a relation between a visible, known person (me) and something completely unknown and mysterious that ultimately "is merely an assumption for the sake of convenience."

According to this new view, the dream is not just the patient's dream, not just his own. Dreaming is not something individualistic, not strictly subjective and personal, despite the fact that dreams are the private property of the dreamer. Just as earlier we had to see that already the *dream experience* is interpretation (and that not only the conscious memory of it is interpretation, let alone the explicit dream interpretation in therapy), so now we see here that both the dream interpretation in therapy and the *dreaming* or producing the dreams in a therapy context are communal work.

The degree to which this is the case is of course greatly dependent on the extent and depth of the therapeutic relationship. Some people enter into the therapeutic relationship spontaneously and connect on a deeper level and more intensively, while for others the relationship remains much more superficial. Some may even be completely immune. In the two latter cases, the dreaming probably happens to a much lesser degree from out of the relationship. Dreams are then much more the individual's *own* dreams than in the other case. Also, there are very severe cases, e.g., patients with borderline personality disorder, who are far too caught up in their powerful pathology to be free and open to the Other on a deep level.

That dreams are dreamt out of what lies between the dreamer and the Other is of course not restricted to the relationship between patient and analyst. It can also apply, outside of psychotherapy, to other intensive relationships, such as between lovers, close friends, at times even to contact with strangers. But it is in no case, neither in analysis nor in other relationships, a fixed law that dreams *must* come out of the relationship. They may also predominantly be the dreamer's own dreams. It is unpredictable and in the same person and in the same therapy may apply to this dream and not to that, or to this dream to a high degree and to that dream to a minimal degree.

Another aspect is the strength and firmness or solidity of the personalities involved in the therapeutic (or in another social form of close) relationship. Confronted with an analyst with a very powerful charismatic personality, it is likely that patients with a weak personality, whose natural deep longing is to psychologically *lean* on a stronger personality, are more apt to dream out of what is between them. In the case of Jung's analysands I even suggested the possibility that some of those analysands who presented model examples of the individuation process or mandala dreams, visions, and paintings may not even have dreamt their *own* dreams at all but really Jung's, or, to be more correct, not Jung's *dreams*, but what Jung as theoretician needed and desired. In the cited letter, Jung explains such phenomena by saying, "Always the more unconscious person gets spiritually fecundated by the more conscious one" (*ibid.*), and he refers to the phenomenon of the guru in India, but we could just as well think of all the followers of the leaders of sects in the West.

I wonder, though, whether the criterion to be applied here is really that of "unconscious vs. conscious." The real contrast seems to me to be that between the more or less vacuous mind on the one hand and strong, impressive conviction on the other hand. The latter exerts a tremendous fascination and, in the case of gurus and leaders of sects, establishes an extremely powerful, often pernicious, dependence of their followers on them. The converse is, of course, also true. The psychologically fuller, stronger personality is less likely to be affected by the therapeutic relationship.

Nevertheless, as the example of Jung himself shows, a very strong personality with powerful psychological convictions can be unconsciously open to the inner-most soul of a patient to a high degree and dream a dream that reveals the patient's psychology. See, for example, his description of "the case of a Jewish woman who had lost her faith" and suffered from a strong father complex, who was mainly cured through dreams that Jung had about her (*MDR* pp. 138ff.).

"Big" dreams

The question of the "mine-ness" of dreams leads to the distinction of the ordinary dream from the so-called "great" or "big" dream. One could think that "big" dream simply refers to powerful archetypal, numinous dreams, to dreams that are concerned with something that far transcends the horizon of the dreamer's person and of personal (psychic as well as external) reality in general. This would certainly have some justification. But I think that it might be better to reserve the term "big" dream to other types of dreams. What limits the "greatness" of such archetypal or religious dreams is that they are still the dreamer's private, personal experience. They may be told to others, but nevertheless they remain important only for them. They are events in their inner, part of the *opus parvum.*

Great dreams in my sense are also dreamed by an individual. Like the arche-typal or religious dreams mentioned they also have very little to do with the indi-vidual himself. Indeed, they are certainly not *about* something that only concerns the individual. Their characteristic is that they do not come out of their own soul at all and as such are dreams that refer to the issues *of a whole people* or maybe even of *mankind.*

This kind of dream was, it seems, common in earlier days, in the days of myth and ritual, and it would have been the kind of dream that occurred most of all to shamans, medicine men or chieftains who, in fact, bore responsibility for their entire people. Let me cite here in full the story of the Pharaoh's dreams that I briefly mentioned above:

> Pharaoh dreamed: and, behold, he stood by the river. And, behold, there came up out of the river seven well favoured kine and fatfleshed; and they fed in a meadow. And, behold, seven other kine came up after them out of the river, ill favoured and leanfleshed; and stood by the other kine upon the brink of the river. And the ill favoured and leanfleshed kine did eat up the seven well favoured and fat kine. So Pharaoh awoke. And he slept and dreamed the second time: and, behold, seven ears of corn came up upon one stalk, rank and good. And, behold, seven thin ears and blasted with the east wind sprung up after them. And the seven thin ears devoured the seven rank and full ears. And Pharaoh awoke, and, behold, it was a dream.
>
> (Genesis 41:1–7)

As the interpretation given by Joseph later in the same chapter shows, these two dreams had nothing whatsoever to do with the person of Pharaoh. They had to do with the common weal of the nation, much as we hear from Jung, when he reported his experience in East Africa, that the medicine man "had formerly negotiated with the gods or the fates and advised his people." One such medicine man (*laibon*) told him: "In the old days the *laibons* had dreams, and knew whether there is going to be a war or sickness or whether rain comes and where the herds should be driven" (*MDR* p. 265, transl. modif.). But beyond such still worldly survival-related concerns they were also responsible for the whole people's relation to the spirit world, the gods. Their dreaming came from their "responsibility for the whole people" as its source, that is, from the soul of the group or tribe or nation as a whole, whereas the ordinary people, who had so to speak delegated this responsibility to the shaman or chieftain or Pharaoh, could normally not tap this source; their dreams would only come from their own psyche and out of their personal concerns, or from more immediate familial or personal relationships (Jung's "what lies between us and the other") as well as circumstances that they were in.

The "big" dreams are not really the shaman's or Pharaoh's dreams. If we raise the question, "whose dream is it?" concerning "big" dreams we would have to answer: it is the tribe's, people's, collective's dream, notwithstanding the fact that it is a dream that appears only in one particular individual. The shaman or Pharaoh is merely the special "empirical" place in which the invisible, transcendental group soul's dreams manifest. Concerning the relation to the divine, the shamans and medicine men were, to say it with Hegel's pointed words, "those solitary souls who were sacrificed by their people and exiled from the world to the end that the eternal should be contemplated and served by lives devoted solely thereto."[9]

Are there "big" dreams today? I do not know, but I think it is completely unlikely, for two reasons. Those people to whom we today delegate the responsibility for the whole people—our politicians and experts—do not carry a psychological, a *soul* responsibility for the community, but instead a technical, practical, political responsibility, a responsibility on the ego level. Our leaders are not shamans or the like any more, not even Majesties by divine right, and this is why they cannot tap the source of "the whole" either. They derive their authority not from Heaven, from the gods or spirits, but from the people (as the sovereign) who elected them from among their own ranks, that is, they remain *decidedly* human-all-too-human. As a matter of course, they do not rely on dreams or visions, on omens or other spiritual signs, but on advice by experts and on rational calculation.

This touches already upon the second reason, which is that the truly important themes or insights for "the soul" would appear in the *form* of dreams only during the times of those cultures that were still essentially "dreaming" cultures— cultures guided by myth and archetypal symbols and the self-manifestations of the divine, cultures the form of whose very (psychological, spiritual) existence was constituted by the fundamental difference between Heaven and Earth, between the "metaphysical" and the worldly. These were the times before the birth of man or, more precisely, before the soul had become born out of itself in the form of the modern reflecting I. With the development of consciousness in modernity, after the birth of man, these times are over. The moment that modern *psychology* came into existence and man has inevitably become psychological man *essentially* living in waking consciousness, "big dreams" as literal dreams have become unlikely, if not impossible.

Today the persons who bear soul responsibility for the whole people are no longer dreaming medicine men, shamans, seers, but poets, artists, philosophers. And the *form* that that which formerly was the "big dream" today necessarily has is that of the fundamental *awareness* expressed in great cultural *works* produced by poets, artists and thinkers. Jung knew that. He said: A "poet or seer lends expression to the unspoken inner depth [or inner truth] of his time [*dem Unausgesprochenen der Zeitlage*]" (*CW* 15 § 153, transl. modif.), he is "a bearer and form-giver of the unconsciously productive soul of mankind. That is his office …" (§ 157, transl. modif.), and "at this level of experience it is no longer the individual who is the experiencing subject, but the nation [*Volk*]" (§ 162, my transl., omitted in *CW*) or, as we could also say, the specific "historical locus." He speaks from that "soul depth" "where the individual has not yet separated itself off into the loneliness of consciousness," but "where the feeling and acting of the individual still reached out into mankind at large" (§ 161, transl. modif.). "It is the great dream which has always spoken through the artist as a mouthpiece" (*Letters* 2, p. 591, to Read, 2.IX.1960).

Above all, in view of these cited far-reaching insights of Jung's, but also in general, it was in my opinion his great psychological mistake to think that we ordinary people could still today have "big" or "great" dreams simply because certain dreams come loaded with strong numinosity and powerful archetypal images, as well as to think that the major concern of dream life was individuation as the development of the individual.

In one paper, Jung first points out that "every individual problem is somehow connected with the problem of the age, that practically every subjective difficulty has to be viewed from the standpoint of the human situation as a whole," but then restricts this general statement by adding: "But this is permissible only when the dream really is a mythological one and makes use of collective symbols." This sentence clearly opens the door for the opinion that still today "big" dreams are possible. The only requirement Jung sets is, as I said, that they make use of collective symbols, that is, mythological or archetypal material. But then Jung introduces a second limiting insight. He says: "Such dreams are called by primitives 'big' dreams. The primitives I observed in East Africa took it for granted that 'big' dreams are dreamed only by 'big' men—medicine-men, magicians, chiefs, etc." (*CW* 10 § 323f.). Those "big" men are "big" because they hold the superior spiritual status in their society of mediator between their people and the gods, and they hold it because they have undergone a real initiation. So, Jung had been fully aware of the exclusiveness of "big" dreams. They cannot be dreamed by ordinary people. About "the ordinary dream of the little man," as we hear elsewhere, he was informed by those Africans quite clearly that "*Little dreams are of no account*" (*CW* 7 § 276, my italics). But this insight is dismissed out of hand in his next two sentences following the former quotation: "This may be true on a primitive level. But with us these [i.e., 'big'] dreams are dreamed also by simple people, more particularly when they have got themselves, mentally or spiritually, in a fix" (*CW* 10 § 324). The dismissal of the fundamental exclusiveness of "big" dreams occurs through the argument that this exclusiveness applies exclusively to the primitive level and not to us.

Jung does not give any reason why the dependence of "big" dreams on the social institution of "big" men, who have direct contact with the spirits or gods, all of a sudden no longer applies in the modern situation. What Jung is not willing to admit is that along with the abolition of the distinction between simple or ordinary people and "big" men the distinction between ordinary (merely "personal") dreams and "big" dreams has also been abolished. The whole vertical dimension objectified and institutionalized in those "big" men, i.e., the direct bond to "Heaven," has objectively disappeared from the logic of the modern world. We live in the age of democracy, equality, non-discrimination and thus programmatically in a horizontal-only world. No doubt, there may nowadays be dreams with clearly mythological, numinous symbols, and it could theoretically also be the case that, as Jung suggests, such dreams appear when people have got themselves in a (mental or spiritual) fix, although so far the causal relation between "being in a fix" and archetypal dreams is just an assertion. But that and why merely "being in a fix" would raise ordinary people to the rank equivalent to that of "big" men and re-establish the vertical dimension with a direct line to the gods or God has not been explained, nor is it plausible, and, above all, the feature that certain modern dreams come with mythological motifs is merely a *semantic* attribute or characteristic of such dreams. It provides no more than the *abstract form* or *external likeness* of " 'big' dream," but in no way alters the fact that *psychologically, syntactically*, such dreams with "collective symbols" are and remain strictly private, personal dreams, of significance only for the individual dreamer and precisely not of significance for the *collective*, that is, for society as a whole, for the nation, for mankind. But "collective significance" was/is the criterion for a dream's being a "big" dream.

What helped Jung out of the (theoretical) "fix," into which *he* had mentally got himself through his longing for the actual presence of higher meaning in modern dreams, was a sleight of hand: the coining of the term "collective unconscious," the "collective" of which could be used equivocally. The equivocation covers up the gap that gapes between the "primitive level" and the "modern level" and obfuscates the fact that mythological motifs or "collective symbols" in modern dreams are modern citations (in quotation marks, so to speak) of what once upon a time, in a distant past, was *really* "collective." In other words, such dreams contain a fundamentally bracketed, sublated, and *privatized* "collective" or "mythological." Modern archetypal dreams present mythological motifs in isolation, cut off from the living mythology to which they originally belonged and in which they were once rooted, as in their native ground. Their uprootedness turns those motifs into something like the cut and dried flowers in a herbarium. One's *personal, subjective* emotional excitement ("numinosity") cannot restore to them lost objective-psychological life and truth.

With respect to Jung's other belief mentioned above, namely that the major concern of dream life is individuation as the development of the individual, his psychological mistake was to take "individuation" literally: as if the subject of individuation would have to be the *literal* individual in his positivity. The real subject of individuation is nothing positive. We are here in psychology, the sphere of the soul, not in the world of positive fact, not in people's psychology. What is the subject that undergoes the process of individuation? It is the (general and objective) *logical form of consciousness*. It is a form change of the general logic of "the world" and not an existential, substantial change of the individual *person*. Psychotherapy is the making of *psychology*, I pointed out. Jung's mistake was that he succumbed to a personalistic view, despite his great insights into the collective psyche and the objective soul.

The dream series

It is a common idea in Jungian psychology or psychotherapy that one should pay attention to dream series, to the development that shows in a sequence of dreams over weeks and months. This view is in conflict with the idea of the dream as a self, and as the soul's speaking. If the dream is a self and if work with the dream begins with a radical closure (the exclusion of anything external), then we cannot view the dream as one element embedded in a series. We have to look at "this dream today" as self-sufficient. It has everything it needs within itself. We would deprive the dream of its individuality, as something in its own right, and reduce it to a subordinate part of a larger whole, a higher, more comprehensive self, if we apperceived it in terms of what preceded it.

To look at the dream in terms of the dream series amounts to *external reflection*. We would not be trying to understand the dream from within itself, but look at it from a superior standpoint. The idea of the dream series would automatically assign the self-character *to the person* who had the dream and ipso facto deprive the individual dream of its self-nature. We would instrumentalize the dream. It would become a mere *means to an end*, namely to the end of understanding the development of this person. With the idea of the dream series a *program* is implicitly set up, a developmental scheme, to which the individual dream would then always already be subsumed. Probably something like the model of *Bildungsroman* (a novel about character development) is somehow at work in the back of the consciousness that focuses on dream series.

It would also mean that we would approach today's dream, this new dream, with a mind *prejudiced* by the images, categories and expectations derived from the previous dreams. Here again it needs to be stressed that the first mental act when approaching a dream must be to empty the mind, to wipe away, as much as is possible, not only all memories from before, but also all implicit expectations, in order to free the mind for the new, fresh experience of this one dream at hand. What I said about the dream series, i.e., the earlier dreams, applies, of course, also to our knowledge of the patient's biography, childhood history, etc. We should free ourselves from this knowledge as far as possible, so that we do not look at the dream through the same old lens of the past.[10] Let us give the dream a chance! Let us grant it the right and the opportunity to be a new, fresh experience and to enrich our thinking precisely through unexpected points of view on life.

"*This* dream today" has to be for us *the* dream, the one and only dream there is. It has to become a world, indeed *the* world, a true whole, all-comprehensive with nothing outside. The dream as a totality. The counterpart to the self-nature of the *dream* is our methodical attempt to relentlessly abandon *ourselves* to the inner world of the dream, to try to get into the dream. Now, for as long as we are working with the dream, the dream is the All for us, and everything else is forgotten. The dream *is* soul. To devote ourselves wholeheartedly to the dream in its eachness is precisely the *therapeutic* obligation and the best service for the patient, too.

Of course, dream work is only one element of all that is going on in therapy. When we have concentrated long enough on a particular dream, then we are again outside the dream. And then, from the resulting standpoint of external reflection, it is, of course, possible to think about the course of therapy as a whole so far, and thus also about the sequence of the patient's dreams.

There is no question about the fact that if a patient brings dreams to therapy time and again they also have a temporal sequence. But does this also mean that this temporal sequence is a series?

For the concept of "series" it is not enough to point to the fact that dreams occurred one after the other. "Series" requires that the sequence also be in some sense meaningful beyond mere succession. There must be an order, an overall sense of coherence; the whole sequence must be, at least loosely, structured by an organizing principle. Jung wrote in *MDR* (p. 196 f., transl. modif.) that "There is no linear evolution; there is only a circumambulation of the self. Unidirectional development exists, at most, only at the beginning." In contrast to the concept of "series," circumambulation does not imply a more or less continuous development. This concept is completely free of a program. It rather suggests that the same may be shown from different angles, that it can be played through in diverse variations, and that different emphases can be put in different dreams dealing with the "same" topic. From this point of view a later dream that presents a solution that seemed still unthinkable in an earlier similar dream would not indicate any progress made by the patient, but simply a different variant. Conversely, a later dream with a "bad" ending after earlier much more "positive" ones must not necessarily mean a serious relapse.

Even the idea of a circumambulation of the self or a center is problematic. Who says that all dreams circumambulate the self, i.e., *the* center? Could it not be that successive dreams "circle" around different centers? In practical reality, dreams during a given time span can be of very different caliber, depth, character, and significance. They may address quite different psychological themes, the one yesterday may have been concerned with a deep soul truth or indeed with "the self," whereas today's seems to be much closer to the dreamer's personal sphere and about a pressing problem in his daily life. Even towards the end of a successful therapeutic development dreams may occur in which the pathological conflict is surprisingly portrayed again very much as during the initial phase of therapy, and conversely, during that early phase there may have been dreams that showed a rather harmonious internal state despite the patient's prevailing disorder. The real danger of our entertaining the idea of "dream series" is that we fall prey to a fiction or construct of our own making rather than looking at an authentic *phenomenon*. It may be the ego's wish to see that the sequence of dreams (and the therapy as a whole) follow a hidden teleological program.

But the biggest problem is that we fall back into personalistic thinking and into thinking in terms of a developmental scheme.

Excursus: Can one learn to interpret dreams?

The first point to be made here is that one cannot learn and teach dream interpretation like one can learn and teach techniques.

This is only one aspect, even if it is a crucial one. The second point is that one has to and can learn a lot, as I had already stated in Part V, chapter "Trap: Dream interpretation as its translation into the terms of one's psychological theory": about mythology, fairy tales, history of religion, ethnology, cultural history, psychopathology, psychological theory, etc. This kind of "technical" knowledge can be taught and learned like in other fields, *but* for soul work it is only background knowledge, nothing to be practically applied directly.

Furthermore, it is important to have practical psychological, therapeutic experience.

But this is still not enough. There is one more thing one has to learn. This is the most important and difficult thing. One *can* make progress with this aspect, but only if one has the necessary personal prerequisites. Like in any field, psychology and dream interpretation require and presuppose also a special psychological giftedness, an aptitude that one either has or has not. To the extent that working with dreams also presupposes some kind of personal giftedness, it cannot be learned.

Some people are musically gifted, some for languages, some for mathematics, etc. and some are definitely not gifted in the one or the other of those areas. Some people look at a painting and are interested only in whether it is true to reality, some think only about paintings in terms of whether they are a good investment or not. However, there are also some who see the truth that shines forth from a painting. In much the same way there are also people specially gifted for psychology and others not gifted. One's having naturally (by temperament, "instinctively") the *potential* to have access to soul, to be reached, touched by it, is precisely what psychological giftedness means. Having a "sense" of soul. Soul implies *depth*, an abyssal depth, and as absolute negativity it has a special relation to death, to "the underworld," to gods, to the metaphysical. What an ongoing psychologist needs to bring to his field of study is a certain depth of personality adequate to perceive and receive the depth of psychic reality.

If this aptitude or potential is there, there can be additional learning: this aptitude can be developed, cultivated, differentiated. What is the thing to be learned *here*? It is nothing else than that the learner's general sense of what soul is specifically about (in contradistinction to the practical, pragmatic ego purposes, desires and categories, or, more generally, to the issues of the daily life and the sphere of the human, all-too-human) becomes more and more explicit, concrete, differentiated. What does the soul want, what are the soul's concerns? What one needs for dream interpretation is that one has really acquired a *conceptual notion* of and a *genuine feeling* or *sense* for the dimension of soul, for what the *psychological* standpoint (or perspective) is, and that all of this is saturated with actual experience. One has to have become quite naturally able to see in terms of the "psychological difference."

One main factor for developing this sense of soul is time and lots of practice, experience. One has to "grow" into such knowledge. It is not merely a matter of an intellectual understanding. It is helpful to learn from good examples of dream interpretation (many examples), and of course one's own working with hundreds or thousands of dreams is also needed. When I started, I simply tried my best, I had some ideas, but judging from how I look at dreams today I would probably say that I was not very good with dreams. I did not understand very much. It has taken me a long time, many years, until I saw a little clearer. Still now I never know if I will succeed. There is no guarantee. But I don't mind if the dream does not disclose itself to me. No pressure. In such a case I have to hold my place in my *not* knowing, my helplessness, and not try to be better than I am, above all, not try to impress the patient, who probably expects an intelligent interpretation from me.

It is very important for the person learning to work with dreams to learn not to mind that he or she feels that he is not so good. That is all right and has to be bravely borne as the beginner's lot. One has to accept one's helplessness, one's *not* knowing (and to be sure not merely as a beginner but throughout!). Humility. Just go ahead, and try your best. But always be honest with yourself: don't pretend to yourself to know and understand more than you actually do. Slowly one develops a certain style, one acquires some insights, has a broader experience with dreams. *Patience* is crucial. Can one wait, patiently "brood the egg"? Is one willing to stick to and stay with the *nonunderstood*, with the *fog*, and treat it like the fairy tale corpses that needs to be warmed, rather than substituting the fog with some quick and easy rational meaning?

A personal test concerning one's own aptitude for soul work and dream interpretation is whether one "catches fire" when one hears a truly *psychological* dream interpretation. Does it deeply speak to you? Do you get excited? Do you get hooked, as if a harpoon were stuck in you? Does it take root in you? Does it suddenly open a truly new dimension for you and a feeling like, "Oh, *this* is important!" "*This* is it!"?

Notes

1. New York (Spring Publications, Dunquin Series 4) 1972.
2. "Since the stars have fallen from heaven and our highest symbols have paled..." (*CW* 9i § 50).
3. C.G. Jung, *Über Gefühle und den Schatten*. Winterthurer Fragestunden. Textbuch, Zürich and Düsseldorf 1999, pp. 22 and 24 f. My translation or paraphrase, respectively.
4. The point of this phrase is that consciousness itself changes its nature, in itself becoming the opposite of itself. The *Collective Works* use in their translation the word "regression." But a regression would be harmless compared to what Jung says.
5. Review by Jane St. Lawrence of: Marion Woodman, *The Ravaged Bridegroom: Masculinity in Women*, in: *Jung at Heart* (News and Views of Inner City Books) no. 7, Fall 1990, p. 3.
6. A quote frequently cited by Jung. The lines are by Friedrich Nietzsche, from his poem "Sils-Maria," in: *Lieder des Prinzen Vogelfrei*.
7. See *CW* 11 § 463.
8. Heino Gehrts, "Jacob Dürr aus Kirchheim (1777–1840). Der letzte deutsche Schamane" and "Der Schneider von Kirchheim," in: Ders., *Justinus Kerner und die Zeit der Aufklärung, Gesammelte Aufsätze* vol. 2, ed. by Heiko Fritz, Hamburg (Igel-Verlag) 2015, pp. 183–192 and 193–207.
9. *Hegel's science of logic*, tr. by A.V. Miller, London (Allen & Unwin) 1969, paperback reprint Atlantic Highlands, NJ, (Humanities Press International) 1989, p. 26.
10. One may recall here the later parallel of Wilfred Bion who advocated starting every analytical session without memory.

Part IX

The ulterior purpose of and assignment for dream interpretation

From *Natura* to *Ars*

What follows in this Part is a meta-reflection about the deeper function and purpose of dedicated work with dreams.

We have discussed the Jungian view of the dream as a self, as its own interpretation, and as having everything it needs within itself. We have also subjected ourselves to the narcissistic blow that Jung's dictum, "It has a say now, not you!" amounts to and seen that the methodological consequence of this dictum is the necessity of our going under—of our circumambulating the dream and interiorizing ourselves into the dream. When I now turn to a thoroughgoing discussion of Jung's late statement,

> We have simply got to listen to what the psyche spontaneously says to us. What the dream, which is not manufactured by us, says is *just so*. Say it again as well as you can. *Quod Natura relinquit imperfectum, Ars perficit.*
> (*Letters 2*, p. 591, to Read, 2 September 1960)

we will see that it expresses a dialectic and that inherent in a truly Jungian dream interpretation there is not only a move in the direction of our own "going under," but also a definite countermove to the "not you!" move, namely a move precisely to "YOU!" (or "I," the subject). This may be surprising, but it is a consequence of this dialectic.

The beginning of Jung's dictum clearly confirms the stance that we have worked out previously: "We have got to listen," that is to say, we are to be recipients of what shows itself of its own accord ("spontaneously") and what "is *just so*." The *soul* is the one who speaks. *We* have to be silent, nothing but listeners.

But then comes: "Say it again as best as you can." At first glance we could perhaps still think that this means nothing more than sticking to the text: we are *not* supposed to bring any innovation, expansion, addition, modification to it, but be absolutely faithful to the dream text. What is demanded is a commitment to strict sameness, "just so"-ness. As the attached phrase, "as well as you can," indicates, this "saying again" does not mean simple repetition either, such as our reading the dream text out loud, reciting it. Jung does not invite us to such a thing as chanting the dream like a mantra. Nor does "saying it again as best you can" suggest—it hardly needs to be mentioned—that we translate the dream images into the jargon of psychological theory, replace them by terms and categories of the psychoanalytical school we belong to (whichever one it may be), for example, by identifying dream motifs as manifestations of the "Oedipus complex," "resistance," "good or bad breast," "feeling function," "anima," "shadow," "self," "mother complex," "hero archetype," the various "gods" and "goddesses," and so on.

That all this is excluded becomes quite clear from the sentence Jung added after the beginning of his statement, namely the alchemical dictum, "*Quod Natura relinquit imperfectum, Ars perficit.*" It implies that *our* "saying it again" has to provide added value, and this added value has to consist in bringing "perfection" to the dream, a perfection obviously thought to be lacking in the way the dream originally comes to us (or the way it is remembered and perhaps written down as text), in other words, the dream as "*Natura*"! This is absolutely astounding: The dream's perfection is supposed to be our own active, artful contribution and addition to it. And so at second glance we realize that "Saying it again" is in a certain sense in radical contrast to the passive and receptive "We have simply got to listen." It demands our own *speaking*, our actively taking the stage, bringing ourselves into play.

Of course, our own speaking in this case is not totally our own. For contentwise we are, as we know, not supposed to put in our own two bits. All we need and are allowed is to say "*it* again." Semantically, we must feel bound by what the *non*-ego,[1] the psyche, has spontaneously said to us (or to the patient, if he is the dreamer). We are not to add new content that we feel is missing, nor new insights, but only the otherwise unaltered dream's *own* "perfection." Here the question arises in which sense such a simple "saying it again" can bring perfection to the dream when the dream itself, the way it came to us from the psyche's spontaneous, "natural" speaking, is declared to be still fundamentally imperfect and in need of being perfected? How is it possible that the dream, if it is considered as a self and as having everything it needs within itself, can nevertheless be said to be imperfect?[2] What can it lack? Or, asked from another angle: What kind of, what sense of "perfection" is meant here?

As the phrase "as best as *you* can" implies, the sense of "perfection" brought by "saying it again" is not the abstract-universal one of absolute faultlessness and supreme excellence, but it is tied to, and thus relative to, each individual who "says it again." And of course, people can always be psychologically more or less gifted, deeper or not so deep. Different individuals will produce better as well as poorer, more simplistic as well as more penetrating or more convincing versions of "saying it again." All that the perfection intended here requires is each person's doing *his* or *her best*. As such, precisely *as* being *relative to* the concrete individual as well as to the concrete instance of his or her "saying again," "perfection" here is *absolute* perfection in Hegel's sense of "absolute" and in contrast to a positivistic sense. In other words, the perfection that psychology inspired by alchemy has in mind does not aim for the ultimately best interpretation and dismiss the less good ones. It does not imply a ranking of interpretations. It does not apply an a priori objective standard for "top performance" and "achievement of the optimum."

What alchemical "perfection" is really concerned with is something completely different, namely the transition or transportation from the *"Natura"* state to the *Ars* state. Perfection is the achieved *status* change, the accomplished transferal of the dream from its original status of primary givenness, its having spontaneously come to us (= *Natura*), to the status of *reproduction*, of *having been reborn again* by the individual human subject. This is why even a relatively poor interpretation might nevertheless well make the dream "perfect" (in this special sense), provided only that it is one that "says the dream again *as best as this particular interpreter can*" say it. The perfection it brings is that it *re*-presents the dream *in the human subject's own words*, but in its sameness (that is, with its content and idea painfully preserved unaltered). The perfection lies in the transition to *subjectivity*, to the re-production of the received dream through an artful and "artificial" *human intervention*! This is what *Ars* here means.

Ars ultimately amounts to the subject's wresting the dream (again: in the intactness of its What) from nature, from the status of givenness, of being empirically found as a happening or existing content, and giving, secondarily, birth to it from within the subjectivity of the interpreting subject. Thus it means giving it a new source, a new ('artificial') origin, a new "mother ground"! It is a revolution from → to ←.[3] The dream *returns* to itself from the other, the subject's side, is thrown back to itself much like a mirror image is a reflected image.

If the dream as it comes to us of its own accord as a *Natura* product is in itself imperfect and has its perfection outside of itself, being dependent for its perfection on its being reflected in human consciousness, we have to conclude that the dream in its original form *is only one half of a full-fledged dream*, like a question without its answer. The full reality of the phenomenon "dream," in other words, is a two-part reality, a kind of twin phenomenon, but such a one whose own other half is at first missing and needs to be supplied.

From here we can also better understand what "dreaming onwards" means in Jung's view that "[What we do when we interpret a myth is] at best [that] we *dream* the myth onwards" (*CW* 9i § 271).[4] What this sentence implies is only the preservation of the semantic content, the idea and spirit presented by the dream. But it does by no means imply a continuation of the dream *mode, our* staying in the imaginal and fantasizing mode. No, *we* have precisely to fully wake up from this mode of dreaming innocence, we have to leave the innocence of *Natura*, break our loyalty to it much the same way that an adolescent has "to leave father and mother" in order to establish himself as an individual standing on his own feet.

To become "perfect," the dream must already have been negated, brought into a distance, turned into a mere memory. It must have become, as it were, *historical* for us, a text, a "corpse." The rupture must have happened. No continuation of the imaginal sphere and aura created by the dream: the spell of, and our enchantment with the dream must have been broken. The subject must clearly *stand vis-à-vis* the dream and now see it from outside (which may appear as paradoxical but is precisely the necessary precondition for one's being able to learn to *methodologic-ally* see *from inside*, to interiorize the dream absolute-negatively into itself and to take a *professional* stance toward it). What "dreaming onwards," be it the myth or the dream, means is explained in Jung's comment right after his "dreaming onwards" sentence, namely, that we "give it a modern dress." Two aspects of this phrase are noteworthy: (1) We *give*, which is equal to "our *saying again*," and (2) *modern* dress (which is in opposition to the frequently archaic, mythological, archetypal character of dreams that Jung was particularly interested in). A discussion of what the reference to modernity involves will have to wait a while. For the time being let me point out that modernity is the age of subjectivity, of "I."

The *Natura* status, by contrast, means that the human subject remains the passive and faithful recipient of the dream as the image that appeared of its own accord and lets it reverberate in the subjective psyche and continue its life there undisturbed. If this is the prevailing attitude, then the dream as well as other soul productions (symbols, religious ideas, etc.) have the status of a "revelation" in the colloquial sense of the word (from "*the* unconscious," from "*the* psyche"), just as the proclamations of the Prophets, the texts of the Bible and other holy books, and the Dogmas of the Church have the status of a Revelation in the emphatic sense (directly from God). In both cases Jung's "It [exclusively *It*!] has a say now, not you!" applies. The *Natura* status is maintained as long as the primary sympathetic oneness—the *unio naturalis*, or *participation mystique*—with the pronouncements is preserved. This is most obviously the case when the human subject stands in awe in front of them, is impressed by their "numinosity," perhaps considers them even as manifestations of "the sacred," and accepts them, sort of sight unseen, as unquestionable truth. But this retained sympathetic oneness also prevails in other, much more sober, more "mechanical"-looking areas, for example, wherever religious texts or dogmatic ideas are chanted, wherever they are sung as hymns, recited as the creed, in adapted form repeated as personal prayers, or performed as ritualistic acts. Furthermore, it is also retained in such widespread ardent efforts, as in the monastic traditions, through meditation or contemplation to completely immerse and envelop consciousness in the holy texts and their truths, in other words, to make consciousness go under in the interiority of their depth in total devotion and thus to bring about an as complete as possible *adaequatio* of consciousness to them. The whole liturgical use of them is, to be sure, a "saying them again," but precisely *not* "as best as YOU can" in Jung's sense, with the crucial alchemical distinction between "imperfectum" and "perficere" clearly kept in mind. Consciousness, the subject, stays immersed in them or keeps itself out of it, playing dumb.

So far, the preservation of the *unio naturalis* with the "documents of the soul" or the holy texts of religion was connected with cases where "saying it again" remains primitive *literal repetition*, entirely pre-rational, not intellectual, and undifferentiated. But it would be an error to confine it to such modes, to what I even denigrated as "playing dumb." No, what is "to be said again" can very well also become an object of deep conscious meditation and thus of a subject's intensive process of disciplined concentration, indeed, even of an active *intellectual* processing and refining, a thorough thinking it through, as in theology, and yet, against appearances, *nevertheless* amount to a continuation of primary sympathetic oneness. For we have to realize that, although all this intensive effort may lead to amazing higher awareness, it does not in the least disrupt the continuity with the original *givenness* of the inherited religious wisdom that it tries to faithfully elucidate and unfold. We must realize that the intellectual penetration of religious ideas can be another form of bathing in their waters. For this reason, the tradition of highly developed, intellectually sophisticated and deep commentary on doctrinal contents is, as a kind of "*dreaming* onwards," in no way incompatible with the perfectly retained *unio naturalis* with them. A good example would be much of medieval Scholasticism. It certainly exercised in an exemplary way a disciplined and thoroughgoing rational "thinking through." But it did not start from scratch; it relied on transmitted authorities. The basic content to be thought through was given to it and received by it from the Bible, the doctrines of the Church, and the ancients.

Even if a tradition of highly sophisticated thought must not always be incompatible with the preservation of the *unio naturalis*, any such tradition or activity that indeed retains the *participation mystique* certainly is incompatible with the surprising, if not shocking alchemical conception that what has come spontaneously from *Natura* is fundamentally *imperfect* and *in need* of an artifex (!), and his active human intervention as that which alone can bring perfection to it. The idea that that which comes from *Natura* (no matter whether this means directly from "the unconscious," from "the soul," or from God) is imperfect deals consciousness a narcissistic blow! However, this narcissistic wound is the precondition of *Ars*. *Ars*, as artificial and deliberate intervention, indicates the logical status of reflection. And "Reflection," Jung once rightly noted,

> should be understood not simply as an act of thought, but rather as an attitude. It is a privilege born of human freedom in contradistinction to the compulsion of natural law. As the word itself testifies ("reflection" means literally "bending back"), reflection is a mental[5] act that runs counter to the natural process, an act whereby we stop, call something to mind, form a picture, and take up a relation to and come to terms with what we have seen. It should, therefore, be understood as an act of *becoming conscious*.
>
> (*CW* 11 § 235, fn. 9)

For Jung, reflection is not the event of one's performing a particular act of reflection, but it is "an attitude," that is to say, a general *status* reached by consciousness, a decidedly "counternatural" and in this sense "artificial" status, one that consciousness has only reached by its having freed itself from another previous or underlying naturally given status. The given status is the status of the *human animal* or "natural" man in which it was unquestionably *determined* by the natural process and natural law, by man's own instinctual impulses, by the external stimuli and impressions he receives, by the constraints imposed on him by the familial, social customs and cultural dominant ideas and expectations. Reflection is, Jung claims, a privilege, and it has its origin in human *freedom*, in man's active subjectivity, and it concretely means that the thinking subject maintains itself, itself as free, vis-à-vis that which is to be thought.

Only through freeing itself from being conditioned by what comes naturally and spontaneously has consciousness come home to itself and ipso facto entered the privileged position of standing over against the natural world and thus being free to choose, on its own responsibility, the relation or stance it wants to take towards it. Its freedom means that, by definition and on principle, it is (psycho) logically its own master, of course not empirically or literally, in other words, only with respect to the attitude it takes to reality.[6] Only when this freedom has been attained has the subject become veritable *subject* (in the sense of modern subjectivity), and only as veritable subject can it be *artifex* and bring "perfection" to the *Natura* product. According to the cited Jung passage, the very concept of *consciousness* (truly *psychological* consciousness in contrast to merely psychic consciousness[7]) is rooted in this freedom of subjectivity.

Our working with dreams, with devotion to their details, has the purpose to broadly unfold what is inherent in and implied by the images and words they contain so that it becomes explicit, is spelled out, and this means conceptually comprehended, understood. The perfection that our saying it again, our *Ars*, brings to the dream as natural product is the conscious conceptual comprehension of it in a concrete human mind. Our task is to return the dream to itself a second time, namely *as reflected* in our consciousness and comprehension, and thereby complete it, to supply its own other half that was missing in its original form. This is what "giving it a modern dress" means. Comprehension here does not mean that *we*, high-flying above dream details, comprehend "its meaning," "its message" as its *extracted essence*, which would make the dream only serve our egoic purposes and interests. *We* as ego-personalities, as civilian man, have a strong interest in understanding what "it means" and what it says about ourselves (or the patient) and how the dream can help. But comprehension here means something else and more modest, more basic: bringing the light of conscious reflection to all its details.

After having clarified how our "saying again" can bring perfection to the dream, I have to add an additional insight about the dialectic of this process. Alchemy's "*Quod Natura relinquit imperfectum, Ars perficit*" makes us think that the *Natura* form of the dream (together with our listening to it) comes first, and perfection through *Ars* second, which on a first level of understanding is, of course, correct. But in order to do full justice to this alchemical dictum, we also have to reverse the order between "listening" and "saying again." *First*, we need to be *standing objectively vis-à-vis* the dream as a mute text, a "corpse," and arrive precisely at the zero point of *not* hearing and *not* knowing. And only then, *secondarily* and not immediately, can we try to *methodologically*—that is, consciously and deliberately, as veritable *artifex*—slowly work ourselves into its details and start saying it again as best we can. Only by saying it again as best we can we become able to begin to truly listen to the dream in the first place and can *it* begin to have truly *its say* for the first time. Our truly listening to it becomes possible only after our having "said it again."[8] Paradoxically therefore, it is the *Ars* that gives birth to the true *Natura*. Only through the *Ars* and the process of our interiorization into, and our bringing our conceptual comprehension to, the dream can we at long last arrive at the dream's speaking as what really is *just so* (as Jung had put it).

Perhaps this is the same as what Heidegger wanted to convey when he said the following about poetry interpretation. It is just as pertinent to dream interpretation.

> Whatever an elucidation may be capable of and what it may not be capable of,[9] the following always applies to it: in order for the pure poetic core in the poem to stand out even more clearly, the elucidating speech must in each case shatter itself and what it attempted to achieve. For the sake of the poem, the elucidation of the poem must seek to make itself superfluous. The last, but also the most difficult step of any interpretation is to disappear with its elucidations before the pure "standing there" of the poem.[10]

This pure "standing there" of the dream (to return to our topic) is no longer the same that it was in the beginning when it was a mute *Natura* phenomenon. Its words and images have now been opened up to resonate with all the implications discovered in them by our work. The dream has thus been enriched, "enlightened," it has absorbed the reflection brought to it into itself. It now *speaks* to us. It has become "perfect."

Notes

1. Jung emphasizes explicitly: "the dream which is *not* manufactured *by us*."
2. In Part V above I insisted repeatedly on the dream's *perfection* (chapter "The dream-I" and "5. Opposition as obvious conflict between the Two ...")! But now it comes out that despite its perfection in this sense it is still imperfect in another sense.
3. Here we can remember that the move from *Natura* to *Ars* should in Jung's eyes not only happen to dreams, but also to man himself. Cf. the motif of man as *twice-born* in his thinking, of our being "*made* into sons of God," that we are "more than autochthonous *animalia* sprung from the earth, but as twice-born ones ha[ve our] roots in the deity itself" (*MDR* p. 333, transl. modif.).
4. Jung's statement, more accurately rendered into English, would read, as given by me above: "What one does is at best one's *continuing to dream* the myth." I stay here with the *CW* translation because it has been used a lot in Jungian literature. The same as to "dreaming onwards" applies to my metaphor of "sleepwalking."
5. The *CW* translate Jung's "geistig" here with "spiritual" rather than with "mental," but "spiritual" brings in false connotations.
6. This is reminiscent of the relation of the dream in its *Natura* form and the perfection brought to it by *Ars*. As pointed out, content and substance of the dream must be maintained intact. Perfection refers only to a different, new *status* given to the dream.

7. I will touch on the topic of truly psychological consciousness in the next Part.
8. Before our "saying it again" the dream is merely a dead text, a "corpse" that needs to be brought to life.
9. The simultaneity of "capable" and "not capable" can remind us of Jung's "as well as you can."
10.

> Was immer auch eine Erläuterung vermag und was sie nicht vermag, von ihr gilt stets dieses: damit das im Gedicht rein Gedichtete um einiges klarer dastehe, muß die erläuternde Rede sich und ihr Versuchtes jedesmal zerbrechen. Um des Gedichteten willen muß die Erläuterung des Gedichtes darnach trachten, sich selbst überflüssig zu machen. Der letzte, aber auch schwerste Schritt jeder Auslegung besteht darin, mit ihren Erläuterungen vor dem reinen Dastehen des Gedichtes zu verschwinden.
>
> Martin Heidegger, *Gesamtausgabe* vol. I.4,
> Frankfurt a.M. (Klostermann) [2]1996, p. 194, my translation

Part X

Beyond working with dreams

Pushing off to the dimension of the soul's real life

It would seem that we could fairly say that with the last Part, IX, this book on working with dreams has been concluded. But in the context of a psychology conceived as a psychology *with* soul, one final task remains to bring about the real conclusion. The real conclusion is something paradoxical since it amounts to a negation, to our pushing off from working with dreams! At the very end of our psychological interpretation of one dream by way of example (Part VI) we said that the interpretation presented has to be left behind in order to give way again to the dream text itself, just as Heidegger expressed the corresponding necessity in the case of the elucidation of poems (see the end of the preceding Part IX). Here now the demand is similarly to leave the entire topic of dreams behind and to allow it to self-sublate—for no other purpose than to do full justice to the topic of dreams. This is the paradox I hinted at.

We are psychologists. We need to put the dreams themselves and our working with them in perspective, assign to them their proper place. As far as that is concerned, I hope it has become clear from the discussion in this book that dream interpretation or working with dreams as described can be most helpful for practical psychotherapy and provide a real access to some depth. But our working with dreams inevitably takes place in the consulting room, the latter understood not only as literal place, but also as mental horizon. Even when we are alone and think about our own dream of the previous night we have unawares entered, or put ourselves into, the imaginal topos and frame of mind of the consulting room inasmuch as we are focusing on our inner, on the private psyche. We have already seen above that for historical reasons, because of fundamental changes in the logic of modern reality over against archaic times, there can generally be no "big" dreams any more. Dreams and our working with them take place exclusively in the sphere of what I have called the *opus parvum*. They are relevant only for the individual dreamer. Even if impressive mythological, archetypal motifs or initiation tasks appear in them, these are nevertheless merely "citations," as it were, of *former* soul truths, contents of the *historical* soul, sedimented cultural goods sunken to the level of the atomic individual's inner. Dreams are concerned with the *psychologically* obsolete, with what is *psychologically* past: once and for all fenced in within the subjective psyche and as such a priori checkmated. About "the ordinary dreams of the little man" Jung's East African informants had told him that "little dreams are of no account" (CW 7 § 276). No doubt, for the individual and his personal development, for the cure of his symptoms and thus *psychically*, dreams can be extremely helpful. In addition, for psychology itself our work with them can be a wonderful way of training ourselves in the truly psychological mode of looking at phenomena. As such, this work has a propaedeutic function in psychology, like finger exercises in music in contrast to playing music or like sparring compared with actual combat. Dreams do *not* give us the actual content or substance of *soul*; they are *not* the place where the *soul's* real action is. Because the soul is always cultural, always concerned with the generality. It appears as the *opus magnum*. Dream interpretation does not connect us with the truly objective soul, with the real soul issues. As long as psychology concentrates on dreams, it is ipso facto at bottom still personalistic psychology, even if it includes archetypal perspectives and uses mythology and archaic initiation rites as its frame of reference for understanding dreams.

Without explicitly naming the difference between the *opus parvum* and the *opus magnum*, Jung nevertheless stated clearly enough: "It is the smallest part of the psyche, and in particular of the unconscious,[1] that presents itself in the medical consulting room" (*Letters 2*, p. 307, 17 June 1956, to Nelson); "analytical psychology has burst the fetters which hitherto have tied it to the consulting-room of the doctor. It transcends itself" (*CW* 16 § 174, transl. modif.), namely in the direction of the sphere of supra-personal generality ("*Allgemeingut*" is the word Jung uses in this context).[2] True psychology has to move out into the open, into the soul's wilderness. Working with patients is not the main vocation of psychology. As far as psychology as a discipline is concerned, this work is no more than a sideline. We can see from the predominant focus of Jung's own studies that psychology's "main business" is something else (just think, for example, of his *Psychology and Alchemy, Mysterium Coniunctionis, Aion*, or the manifestation of psychological types in Patristic theology, works of philosophy, literature; or Jung's studies of the psychology of Trinity and of the Catholic Mass, the psychological examination of Nietzsche's *Zarathustra* and the *Exercitia* of Ignatius of Loyala, and so on). Psychology "is something broadly human, [...]. Nor, again, is it merely instinctual or biological. *If it were, it could very well be just a chapter in a text-book of biology*. It has an immensely important *social* and *cultural* aspect [...]" (*CW* 16 § 52, my italics). "Psychology, however, is neither biology nor physiology nor any other science than just the knowledge of the soul" (*CW* 9i § 63, transl. modif.).

Now it is true that Jung also said that we must simply listen to what the dream, what the psyche spontaneously says to us in dreams, and he said this precisely in a context where the issue was the future general cultural development of the modern world (*Letters 2*, p. 591, to Read, 2 September 1960). Even in old age Jung obviously still held that dreams are the foremost place where the *objective* soul expresses itself for modern man and about "*collective*" necessities. But this does not make sense. This critique needs to be clearly stated. Despite his essential insight that the poet or philosopher (and, I add, *not* the dream) is the "bearer and form-giver of the unconsciously productive soul of mankind. That is his office ..." (*CW* 15 § 157, transl. modif., see chapter " 'Big' dreams" above), Jung refused to see that dreams, even those with mythological motifs, for modern man inevitably belong to the subjective psyche and ipso facto in the "consulting room." Dreams are not the answer, not the solution, *if* it is a question of the *opus magnum*, of the soul's logical life, of what Jung ultimately had in mind with his concept of the "collective unconscious." Dreams are not the language in which the objective soul expresses itself in modernity.

The objective soul is at work in the invisible logic of the REALITY *in which* we live,[3] not in individual, personal phenomena, such as dreams that emerge *in us*.

Therefore, in order to connect with the objective soul we have to return to that other Jung who said: "My problem is to wrestle with the big monster of the historical past, the great snake of the centuries, the burden of the human mind, the problem of Christianity," "with the great battle between the present and the past or the future. It is a tremendous human problem. ... Certain people make history and others build a little house in the suburbs" (*CW* 18 § 279). Psychology has to expose itself to where the wind of history blows. This is where the real soul manifests itself. And this is also why psychology must burst the fetters that tie it to the consulting room as its logical horizon.

This is why Hillman was right to demand: "From mirror to window."[4] The problem with his move was, however, that he literalized it. He acted his insight out by giving up work in the consulting room altogether and becoming instead active in *the social arena* (in a popular movement, a working with *people*) and a critic of contemporary civilization with an *educational*, world-reforming, rather than psychological impulse.[5] But there is no need for us to literally leave the consulting room, literally leave dream interpretation behind. We need to leave them *logically*, simply by adhering to the psychological difference between the *opus magnum* and the *opus parvum* and by conceptually assigning dream-work to the latter, to the privacy and "collective" or cultural insignificance of the *subjective* psyche. With our dedication to dreams we do something important for the *people*, the patients, who have these dreams (and we on our part busy ourselves with something that is in itself interesting, stimulating, and often allows us to go into a certain depth). But all this has nothing to do with the objective soul and its real life.

I want to illustrate the complexity of the move that needs to be made by using as a model the movement described in Plato's Parable of the Cave, that is, only the abstract-formal movement pattern, not the philosophical issues with which it is involved. The starting point is the situation of people in a cave who, fettered, can only look at the back wall of the cave, upon which they see the shadows of objects in motion behind them. For one of these cave-dwellers the fetters are burst, and he is made to leave the cave with a radical about-face and now for the first time sees the real world outside. Interestingly enough, this move does not end with liberation from narrow enclosure in the cave and fixation on a display of fundamentally secondary shadow images and an ensuing revelational confrontation with the concrete three-dimensional, tangible things out in the open. The last stage of the movement is a return into the cave. This is, however, by no means a return to point zero, but a return based on the achieved fundamental expansion and enrichment of consciousness.

The partial analogy of this story with Jung's idea of psychology stuck and chained in the consulting room is obvious. The consulting room is the place of the endless loop of case histories, the repetition–compulsion of psychotherapy's revolving around one personalistic psyche after another. It is the place that imprisons psychological experience and thinking in a fundamentally constricted, limited, indeed reductive, horizon, while at the same time making psychologists believe that they are busying themselves with the real thing, because they know nothing wider and greater.

The fetters that hold the psychologists in "the cave" of the consulting room are not actual chains. The real fetters are, much as in Plato's cave (as it turns out in the end of his parable), their own *delight* in confinement within the personalistic, naturalistic horizon and in the secondary shadow images[6] of psychological reality, delight in all that material that as private material is a priori sublated, passé. We also see why these fetters need to be burst and the psychological mind needs to push off from the consulting room as psychology's horizon and penetrate to that other dimension out in the open, in the wilderness, as I called it, that is the home of the objective soul's real life. But once his eyes have been opened and his horizon *fundamentally* widened, the psychologist can also return and devote himself to dreams again.

We should not read the liberation from the cave and the return into it as two separate consecutive acts. Rather, with our earlier insight about the difference between two types of narratives we can here say that it is only the *narrative genre* that forces Plato's parable "to represent in sequence what actually is a permanent simultaneity of becoming and being," as Plotinus worded it (*Enn.* IV 8 [6] 4, 40–42). What appears in the narrative as two independent, opposite movements is in reality the inner dialectic of a truly psychological approach. Psychology's methodological stance is in itself and at once the contradiction of having broken out of the consulting room *and* having returned to it, whereas conventional psychology, on the one hand, stays firmly settled in the "consulting room" with its positivistic notion of the psyche as its horizon, without any thought of leaving, and whereas Hillman, on the other hand, has undialectically broken with the "consulting room" in favor of the social arena or the naturalistically perceived "world" with its hypostatized anima mundi and makes his psychology dwell there. Both isolate and stay at one of the two endpoints or poles: mirror (consulting room, Plato's cave) and window (world), instead of getting into the motion itself.

Since for us leaving and returning are not literal acts, but moments of one and the same methodological attitude, the fixed endpoints or locations lose their importance. What is left and only counts is the dialectical movement itself, the distance, difference, and *living* tension (contradiction, dialectic) between them, the "psychological difference" as methodological stance, as the openness between the opposites, as "the wild." This, in turn, has the consequence that the return does not go back to the literal consulting room. Or rather, the psychologist who has left the consulting room and ventured forth into the open field of the objective soul in its opus magnum will not have the mental horizon of the consulting room even if he happens to be in the literal consulting room. By the same token, pushing off from the consulting room does not mean entering the literal world with its "anima mundi." Both movements are absolute-negatively interiorized into themselves and into each other into a methodological *style*. They have become distilled and only in this way truly psychological. Psychology is not defined by existing *objects*, be it people's psyche (consulting room) or the anima mundi (what is seen through "the window"). Psychology is only defined by interiority, by the inwardness of *psychological SEEING*, by a certain style in the absolute subjectivity of the psychologist's mind. The soul is not outside, not in the other, nor is it in us. It is not an objective reality (does not have "object" character). There is no anima mundi for a true psychology. The soul is in psycho*logy*, in the psychologist's *seeing* "the soul" (the deep inner logic or better logical life) at work in whatever phenomenon, regardless of whether it is personal or collective, archaic, ancient, or modern, obsolete (historical, present only in *Mnemosyne*) or actual (a present reality). It is rather in the psychologist's *speaking*[7] this *unspoken* logic of the soul (or in any recipient's hearing it spoken).

Part X, "*Beyond* working with dreams," is the last part of this book. But what it is about, psychology's breaking out of the consulting room and its positivistic presupposition, is not at all a final move, coming at the end of *Working with dreams*. On the contrary, it needs to be understood as lying behind the very beginning, behind the starting point of *psychological* dream interpretation: as its *sine qua non*. In fact, it has been the underlying premise and guiding principle of our approach to dreams. For it alone makes it possible for the psychologist to come to dreams with the notion of "the river that needs to be crossed" in the structure of his consciousness and with all the other necessary notions about the proper attitude towards the dream, the dream interpreter and the interpretation of dreams discussed in this book. It alone lets us do real justice to dreams, give them their due, because having acquired an authentic access to the dimension of the soul's logical life as present reality, we no longer need to inflate dreams with alleged veritable soul importance and as a kind of initiation into the (perhaps even divine, sacred) mysteries of the soul, but can appreciate them for what they are, interesting, precious little elements of the private psyche and "*only* that!" We owe it to the dreams that we *relativize* their soul significance as irrevocably *sublated* and *fenced-in*, *museum-piece* soul phenomena, although nonetheless *soul* phenomena.

In this sense "*Beyond* working with dreams" is and has all along been an integral moment of "Working with dreams." But inasmuch as "*Beyond* working with dreams" is the very premise and unspoken presupposition of this whole book, it also needs to be made fully explicit in it. Just as we began with the *return* to the "consulting room" (by devoting ourselves to working with dreams), so now at the end of the book we turn explicitly to the implicit beginning, so that the circle closes and the tacit underlying presupposition is caught up with.

The logical beginning—the bursting of the fetters that tie psychology to the consulting room, the ascent to daylight from out of "the cave" of the sleeping soul, the move out into the open—must obtain an explicit presence in this book in order for the latter to come to a real conclusion, even if only in the form of an invitation to future work. Just as a dreamer *wakes up* from his sleep and his dream, so psychology itself must also wake up from being spellbound by its idea that dreams of people are the *via regia* to the soul and the "main business" of psychology. It has to push off from the *sleeping* to the fully waking, *conscious* soul. It must awake from what Jung once called "primitive awareness" as "merely perceiving consciousness" and as an "inferior state of being conscious" (this is our usually prevailing consciousness!) in contrast to veritable "psychological consciousness" (which is still very much a matter of the future). But this is a topic for another occasion.[8]

Notes

1. I.e., the "collective unconscious," the "objective psyche," or what I call the soul.
2. Interesting in this regard is also Jung's statement: "I have therefore refrained from expositions of case histories" (*Letters 2*, p. 56, to Kostyleff, 25 April 1952, transl. modif.). At the beginning of Part VI I already quoted: "I omit personal details intentionally, because they matter so little to me" (C.G. Jung, *The Visions Seminar*, From the Complete Notes of Mary Foot, Book One, Zürich (Spring Publications) 1976, p. 2).
3. And in this sense we could even appropriately use Jung's term "collective unconscious" for it.
4. James Hillman, "From Mirror to Window. Curing Psychoanalysis of Its Narcissism," in: *Spring 49*, 1989, pp. 62–75.
5. Whereas Hillman's original main project was re-visioning *psychology*, the *field* of psychology, his later main concern and longing shifted away from psychology to the cure or rescue of the *world* (*We've had a hundred years of psychotherapy and the world's getting worse*). One of several problems with this concern is that it inevitably constellates the person who pursues it as *civilian man*, even if he factually brings psychological training, experience, and expertise to it and tries to justify this new concern by re-introducing the idea of an *anima mundi*.
6. What I called the sedimented cultural goods sunken into the inner of the atomic individual.
7. "Speaking": giving voice to, manifesting, making accessible, giving explicit expression. Soul has to be *made*. Only through this "speaking" (and in the specific moment of this "speaking") is soul a *present reality*.
8. See my *The Historical Emergence of the I*, London, Ontario (Dusk Owl Books) 2020, chapter 4.

Index

interiority 106, 108, 111, 114, 149, 176, 177, 189, 209, 218; psychology as discipline of 2, 3

Jaffé, Aniela 4, 8
Japan, Japanese 22, 27, 41, 42; and shamanistic tradition 186
Jung, Carl Gustav, *passim*; disappointed by his disciples 4; dream of customs official 8; in dream, led into the highest presence 122, 136, 164; logic of difference and otherness excluded 114; pre-/post-alchemy J., mature J. 3, 4, 5, 36, 37, 96, 114, 135, 192; as shaman 56; "then I *happened to myself*" 169

Kafka, Franz 57, 159, 179
Kant, Immanuel 4, 30–2
Kast, Verena 4
Kawai, Toshio 5
Kena Upanishad 59
known *vs.* really new 101

Lange, Friedrich Albert 2
Lichtenberg, Georg Christian 38, 50
listening: importance of 77, 113, 119, 120, 127, 162, 178, 206, 207, 211, 212; *listening cure*, psychotherapy as 77, 163
logic of difference and otherness (*see also* sameness) 114
Lucretius, Carus 70
Luther, Martin 92, 97, 108, 113

Mercurius, spirit 65, 107; *duplex, utriusque capax* 84; fugitive 107
methodological *vs.* metaphysical 53, 107, 153, 194, 217, 218
modernity 65, 76, 132, 145, 185, 186, 191, 194, 195, 199, 209, 216; cultural rupture since Industrial Revolution 124; distinguished from all other times 132
Mogenson, Greg 80
Molière, Jean-Baptiste Poquelin 178
myth (contrast: fairy tales): *narrative* sequence but *logical* simultaneity 138, 217

narrative structure, two forms of *see* fairy tale, myth
Nasreddin, Hodja 59–61

Natura 206–12; and the preservation of the *unio naturalis* 209; is fundamentally imperfect 210
naturalistic stance 3, 4, 10, 18, 19, 60, 65, 105, 107–9, 115, 217
nature: blind and mute 21
Neumann, Erich 121
Nicholas of Cusa 103
Nietzsche, Friedrich 80, 143
night world/day world (*see also* "impressions of the daily life") 14, 17, 22, 33
nightmare 186
not knowing, zero point of knowing 73–5
Now, the 94–6
numinous, the 57, 64, 65, 159, 189, 191–3, 200, 201

object level 98, 99
objective feeling 121, 132
objective soul 36, 37, 42, 60, 61, 80, 83, 98, 100, 201, 215, 216, 218
oportet me adesse / oportet operatorem interesse operi 91, 92, 108, 113
opus magnum / parvum 191, 197, 214–16, 218

patient: "disregard the patient's association" 128; does not know best 130, 131; does *this* patient need soul work? 54; "Forget the patient!" 83; has no dreams 45, 48; his absolute-negative interiorization into the dream 179; it is his job to do the entering 55; needs to be wounded by his truth 183; patient narratives 43–5; "patient" *vs.* "client" 81; what *they* feel about dream images/who cares what the patient says 82
people's psychology 57, 58, 201
perfection: of image, dream 88, 89, 148, 182; perfection through *Ars* 206–12
Pharaoh's dreams 133, 135, 198
Plato: *anámnêsis* 168; parable of the cave 31, 216, 217
Plotinus 138, 148, 217
Pope, Alexander 83
prophetic dreams 186
psychê 82
psychic(ally) *vs.* psychological(ly) 62, 71, 174, 191, 214, 215

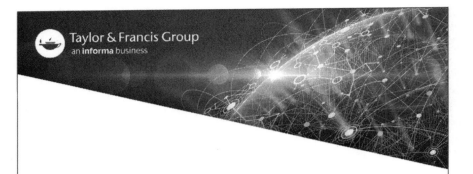